LIFE
AFTER
BILLY

Jane's Story: The Aftermath of Abuse

LIFE AFTER BILLY

Jane's Story: The Aftermath of Abuse

BRIAN VALLÉE

SEAL BOOKS

McClelland-Bantam Inc.
Toronto

LIFE AFTER BILLY
A Seal Book / November 1993

Copyright © 1993 by Brian Vallée
Jacket design by David Montle
Photo of Jane Hurshman by Vernon L. Oickle

Canadian Cataloguing in Publication Data

Vallée, Brian.
  Life after Billy

ISBN 0-770-42556-9

1. Stafford, Jane, 1949-1992. 2. Abused wives -
Nova Scotia - Biography. I. Title

HV6626.V33 1993   364.1'523'092   C92-095282-8

Published simultaneously in the United States and Canada

Seal Books are published by McClelland-Bantam, Inc. Its trademark, consisting of
the words "Seal Books" and the portrayal of a seal, is the property of McClelland-
Bantam, Inc., 105 Bond Street, Toronto, Ontario M5B 1Y3, Canada. This trademark has been duly registered in the Trademark Office of Canada. The trademark
consisting of the words "Bantam Books" and the portrayal of a rooster is the
property of and is used with the consent of Bantam Books, 1540 Broadway, New
York, New York 10036. This trademark has been duly registered in the Trademark
Office of Canada and elsewhere.

PRINTED AND BOUND IN U.S.A.
JACKET PRINTED IN U.S.A.

0 9 8 7 6 5 4 3 2 1

This book is dedicated
to the memory of
JANE HURSHMAN

CONTENTS

❖ ❖ ❖

ACKNOWLEDGEMENTS
✦ ✦ ✦

I WOULD LIKE TO THANK Jane's family, friends, associates, and the many others who helped me gather the information necessary to write what I hope is a thorough and accurate account of her life and death.

The seven poems in this book were written by women who were physically or sexually abused, or both, as children or adults. Two of the poems are by Jane. I wish to thank Linda, Angela Cupido, "Sara", and Linda Cooper Waters for the others.

I wish also to thank Alison Maclean for her guidance, Shaun Oakey for a fine edit, and my companion, Nancy Rahtz, for her patience, support and understanding.

"In a sense, I've been able to put Billy
Stafford, and those years of suffering, away
on a shelf where they can no longer hurt me,
although they do come back to haunt me on
a regular basis."

—Jane Hurshman

(Liverpool *Advance*, Feb. 26, 1992)

PROLOGUE
❖ ❖ ❖

WHEN, IN NOVEMBER 1982, a jury acquitted Jane Stafford of first-degree murder in the shotgun death of her common-law husband, Billy, the packed courtroom rose as one to applaud the verdict. The trial, in the town of Liverpool in rural Nova Scotia's Queens County, had focused national attention on the issue of wife battering.

Before Jane, Billy Stafford had beaten and tortured his wife Pauline, and their five children. They fled to Ontario to escape him. He did the same to his first common-law wife, Faith Hatt. After a particularly brutal beating, when she was pregnant with his child, she fled to western Canada and didn't return to the Maritimes for several years.

Billy was well known as a cop-hater and the resident bully of Queens County. Jane's lawyer, Alan Ferrier, described him in a brief to the court: "Mr. Stafford would not permit a Bible in the home, constantly talked of being sent by the devil, and consistently, over his adult life, was in conflict with the police and, in particular, with members of the RCMP detachment at Liverpool, Nova Scotia. He bragged of having killed a fisherman at sea, pointed and fired weapons in the direction of others without any concern for their welfare, and constantly committed offences under the Lands and Forests Act. In short, Mr. Stafford was an animal who was feared by many, including the police."

Two weeks before Jane killed Billy, the RCMP delivered a summons to the Stafford home ordering Billy to appear in Magistrate's

Court on a charge of shooting deer out of season. Billy wasn't home at the time, and the police asked Jane to give him the summons.

Billy beat Jane and ordered her to return the summons to the RCMP detachment. She arrived at the detachment and begged the duty officer to take back the summons. The officer noticed the bruises around Jane's eyes. Ferrier didn't learn of that incident until after her trial.

The police felt so strongly about Billy Stafford, and the threat he posed, that after Jane confessed to killing him, Sgt. Peter Williamson, the officer in charge of the Liverpool detachment, said Jane deserved a medal and had probably saved at least two of his officers' lives.

Jane came to accept full responsibility for Billy Stafford's death. She believed that if she hadn't killed him, he would have killed her. And on the night she pulled the trigger, while Billy was passed out in the front seat of his half-ton truck, she believed that when he awoke he would carry out his threats to burn out her neighbours, who lived in a trailer at the foot of the Stafford property, and to hurt her son Allen, who was sixteen at the time.

Jane never forgot Billy's drunken words that night: "When Margaret turns her lights off down there tonight, it'll be lights off for her, for good! I got five gallons of gas in town today and I'm going to dump it all around that fucking trailer and watch them burn. They'll never get out. Can't you just see Margaret with her game leg and Roger with his bad heart, running around trying to get out. They won't have a chance."

A fit of laughter followed Billy's harangue but he stopped abruptly and stared menacingly at Jane. "And I'll deal with that son of yours at the same time," he said. "I've waited a long time to deal with him. I might as well clean them all up at one time."

After she killed Billy, Jane, through her lawyer, Ferrier, offered to plead guilty to manslaughter. The judge would then hear the evidence about her horrific five-year relationship with Billy and sentence her accordingly. Jane was prepared for that, whatever the outcome. Ferrier believes the local Crown prosecutor and the police were in favour of accepting the manslaughter plea, but the provincial attorney general's office, in Halifax, rejected it. Charged with first-degree murder, Jane faced the possibility of twenty-five years in prison without parole. She was forced to go through a jury trial and recite, before an overflowing courtroom, the litany of atrocities Billy had inflicted on her and her family.

After a nineteen-day trial, the jury found Jane not guilty. Still numb from her ordeal, she was obviously relieved at the verdict. But Ferrier warned her, correctly, that the judicial system probably wasn't through with her. The Crown was stunned and embarrassed by the jury's decision. It appealed the verdict and won. (Because of issues raised in Jane's case, the laws have been changed, and today the Crown would have likely lost the appeal.) A new trial was ordered, and this time Jane's plea of guilty to manslaughter — offered two years earlier — was accepted. She was sentenced to six months in prison.

The Crown's decision to charge Jane with first-degree murder and to appeal the jury's not-guilty verdict was viewed by many as nothing less than legally condoned emotional battering on the part of the judicial system. There were some in Queens County and elsewhere, however, who didn't share the widespread jubilation when Jane was acquitted. Furthermore, they resented her light sentence. They believed she got away with murder.

While in prison, Jane was allowed to continue her education toward a nursing assistant degree. A light rain was falling on April 14, 1984, when she returned to the Halifax Correctional Centre from her classes two hours away in Bridgewater. Upon her arrival, prison authorities informed her that her release papers had come through. She had served two months — one third of her sentence — and had been granted parole.

Jane signed the papers, picked up her belongings, and headed for freedom.

"I ran to the gate," she recalled later. "It seemed like I waited forever for it to open." The officer on duty smiled and waved to her from behind the glass of the guardhouse as the gate slid open. She heard his voice over the remote speaker beside the gate: "Good luck, Jane, be happy."

I

A BODY

On Saturday, February 22, 1992, between 9 and 10 a.m., a worker with East Coast Towing, a tugboat company on the Halifax waterfront, noticed a lone blue Ford Tempo in an adjacent parking lot. The car was parked near the water a considerable distance from several other cars bunched at the top of the lot across the street from Brewery Market, a collection of upscale shops, restaurants, and offices.

The Tempo was still there at three the next afternoon when Roy and Yvonne Kline drove about two-thirds of the way into the lot and parked their car. Roy, recently retired after forty-five years with a local dairy, and Yvonne, who works with the motor vehicle division of the provincial transportation department, made the mile or so drive to the waterfront two or three times a week to watch the ships in the busy harbour.

There was snow on the ground and a biting wind was blowing from the north as the Klines stepped from their car. Yvonne decided it was too cold to stray very far and she stood near the car as her husband walked toward the water.

"I was just pokin' along, heading south towards the entrance to the harbour, when I noticed the car there," recalls Roy Kline. "When I was four or five feet from it, on the driver's side, I noticed a lady slumped over in the front seat. The first thing that came to my mind was, my gosh, that could be somebody's mother in there and she probably has children waiting for her to come home. I

1

thought maybe she had a drink or something and she was just resting, or else she tried to start the car and it wouldn't go.

"The snow had fallen through the night and I observed there was no marks or footprints around the car. And I took a closer look and I didn't like the colour of her face. I thought, *There's something wrong here*. I thought she might have had the car going and she was asphyxiated."

The cold, meanwhile, got to Yvonne Kline and she was back in the car watching her husband. "He just stood there and looked into that car," she says. "He wasn't moving — wasn't saying a word." She called out, and he returned to the car.

Roy Kline sat silent behind the steering wheel for a few moments. "You won't believe this," he said finally, turning to his wife. "There's a woman in that car."

"What does she look like?"

"She doesn't have very good colour."

"Well, maybe she's dead. We better go call the police."

They drove two or three blocks to a pay telephone but vandals had damaged it. They found another phone booth, and Roy told police about the woman and gave them the licence number of the car. "We decided to come back and watch," he says.

They chose an adjacent lot where snow collected from city streets was being dumped at the water's edge and pushed into the harbour. A bulldozer operator and a truck driver stopped to watch along with the Klines as a police cruiser arrived within minutes, sliding to a stop near the Tempo.

"There were two officers, a man and a woman," recalls Yvonne Kline. "They walked over to the car and looked into it." The officers then moved away and pulled on white surgical gloves before approaching the car again. As they watched, the Klines overheard the bulldozer operator say to the dump-truck driver: "They're putting on their white gloves. That means there must be something wrong."

Another police car arrived a short time later. The Klines decided it was too cold to wait around until the body was removed.

"We may as well go home and see it on the TV," said Yvonne Kline. Roy nodded in agreement.

"I figure they must know who she is by now," he said. "I gave them the licence number. They can tell from that."

Kline was right. The Tempo was registered to Jane Hurshman-Corkum, and police had been looking for her since late Friday after she failed to show up for the night shift at the Halifax County Regional Rehabilitation Centre, not far from her Cole Harbour home, on the outskirts of Dartmouth.

II

. . .

STARTING
OVER

UPON HER RELEASE FROM PRISON on April 14, 1984, Jane
Hurshman had no illusions about what lay before her. The relief
that she would never again have to face the daily, all-consuming fear
of Billy Stafford's irrational anger and unpredictable brutality was
tempered by the knowledge that her emotional scars would never
completely heal, and forgetting the horrors she had lived through
would be impossible.

She knew that she and six-year-old Darren, the son she had with
Billy Stafford, would need long-term therapy if they were to even
begin to repair the damage wrought by five years of extreme trauma
and abuse. Therapy, Jane understood, must be her number-one priority. There were three others — get a job, reunite her family, and
help other abused women.

In the time between her acquittal, appeal, prison term, and
release, Jane upgraded her highschool education and entered the
nursing course at the Lunenburg Regional Vocational School, in
Bridgewater, graduating in June of 1984 at the age of thirty-five. She
and Darren lived for a time in Ontario, but in the fall she was
offered a job as a nursing assistant at the Halifax County Regional
Rehabilitation Centre, in Cole Harbour, Nova Scotia.

The job, working with aged patients with behavioural problems,
was rewarding, and Jane was paid well. She was permanently scheduled on the night shift at her request. Like most battered women
who had suffered severe sexual and physical abuse, she found it dif-

ficult to sleep at night. The night shift also suited her because it gave her time to herself.

"I like the night for its quiet peacefulness," she often said. "For most of my life, nighttime was a living hell. The night shift works out very well, because I sleep much better in the daytime."

The story of Jane's shotgun killing of Billy Stafford and her subsequent journey through the Canadian legal system gained the attention of the media nationwide. Her case was the subject of a CBC documentary, and she agreed, in 1984, to collaborate on a book, *Life With Billy*.

Even before the book, she began speaking to women's groups and gradually gained confidence and self-esteem — attributes that, until then, were alien to her.

"I am sure that as far back as I can remember, I was conditioned to be a victim," Jane once wrote. "My mother always said that someday things will change — someday things will get better. For her, after many years, they did. For me, this is the first time I can honestly say that life is looking good. I survived hell and I feel as if I'm a totally different person. I want to live, and I am trying hard with each passing day to find out how. I am so much more aware of life's gifts than I ever was before. I guess I just *feel* more than I ever did."

Wendy Annand, Jane's parole officer during the four months after her release from prison, saw the gradual transformation. "I really liked her. She was always so natural, with a bright, shining disposition. Knowing a bit of the background and the horror that she'd been through, and seeing what a positive outlook she had on life — it was just a treat."

Annand is a slim, wiry woman who speaks forcefully, and often, against family violence. By the time her supervision of Jane ended in August 1984, they had become good friends.

"Jane's basic personality never changed the whole time I knew her, but her public persona certainly became more polished and her ability to analyze was amazing. She picked things up almost by osmosis. She wouldn't sit down and read a feminist tome on wife battering, and she wouldn't necessarily label her ideas, but just by being around people who held certain views — they came out that way."

Seventeen years as a parole officer have hardened Annand's resolve to seek an end to the brutality that women and children suffer in their homes. It's a problem that in recent years has been exacerbated by a severe depression in Nova Scotia's traditional fishing and lumbering industries.

Jane was not typical of the clients Annand supervised. "Most of them are men who have left school in Grade Six and are basically functionally illiterate and have no trades. In the old days they could go out on the boats and make good money, but now, with the fishing industry basically drying up, they're being laid off and there's no way that they can be retrained. And the guys working in the woods used to be able to make good money as long as their backs held out, but now you can cut all the pulp you want but you can't sell it. The only wood they *can* sell is firewood, but there's incredible competition for it.

"I have no idea what's going to happen to all these men. Most of the work around here now is seasonal and minimum wage."

Families that were relatively stable before the depressed economy are now under increased stress, says Annand. "My guess is, it has caused a slight increase in battering, but battering is so common in this area, it's difficult to gauge."

Annand helped to set up a transition house in the town of Bridgewater, near the rural Nova Scotia hamlet of Bangs Falls where Jane and her son once lived with Billy Stafford.

"The number of crisis calls we get from women who are being battered is unbelievable," she says. "And many of them end up having to go back to their abusive husbands because of the financial reality. The welfare system down here is the pits. To leave a husband when you have children and you're worried about their future and you know you can't even feed them properly . . . it's a dead end.

"The daycare system is terrible, and the kinds of work available to women who do leave is menial at best. People ask, 'Why do they go back?' My response is, what choice do they have?"

Jane knew exactly what these women were going through and she moved to Halifax-Dartmouth with a promise to herself that she would do whatever she could to help them. Wendy Annand encouraged her by inviting her to participate in workshops and conferences on abuse and related topics. "Sometimes I'd ask her to come and do a presentation or sometimes to just attend. She loved it."

Annand was aware that Jane had healing of her own to do and recommended that she contact Ann Keith, executive director of Services for Sexual Assault Victims, or SSAV, in Halifax.

Keith, a soft-spoken, compassionate woman, has been a social worker since the 1960s. Born and raised in Halifax, she has a master's degree in social work from St. Francis Xavier University. She worked in Toronto and Calgary before moving back home to teach social work at the Nova Scotia Institute of Technology. Later, she switched to child welfare and for ten years was supervisor of Family Children's Services, a provincial government agency based in Halifax.

"And then I decided it was time to quit and for a couple of years I just enjoyed life and travelled a bit," says Keith across a long, cluttered table in her SSAV office, in rented space in a north Halifax warehouse.

In 1983, several women at Dalhousie University in Halifax received a $70,000 grant to start a program to help victims of sexual abuse. They asked Ann Keith to develop and run it. "I said, 'Okay, I'll do it for one year.'" Ten years later, she is still there.

The initial grant was seed money to start the centre, now funded by the province, the city, surrounding municipalities, and public donations. SSAV has a paid staff of seven, including two part-timers.

"The heart of this place is the volunteers," says Keith. "They're incredible." About sixty volunteers handle SSAV's crisis line; a dozen more are on the board of directors; and several others help out in the office.

"On the average we help about two hundred women a month," says Keith. "We can't offer long-term counselling because our volunteers would be burned out. If women who call in have been severely damaged, we refer them to other agencies or support groups. What we do is the emotional support. If a woman has been raped, for example, we go to the hospital with her, help her deal with the police, and go through the courts with her if it comes to that.

"We are concerned with sexual abuse and sexual violence. But if someone calls and says their husband or boyfriend is beating them up, then we try to get them the help they need."

Ann Keith has a vivid recollection of her first conversation and first meeting with Jane Hurshman sometime in early 1985. "There were only two of us working here at the time, and when the phone rang I answered it." She was greeted by a "very soft" woman's voice.

"My name is Jane Hurshman and Wendy told me to call you."

The names didn't mean anything to Keith.

"Is it all right if I come in to see you?" asked Jane.

"Okay, sure." There was a few seconds' silence.

"Well, maybe I better tell you who I really am. My name is Jane Stafford."

Once again, Keith didn't recognize the name. "I didn't know who she was, but I was certainly going to talk to her."

They arranged a meeting and Jane came over to the SSAV office. She explained that she had served time for killing Billy Stafford and that Wendy was Wendy Annand, her parole officer. "We just sort of talked," says Keith. "And I guess because it was a sexual assault centre, she decided to concentrate on the sexual abuse she had been subjected to.

"When she started talking about things that really bothered her, I'll never forget her eyes — they were humongous. She would almost dissociate herself. I remember thinking to myself, it was like looking into the pits of hell. What she was carrying around was incredible."

Keith's impression of Jane in that first meeting was that she was like a little girl crying out for help. "She had lost her self-worth and sense of who she was — her identity. From there we established a real comfortable, easy relationship and worked on trying to get her back. I remember one time telling her, 'I'll know you're getting better when your eyes start looking normal.'"

Jane became one of only two women with whom Ann Keith engaged in long-term counselling in her years at SSAV. It was unstructured and informal, with many sessions taking place over coffee or lunch.

"Now that I am seeing Ann and communicating on a one-to-one basis," Jane wrote at the time, "I am able to get objective feedback, and I like the feeling. I don't ever remember having a person that I trusted enough to confide in. As I think back, I wonder how long ago it was that I lost my ability to trust.

"Ann is very compassionate and easy to talk to. My therapy sessions are usually anywhere from two to four hours — but they are helping me a great deal."

Sometimes, however, Jane asked Keith to cancel her sessions. "I asked not to have any this month, as they leave me feeling very drained — and a bit on the depressed side," she wrote. "But all will end up well."

Keith says there were times "when I felt like I couldn't really help her, that it was getting over my head." The counselling stopped after five years, when Keith referred Jane to a local psychiatrist for more advanced help.

As with Wendy Annand, Ann Keith and Jane Hurshman became good friends and continued to see each other socially. On occasion, Jane also talked to battered women who called SSAV seeking support and she sometimes spoke out on behalf of SSAV at events such as the International Women's Day rally.

"We used to go to the movies once in a while and go out for dinner — as friends more than anything else," recalls Keith. "Jane had a great sense of humour and we had some good laughs together."

Jane was gradually fulfilling the goals she had set for herself. She was gainfully employed, she was receiving therapy, and she was helping other abused women. Her other priority, to reunite her family, also became a reality when she and Darren moved into an apartment on Cole Harbour Road, in Dartmouth. They were joined by her sons Jamie and Allen, from her first marriage. Jamie, thirteen, had been living with his father in the town of Milton, near Liverpool. Allen, twenty, had been living on his own.

Jane had also resolved the negative feelings she felt toward her parents, Maurice and Gladys Hurshman, who lived quietly on a wooded lot in the small community of Danesville, between Bridgewater and Liverpool.

The healing between them began after Jane killed Billy. She

wrote about it in her introduction to *Life With Billy*: "The first time my parents ever told me they loved me was when I was arrested and spent the weekend in jail in Halifax. When I came to court from the jail, my dad was there to take me home. He put his arms around me and held me. 'I love you, Janey,' he said. 'Come now, I'm taking you home.' It was while I was staying with them at that time that my mother first said the same three magic words, 'I love you.' I waited thirty-three years to hear my parents tell me that. It's terrible to think that I had to kill someone to get the love from my parents that I always wanted."

Jane drew closer to her parents, particularly her father, during her two-month incarceration. Maurice Hurshman usually drove to the school she was allowed to attend while serving her time and later to a hospital when her program shifted to on-the-job training. He always brought lunch, which they shared in the car as they chatted. Sometimes he brought along Darren, Jamie, or her mom, Gladys.

Although Jane felt closer to her parents than ever before, she was still feeling a lot of anger and hurt from earlier years of emotional abuse, particularly from her father. One of Jane's few childhood memories was of their house in Brooklyn, Nova Scotia, and how cold it was in the winter months. There was no bathroom and no running water, and Maurice Hurshman, who worked in a nearby sawmill, carried wood home on his back each night for heat. He had two children when he joined the Canadian Army at the outbreak of the Korean War and served two tours of duty in Korea before returning home permanently in 1952. Mona was born in April 1953 and Sandy ten months later.

Jane never forgot the day her father stopped physically abusing her mother. The family was living at a Canadian military base in Germany, in the early 1960s, when Jane came home from school and found her mother too ill to get out of bed. She was feverish and her bedclothes were blood-soaked.

Maurice Hurshman arrived home a few moments later and rushed his wife to the hospital. There was no telephone and Jane had no way of checking on her mother's condition. She put Mona and Sandy to bed and waited anxiously. Later, a car pulled up and she could hear her father's voice. She stayed in the bedroom with her sisters, worried that he might be with one of his drunken buddies.

Jane listened intently but could hear only her father's voice. It was then she realized he was praying, and she would never forget his words: "Dear God, let Gladie live, please, I don't know what I'd do without her. I love her and I'll never lay a hand on her again."

Gladys Hurshman almost died that night as a result of massive bleeding from a tubal pregnancy, but she recovered and Maurice was true to his word. The drinking, cursing, and arguing continued but he never struck his wife again.

Ann Keith remembers that Jane talked, during counselling sessions in 1987, about confronting her parents. "We talked about that for a long time," says Keith. "Jane never did anything without thinking about it first. I knew it was really important for her. I said, 'Okay, Jane, if you want to confront them, that's fine.'"

Jane drove down to Danesville and spoke first with her mother in the kitchen and then with her father.

"I took my father into the garage," she told Keith later. "I made sure something was wrong with the car, so he couldn't get out of there. I sat him down and talked to him and he cried."

From that day on, Jane felt an enduring closeness to her parents and she enjoyed visiting them on holidays and on her days off.

The quiet time Jane spent with her parents was particularly important to Maurice Hurshman because it allowed him to make up for the lost years, while his children were growing up, when he was an abusive heavy drinker.

"It was so hard for him," says Jane's sister Mona Donnelly. "I thought a lot about it, and you know, a person, to a degree, is a product of their environment. When he was eleven, he built a little addition on the side of the house. It wasn't much, but it was his spot and that's where he used to live. He was thirteen when he left home.

"The things that he went through as a child weren't very pleasant and sometimes people don't know the whole story as to why a person becomes what they become."

Mona says Maurice Hurshman worked from the time he was thirteen just to survive. He was married at the age of seventeen, a year older than Jane was when she married Milford Whynot.

"You have four children, you're in the service, and believe me, they don't discourage drinking — unfortunately for him," says Mona. "It's been thirteen years since he smoked or drank and certainly much longer than that since he hit my mother.

"I remember one time when I was at university and I'd come home to visit them, and he said how life could have been so different for everybody and how sorry he was for all the pain he had caused because of the drinking. He realized how much he'd missed and how much was lost.

"At least he made an attempt to change his life — and did change his life."

Ann Keith says Jane felt very good after she confronted her parents. "I believe if she hadn't confronted them, she never would have been able to go back down there."

Jane wrote around that time that her healing was far from complete and that she still had hurts and some wounds that would never heal, but life was improving for her.

"I was always so dominated — first by my father, then by my first husband, but mostly by Bill. There didn't seem to be any way that I could break away from it. Now I am finding I can talk about it, then walk away from it. I am not detached — I still hurt — but I am not controlled by it anymore.

"I cannot rewrite my past and I cannot forget, but I can get on with the rest of my life."

III

CARRIE

CARRIE RAFUSE FELT UNCOMFORTABLE the first time she met Jane Hurshman, in 1983. It was after the Crown won an appeal of the not-guilty verdict and Jane returned to Nova Scotia from Ontario to await a new trial. Both women were enrolled in a government-sponsored Job Readiness Training program in Bridgewater. It was there that Jane upgraded her education, completing Grade Twelve, enabling her to enroll in a nursing course.

Since 1988, Carrie Rafuse has been a crisis counsellor at Harbour House, a Bridgewater transition shelter for battered women. "The JRT course is supposed to help you get back into the work force," she says in an interview at the kitchen table in her Bridgewater home, where she lives with her two grown daughters.

Carrie is an outgoing, pleasant person with smiling eyes. She likes people and she couldn't understand the source of her negative feelings toward Jane when they first met. "I had a funny feeling about her. It was like she was looking through me and I thought, *I wonder why I don't like this woman.* I could sense something about her. She always talked to me, and seemed to like me, and I was nice to her, but there was something about her . . .

"Then one morning I had the radio on and was getting ready for school when I heard on the news — 'Jane Marie Stafford' and her second trial coming up. And all of a sudden — that's Jane! No wonder I'd been getting weird vibes. I realized then, she had a lot on her mind."

Jane did have a lot on her mind. In a radio interview three years later, she said the JRT course helped "build up some self-esteem and some confidence. That's when I started to realize that I was a human being, but I was still carrying all the guilt around and I felt like I wore a sign on my head that said, *You're a murderer.*"

The day Carrie Rafuse heard the radio report she told Jane about it at school. They talked for a while and their friendship grew from that day on. A short time later, Carrie, a Seventh-Day Adventist, invited Jane to attend a church meeting in Liverpool where a visiting preacher was speaking.

"She said she'd love to," recalls Carrie. "We had dinner first and after the church meeting we chatted and chatted, and that was it — we just hit it off."

Like Jane, Carrie was pregnant and married in her mid-teens. The marriage was an unhappy one and she and her husband separated in January 1975, three weeks after the birth of her second child. Carrie's husband, like Billy Stafford, was a scallop fisherman, and in 1976 he died in a storm at sea. That was in March, the same month, six years later, when Jane shot Billy.

"Jane could relate to me," said Carrie. "Maybe because Bill and my husband were both dead. We became very close friends. And between her first and second trials I'd go out to Bangs Falls where she was living and we often sat up talking and having tea until three or four in the morning."

One night, Carrie surprised a burglar in the trailer where she lived. He was wearing a mask and he screamed and charged at her, but she fended him off with a lamp and he ran out the door. "I think he was frightened and he just wanted to get out of there." Carrie told Jane she was scared and Jane offered to come down with Darren and stay with her for the weekend. "The first night I suddenly realized, here I am worried about a burglar and yet I'm sleeping beside someone who killed somebody. It took me two years to tell Jane about that, but we had a great laugh."

◆　◆　◆

Carrie Rafuse was in the Liverpool courtroom on February 14 — Valentine's Day — 1984, when Jane was sentenced to six months in prison after pleading guilty to manslaughter. Jane had packed a small bag and said her good-byes to her family the night before. She was ready to go to jail, but her main concern was the nursing exam she was scheduled to write the next day. She did well in school and her sentence included a provision allowing her to continue her education.

"After she was sentenced," recalls Carrie, "they took her into the back of the courtroom and she asked if I could come back to see her for a moment. Here she was going to jail for six months and all she was worried about was her books."

"Carrie, you've got to get me my damn books," said Jane. "I've got a test tomorrow."

"Okay, tell me where they are and I'll bring them over to the jail."

Jane arrived at the jail on a Tuesday. On Thursday she was permitted to drive to Bridgewater to attend classes and write her exam — a day late. She passed with high marks.

Jane quickly discouraged family and friends, including Carrie, from visiting her in prison. She found it too stressful.

"I wanted to visit her but it wasn't good at all," says Carrie. "It made her feel really bad. It was an awful place. So we decided to meet after school whenever we could. We'd have about ten minutes to talk. She loved Big Turk chocolate bars. She was addicted to them and I always took them to her.

Tears well in Carrie's eyes when she recalls a conversation she had with Jane about a year after the church service in Liverpool.

"That night in the church," said Jane, "I was looking at you and I decided, 'I want to be just like her — friendly, open, and nice. And she's got lots of friends and she knows where she's going.'"

Carrie was taken aback, and Jane's comments made her feel sad.

"You know, Jane," she said, "you don't have to be like anybody. Just be yourself — you're great."

Like Jane's other friends, Carrie witnessed her friend's self-esteem and self-confidence blossom after she was released from prison and began speaking out on behalf of other abused women.

"She had no identity before, and now, all of a sudden, she became this person," says Carrie.

NIGHT DEMON

Daytime innocence
Demon-filled nights
Deadly silence
Creeping,
    creeping
        slowly creeping
Nightmare coming,
        coming
Time to close my eyes
Drift away, disappear
Silent night, silent night
It's all right, all right
Crossed legs, stiff as a corpse,
separating
Demon, demon, you came back
Scissors
    straddle
        splits
TRAPPED
Silent night, silent night
It's all right, all right
Demon, demon, you came back
Fingers
    tongue
        snake
Slicing, slicing
Stabbing, stabbing
Burning, burning
A hole in my gut
Nightmare
    nightmare
FADE AWAY
Disappear in morning day
Frozen tears
Paralysing fears
Silent years

— *Angela Cupido, 1987*

ROAD TO
BRYONY

JANE HURSHMAN'S SUFFERING at the hands of Billy Stafford was not unusual in the nether world of spousal abuse, as the staff at any shelter for battered women could attest. And horror stories of domestic violence can be found on police reports in almost any North American city or town.

Jane felt a special kinship with the women caught in the same web of despair, degradation, and depravity that had entrapped her and driven her to kill Billy. In late November of 1986, shortly after her first visit to Bryony House, a Halifax shelter for battered women, she met a terrified woman who was to become one of her closest friends. (Pseudonyms are used in this account to protect the woman's identity and that of her children.)

Donna Smith grew up in a medium-sized Ontario city. Her father was abusive, and she was six when her mother left home after a brutal beating, never to return. Donna, her younger brother, and her older sister were left with their father.

"I know now that she didn't hate us," says Donna, now in her mid-thirties. "I used to blame her a lot for not taking us with her. But she couldn't have supported us, and if she had taken us, he would have found her. I don't know if she's alive or dead."

Donna's father turned to his daughters for sexual gratification. "He started with my older sister. He used to beat her and abuse her sexually. She became a runaway and left for good at the age of thirteen."

On Donna's tenth birthday, her father sent one of his male friends into her bedroom. "This guy raped me with my father out in the kitchen laughing," says Donna, anger in her voice. "All my life he said I owed him this and that because he could have sent us to Children's Aid when my mother left. He and his friends sexually abused me from age ten to seventeen."

One night, in 1977, Donna was waiting for a bus on a main downtown street when a man dragged her down an alley at knife-point and punched and kicked her before raping her. "People heard me screaming but nobody tried to help me." The rapist was eventually arrested when he attempted to attack another woman.

Every day for two weeks after the rape, Donna's father forced her to go with him to the scene of the attack. There, he verbally abused her, blaming her for the rape. Donna tried to kill herself, swallowing a deadly mix of pills. She was taken to hospital, where her stomach was pumped out. "I told them that if I was forced to go home, I'd do it again," she says. She stayed with friends for six months until her father found her and forced her to return home. His sexual assaults, however, had ceased.

It was at this point that Robert came into her life. He was nineteen years old and in the military. She found a good job at a local hospital where she worked for five years. She and Robert were inseparable and they were married in the summer of 1982. She was twenty-three and he was twenty-four. That fall they moved to military housing on a Canadian Forces base in Ontario.

Using words chillingly similar to those Jane Hurshman once used to describe her first months with Billy Stafford, Donna described Robert as "my knight in shining armour." He had rescued her from an abusive father just as Jane believed Billy saved her from a bleak, monotonous marriage to an alcoholic. "I was full of hope for a new and better life when I went off with Bill," Jane said. "He was my knight in shining armour. He was always telling me he loved me." Jane didn't learn until later that Billy had severely abused his first wife and five children and, later, a pregnant common-law spouse.

Robert, the oldest of four children, also had a dark, violent past and in his mid-teens was sent to a correctional centre after he had tried to kill his parents. "Everybody was terrified of him," says Donna. "But in those first five years I was with him, I never saw any of this."

The fairy-tale view of romance, coveted by Jane and Donna, proved illusory. For both, pregnancy triggered the end of their dream. Billy Stafford's verbal and emotional abuse toward Jane increased as her pregnancy progressed. The physical abuse came later, after Darren was born. Robert didn't wait that long. His first attack came when Donna was six months pregnant. "He had wanted me to bring him a chocolate bar, but he didn't tell me that and because I didn't read his mind he kicked me down the stairs when I came back from the store. I didn't say anything when I went to the hospital. I just told them I fell."

To those familiar with the dynamics of violence against women, the conduct of Billy and Robert wasn't surprising, given that 40 percent of spousal assaults occur during a first pregnancy.

Donna spent three days in the hospital after the assault. Like most first-time abusers, Robert offered a tearful apology and promised it would never happen again. His mea culpa and promise were hollow, the usual pattern for batterers. The abuse continued, escalating in frequency and severity.

Mary, Donna's first-born, was a breech birth, delivered by Caesarean section. On her first night home, Donna was exhausted and bleeding after two weeks in hospital. When Robert had to get up with the baby at 3 A.M. he called her, "That fucking little bitch." And when Donna tried to leave three months later, Robert threatened to kill Mary. (Billy Stafford had threatened to kill Jane's family one at a time if she ever left him.)

At five-foot-two and 110 pounds, Donna was no match for her husband, who was a shade under six feet and over two hundred pounds. And she was angry that the military police on the base did nothing to help her. "The first time I called them he told them, 'Get the fuck out. It's none of your goddamn business,' and they never came back after that. They were afraid of him. So I would end up in the hospital, covering up, lying."

When Mary was six months old, Robert tied her to her crib and threatened to sexually abuse her if Donna didn't agree to participate in degrading sexual acts with him. Donna, terrified for her daughter, went along and from then on bondage and beatings, with Donna as the victim, became routine. It was a pattern that paralleled the sexual abuse Jane Hurshman was subjected to at the hands of Billy Stafford.

"That's when I got addicted to Valium — to get through it," says Donna. "My doctor knew what was going on. He didn't report it or anything, just give me Valium."

Donna was four months pregnant with their second child when Robert was transferred to a Canadian Forces base in Nova Scotia in the spring of 1985. "I almost lost Bobby," says Donna. "I was in the hospital for two and a half months before I had him because Robert kicked me so hard."

One night, three weeks before the baby's due date, Robert arrived drunk at the hospital. "I'm going to make sure that fucking kid won't be born alive," he said, lashing out with a punch that left Donna with a black eye. She screamed and the nurses called security to remove him. The trauma caused Donna to go into labor that night. Bobby was born twenty-three months after Mary.

Donna now fit the classic mould of those trapped in the battered-wife syndrome. Her senses dulled by excessive use of tranquillizers, she was living a robotic existence, cowering in fear of the man she once loved. Indiscriminate beatings and sexual assaults had become commonplace. Her self-esteem was non-existent and her only motivation for day-to-day survival was to protect her children as best she could.

Robert, like Billy Stafford, was prone to fits of rage for no apparent reason. In this state, both men's faces would redden and their eyes would bulge wildly.

Robert kicked Donna so often she eventually required arthroscopic surgery on one of her knees. After the operation, he came home from an evening of drinking to find her sitting with her leg propped up on a table. "You bitch!" he sneered, raising his foot and stomping down on her knee with such force that it snapped. Donna fell to the floor screaming in agony and had to crawl to the telephone to call for an ambulance.

"At the hospital, I lied and told them that I fell," she says. Since that injury, she's had several operations on her knee and still has bone chips floating under her knee cap.

At one point an army social worker from the base's Family Support Services visited Donna. "He left crying," she says. "He handed me some money to get groceries and said he couldn't do anything."

Young Bobby had a chronic respiratory problem that, in November 1986, by chance led to their escape from the torture-chamber they called home. Jean (a pseudonym), a friend and neighbour who was aware that Donna and her children were being abused, accompanied her and the boy to the hospital. Bobby was admitted, and the two women went to a private office where a doctor began asking Donna routine questions.

"What does your husband do for a living?" he asked.

Jean jumped to her feet. "He beats her!" she exclaimed. "He beats her and he rapes her! Look at the marks on her arms and neck."

Donna and the children were kept at the hospital for a week. Social workers were brought in and she was given an ultimatum — either enter a battered wives' shelter or be forced to give up her children.

Donna wasn't about to give up her children and she reluctantly agreed to move into Bryony House, a Halifax shelter for battered women. Donna was fearful and uneasy when she and her children arrived at the transition house.

"The counsellors were excellent, but I didn't trust anybody and I wouldn't talk to them. I kept to myself. I was forced to be there but I was sure I'd be going back home. I believed I had no place else to go."

She was certain Robert would find her and come after her as her father had done years before. That fear was magnified when Robert began telephoning the next day. The staff refused to acknowledge Donna's presence to him.

The location of Bryony House, like other shelters and transition homes across North America, is supposed to be confidential, but within a day or two, Robert was parked across the street.

The police were aware of Robert's presence, but he was on public property and there was nothing they could do. There were no laws against stalking. Robert continued telephoning, asking first for Donna and then for Mary. "I know my kids are there," he would say, angrily.

Donna remained totally withdrawn. Her father had cursed her and cut her off from the rest of the family when she told him she was in a shelter. She seldom slept and spent most of her time on a couch in the living room at the shelter. She didn't realize it, but she was also suffering from Valium withdrawal. "Every doctor I went to prescribed it. At Bryony House they lock up all your drugs and give them to you only as prescribed on the bottle. They were giving me two or three a day, while I was used to fifteen or twenty a day. I was shaking and my nerves were shot. I never slept."

At the end of Donna's second week at the shelter, Jane Hurshman happened to drop in to see the place for the first time. She didn't see Donna on that visit, but the counsellors told Jane about her, and Jane left her phone number.

"I didn't know anything about her," says Donna. "I wasn't from Nova Scotia and I hadn't read *Life With Billy*. It took me about an hour to get up the courage to call. Jane told me she had been through an abusive situation somewhat like mine and maybe she could help me. She asked if we could possibly get together and I agreed. After I hung up they told me who she was and that she had killed her husband."

Jane returned to Bryony House the next day, and the two women went into a private room to talk. "It was amazing," says Donna. "I didn't have to say anything at first. She talked and it was as if she was reading my mind. It was the first time that anybody understood how I really felt.

"She wasn't judgemental. If I told other people about my life they would be shocked, or start crying, or feel sorry for me, or start saying something stupid like, 'If my husband ever hit me just once it would be the last time he ever hit me.' You just want to take them and shake them when they talk like that."

Jane was stylishly dressed, and Donna was impressed by her composure and self-confidence. "She just knew how to express herself and she made me feel so comfortable and at ease."

"You're worried that there's not enough protection — that

Bryony House isn't safe, aren't you?" asked Jane. Donna nodded.

"Don't worry," said Jane. "It will be okay. They didn't have safe houses when I was with Billy. At least none I knew about."

Jane talked about Billy and some of the abuse she had gone through. "See, I came out of it," she said. "You can do the same. You *do* have a chance."

"You don't even know me," said Donna.

"I have a feeling we're going to become really good friends," said Jane.

When the two women came out of the room, Donna was smiling. It was the first time counsellors and residents at Bryony House had seen her smile.

Despite the abuse that Donna had suffered, Robert had a legal right to see his children. A lawyer was arranged for Donna and she went to court to seek interim custody until a final hearing could be scheduled. Donna was terrified at the thought of being in the same courtroom as Robert.

"Do you think he'd bring a gun in with him?" asked her lawyer on the way to the hearing. His question deepened her panic.

"I just froze on the witness stand," says Donna. "I couldn't even talk. The judge said he'd never seen such fear in a woman." He awarded her interim custody of the children.

Robert always went to bed at night with a pistol on his bedside table, and his gun collection outdid that of Billy Stafford, who had kept seven rifles and shotguns on a rack in the house in Bangs Falls along with a belt full of shotgun shells and a full ammunition box under the bed. Robert had at least a dozen guns, including pistols, rifles, and shotguns. He also kept a large collection of knives.

With the custody hearing behind her, Donna was feeling much better, but shortly after, she was confronted by a new crisis. One of the two child-care workers at Bryony House came upon three-year-old Mary masturbating in a loft in the basement playroom. The child told the counsellor, "Daddy does that to me." Donna suffered an emotional breakdown when she was told about Mary.

"It was absolutely devastating because I thought I had protected her by doing everything he asked me to do," she says.

Because of Donna's emotional state, it was decided to put the children into temporary foster care. The thought of her baby daughter being sexually molested was unbearable, and Donna contemplated suicide. Bryony House counsellors found twelve bottles of extra-strength sleeping pills that she had hidden.

Jane was informed of Donna's condition and spent as much time with her as she could. *Life With Billy* had been released a few months before, and Jane was caught up in a flurry of promotion events and interviews.

"She had to go to Yarmouth to do a book signing and radio interviews," says Donna. "She got special permission from Bryony House for me to go with her."

The two women left Halifax in Jane's car before 8 A.M. They listened to music "and talked and talked and talked" on the 190-mile trip to Yarmouth, recalls Donna. "It was just great."

They were to stay overnight in a private home. "The location of the house was supposed to be a secret," says Donna. "But when we arrived the woman who lived there was frightened and told us a man had called and threatened Jane. He told her he was going to do to Jane what Jane had done to Billy. I got really scared. Nobody could figure out how he knew we would be staying there."

An RCMP officer was assigned to stay overnight in the house with the women. "He and Jane started joking around," says Donna. "He said maybe Jane should be protecting us because she probably had better aim than him. They both laughed. At first I couldn't believe they would joke about something like that, but then I realized it made us feel at ease."

The Mountie stayed on the main floor while the women slept upstairs. There were only two bedrooms, and Jane and Donna had to share a bed. Before they went to sleep Jane told the story about staying with her friend Carrie Rafuse, who had been worried about a burglar but who suddenly realized she was sleeping in the same bed as a murderer.

"We laughed about that," says Donna, "but then it made me think — I'm in the same bed as a murderer too."

During their stay, a newspaper reporter interviewed Jane and the women visited Juniper House, a Yarmouth shelter for battered women. At the shelter, Donna was asked to introduce herself and

Jane gave a short address to the staff and residents.

The round-the-clock police protection continued and there were two officers with them when they went to a bookstore at a small downtown shopping centre.

"They set up two white wicker chairs for us and there were flowers on each side," says Donna. "People must have wondered who I was."

She says there was a steady line-up and Jane signed books for two or three hours. "It was non-stop. It was mostly women, but there were some men. Most of them wished her well."

From the bookstore, Jane went to a local television station for an interview.

On the drive back to Halifax, Donna thought about the anonymous threat. It would not be the last time she heard about Jane's life being threatened.

· V ·
SPEAKING
OUT

THE MEDIA ATTENTION Jane Hurshman was subjected to during and after her trial, and before the publication of *Life With Billy* in the summer of 1986, was overwhelming and distressful for a person who had lived such an isolated, tortured existence in her years with Billy Stafford.

In a thirteen-page self-analysis, written in 1985, three years after his death, she wrestled with her feelings about the media, her privacy, and what she wanted out of life. Many of the themes would surface later in her public speeches.

"In the days, weeks and months following Bill's death, the world felt different," she wrote. "I was guilty! The world looked and sounded uglier and more cruel than it was before. The reporters and others wanting stories — demanding. I felt invaded, harassed and used. Why was anyone interested? Why did they care? Why didn't they leave me alone? I was bewildered and frightened.

"An ache began in my chest — and it didn't go away. I had never sought the limelight. My past is always present. Bill's life was as violent as his death. Mine had been one tragedy after another. I've lived a life of pain that has left many scars. Often I still cry within and a knot forms in my throat."

The public exposure took a physical as well as an emotional toll.

"At times," wrote Jane, "I couldn't believe it was really me all of this was happening to. I wasn't me anymore. I was somebody I didn't know, somebody lost and scared; somebody whose life

26

seemed to have no focus. I just couldn't believe it. I felt like I was falling apart right before everyone's eyes and nobody noticed.

"I was unable to sleep and barely able to eat. I was still frightened and scared. I felt cut off from everyone — the outside world, my family, myself. The only thing that had changed was that Bill was dead.

"When I was told that Bill was dead, I was in my own world. I heard no noise — the world was soundless. I felt like I was floating, my head somewhere near the ceiling. No turning back. I kept going, fighting to hold on to the rational me, trying to let everything sink in. Bill *was* really dead. Maybe now there would be peace. I couldn't cry. I don't know if I wanted to, but I couldn't.

"When Bill died, I thought it would be over. It wasn't over — it's still not over. It keeps coming back at me. I am a private person. I need my privacy. It was very rough and still is."

In the document, it becomes obvious that Jane Hurshman's desire for privacy was in conflict with her determination to help other battered women, but it was a problem she was working through.

"Success has a new meaning to me," she wrote. "Personal accomplishment, doing well in school or business, used to be important to me. It's not anymore. Making a positive difference in the lives of other people is now the way I define accomplishment. That's what makes me go."

Some of Jane's friends and family were opposed to her collaboration on a book about her life. She addressed those concerns in the document. "I have told them, to me, it is necessary. And hopefully, some day, they will understand why. I used to be so dominated by Bill, there was no way I could break away from it. Now I can talk about him and walk away from it. I am not detached, but I'm not controlled by it anymore."

When Jane began to speak out against family violence, she and others were surprised at how good she was. Her voice didn't waver and she spoke with a forceful passion that held her audience.

It was her parole officer, Wendy Annand, who encouraged her to speak out, and her first address was to a Criminal Justice Workshop, in Lunenburg County in February 1985. Jane was on a victims' panel and Annand was the moderator.

"There were about seventy-five people there," says Annand, "and a lot of them were very impressed with Jane. There were a lot of teary eyes. She was nervous at first, but once she got into it she was just fine."

It was particularly emotional when Jane talked about the scars she and her sons, particularly Darren, were left with after the brutal years with Billy Stafford.

"Not too long ago," she said, "Darren, who was then seven, came into the house and said something sassy to me. Without thinking, I turned and slapped him. With eyes as big as saucers, he looked at me and said, 'Mom, don't you think I've had enough of that?' I reached out and I hugged him and I said, 'I'm sorry, Babe, I'm sorry.' So you see, that one slap brought back years of painful memories — memories that are his for life."

Jane told the workshop that she believed Billy was jealous of his son. "Taking Darren to the sitter and me going to work was our only refuge from this monster. From the time Darren began walking at a year old he was not allowed to cry. As Bill said, 'You're a man now — men don't cry.' If Darren cried, he was beaten. He was beaten until he lay there and didn't make a sound.

"Once Bill gave him a lit cigarette and told him to puff on it. After Darren did he was beaten with a broom handle until he was black and blue from his head to his feet — and still not allowed to cry.

"There were times when Bill came in and picked him up by the hair and held a knife to this throat — or picked him up by the feet and held a fully loaded gun to his head and told him, 'This is just a warning — look out if you do anything wrong.' What kind of memories does that child have?"

Jane did not have kind words for psychiatrists.

"Darren and I saw a psychiatrist for two years," she said, "and for me, I don't think it helped. It was like sitting and talking to a brick wall. They're cold; there is no emotion. Sometimes you get a *yes*, sometimes a *no*, or maybe just a grunt. There was no feedback. I needed somebody to respond to me. I was guilty, I carried that guilt for two years before I even started to get any answers."

Billy Stafford had flouted the law and bullied and beat friends, family, neighbours, and others, always managing to get away with it, said Jane, explaining why she never reported his abuse to the police. "Once I purposely attended a court hearing in Bridgewater for a guy who beat his wife and put her in the hospital. He got a $200 fine and a peace bond against him. Seeing that, I knew I would definitely not ever try to report Stafford because to him that would be the same as a pat on the back."

Jane described her state of mind when she fired the shot that killed Billy Stafford. "At that point there was no past, no present, no future — only the moment. I just stuck the gun in the window and pulled the trigger.

"I can look back on it all now, three years later, and I can say I'm sorry it ended the way it did, because no one has the right to take another person's life, no matter what, but I will *never* be sorry that Stafford is dead."

◆ ◆ ◆

With the publication if *Life With Billy* in 1986, Jane Hurshman became as much a celebrity as she was an activist against domestic violence. She appeared on CBC's "The Journal," "Front Page Challenge," and on the national radio program "Morningside." She also did dozens of interviews with television, radio, and print media and was in demand as a speaker.

Jane soon discovered that the people she felt most comfortable speaking to were battered women, and her favourite venues were the shelters that offered them refuge.

"It is therapeutic for me to be with others who have suffered what I suffered," she once wrote. "When I'm with them, I don't feel like a freak anymore. We don't shock each other. We don't get embarrassed. We don't feel set apart. We feel safe enough to share, to cry, to laugh. We don't just sit around airing our grief. We also reaffirm life. We say that we are ready to live again and what we want is to find out how."

In a speech at Hestia House, a shelter for battered women in Saint John, New Brunswick, Jane said she had to learn to communicate "in order to get past my fears, my hurts, my injuries, and my insecurities."

"I am a survivor," she announced proudly. "I want all of you to be aware that you have a trap door that is on hinges, and if you choose to draw that door shut, then no one can get inside. I am here to open those doors and to allow other women in violent situations to realize that they are not alone.

"It is wrong to ignore battering, thinking it will go away. That does not work. If you ignore it, it continues to spread like a cancer.

"By relating my feelings I hope to help other battered women realize they are victims and they are not alone and they don't have to blame themselves. It was a long time after Stafford's death before I began to realize I was a victim, and even longer to understand that I was not to blame, nor did I have to carry the guilt for his actions.

"I knew nothing of transition houses or support groups. I felt totally isolated and trusted no one. In my community, everyone knew I was being abused, yet no one acknowledged the fact. No one spoke about it out loud.

"Battering isn't the taboo — talking about it is. And it can only continue if we keep silent. I was born in a period when people did not reveal their personal problems, everything was kept secret, as though if you spoke out about it, then it would be a negative reflection on you and the family.

"We all keep up appearances and tell our social lies — that's deep-rooted, early conditioning. As time goes on, and the abuse continues, bitterness piles up and emotions turn up hate. *You* feel like an outcast. *You* feel like the criminal.

"In my opinion, I was a hostage in my own home, living with the threat that others than myself would be killed unless I obeyed my captor. Stafford was my captor and he used guns, knives, and fists to control my every move, to isolate me, to degrade me, and to keep me totally captive and eventually destroy me.

"If society would accept domestic violence for what it is — a crime — then I am sure my life would have turned out differently. Instead, it is accepted behaviour."

The one question that Jane was most often asked was why she stayed all that time with Billy Stafford. Other severely battered women knew the answer, but even when she spoke in shelters such as Hestia House she felt compelled to repeat it.

"The first and foremost reason women stay is fear," she said. "I lived in a world where fear was my reality. It was fear that immobilized me and ruled my every thought and decision. My guts and my mind were so full of fear that I was incapable of feeling anything else. I want you to understand that in the mind of anyone who has been severely beaten, fear blots out all reasoning.

"Also, my fear of not being believed kept me in my situation. My own personal story is shocking and unbelievable, yet it's so very, very true.

"When you are a victim, each day of existence takes its toll. I became an empty shell. I was like a terminally ill patient waiting for death, yet hoping for a magic cure, always thinking as long as I stayed alive, there might be a slight chance of survival for my sons and myself.

"Women in violent situations are in a state of helplessness which incapacitates them. You're in total isolation. I felt — as I know other battered women feel — that I was the only person in the world living like this.

"Battered women need to know that they are the victims and they are not the cause of the abuse, nor do they have to stay and put up with it. Domestic violence is not a sickness, nor a symptom of a problematic marriage — it is a crime."

Jane warned the women that healing takes time and that some scars would never disappear.

"I still have my down times and not so long ago while feeling down I took a drive. During my drive, I saw a farmer and his horse ploughing up his field. Most people looking at this scene would have thought, *My, what a peaceful setting.* But when I looked at it, I saw my life in front of me, I saw that the horse had blinders on and the purpose of blinders was to ensure that the horse moved straight ahead without seeing what was happening around him. As I watched I realized that my whole life had been lived with blinders on. I had been able to move in only one direction, because someone else had always been in control and made my decisions for me.

"Now, for the first time, I do not have blinders on. I am in control of my life. I can make my own decisions. I do have a choice and I want all of you to take your blinders off and open that trap door and give all of us victims the right to have a choice. Help us to have a life without violence.

"I know that by my reaching out and trying to help other victims, I am also helping myself heal. My emotional scars are very deep. Eventually, with time, my feelings of fear and anger and pow erlessness have lessened and a sense of purpose has replaced them."

Society's role in the healing process, Jane said, must be to provide safe haven and solid, timely support when battered women decide to break from an abusive mate.

"For somebody abused over a long period of time, it's usually a spur-of-the-moment decision to leave," she said, "and they need the help right then and there — not two hours from now, not tomorrow, not next week. When they make that decision they are ready to go, they've made up their mind, they need the help from the outside from that point on."

That help and support, she said, must extend to the legal system. "A courtroom is a very cold, intimidating place, it is scary and its people — the judges and lawyers and the Crown — are very dominating and powerful. Victims need courtroom support."

In a speech to Bryony House residents and staff in late 1986, Jane expanded on the theme of why battered women stay in abusive situations. "Another reason women stay is because of shame — you feel like an outcast. And others stay because they want to make the marriage work and they hope things can improve."

Fear of the unknown was also a factor, she said. "Being on your own is scary, and when choosing between two evils, you usually choose the devil you know, not the one you don't know.

"Others stay because they don't have the money or the means to leave, and repeated beatings are like electric shocks, they take away your ability to respond to any form of stimuli or to think clearly.

"There are a lot more Janes out there — too many. When I pulled that trigger, it was too late for me to turn back, but it will never be too late for me to reach out and help others."

In a 1987 radio interview Jane was asked if witnessing her father abuse her mother had affected her later in her life.

"It was a major factor," replied Jane. "Girls seeing that in a home generally become passive and submissive, and that's exactly what I was, with the thought in the back of my head that, you know, someday this might get better. In the meantime you just sort of put up with it and live with it. It's what my mother did. She put up with it and lived with it and she said that someday things would get better. Well for her they did. In my case and in most cases, it never does, it just goes from bad to worse.

"You're conditioned to be a victim, vulnerable to this sort of thing. On the male side, it's a learned behaviour also, except the male usually comes out the aggressor and the female, passive and submissive."

Over and over, in her interviews and speeches, Jane urged women not to be "silent screamers behind closed doors. You're worthy of being heard." She urged women to leave the first time they are assaulted. "If it's a just-starting situation, pack your bag and leave — get out."

◆ ◆ ◆

In a radio interview with Kelly Ryan of *Maritime* magazine after *Life With Billy* was published, Jane admitted that collaborating on the book had been very difficult for her.

"I had to go back into the situation and relive everything. There were times when I didn't think I was going to get through it at all. Until I got the book in my hands about two weeks ago when the courier delivered it, I'd never seen it. I was just so overwhelmed when I held it in my hands. And I opened it and I read it through from cover to finish and I just closed it up and I was still looking at it and I thought, *It's really over — it's really over — it's somebody I used to know*, and it was such a nice, nice feeling. In the end, the heartaches I went through were worth it — it was the best therapy I could have had."

Carrie Rafuse noticed a change in Jane about the time she began collaborating on the book. And after it was published, she glimpsed, for the first time, her friend's troubling dark side. "I know she was pleased with the book. But after it was finished she told me she didn't want to live."

"I feel like a kid on Christmas Eve," said Jane. "You're all excited and waiting. But after the gifts are opened and dinner is over, there's a let-down. That's how I feel."

It would not be the last time Jane told Carrie she didn't want to live.

ROMANCE

JANE HURSHMAN WORRIED that after the physical and sexual abuse she had suffered, a normal relationship with a man might be impossible.

"The abuse was very humiliating and disgusting," she wrote to a friend. "I felt very used and degraded in the worst possible way. Those are memories that I will have to carry the rest of my life. I have been sexually abused, hurt, and raped, and I hate men. I doubt if I will ever again trust any man enough to have a physical or sexual relationship."

That trust eroded further when Jane learned that a prison inmate who had written and telephoned her regularly between her trials had misled her about the details of his crime. He was serving life for a double killing in Nova Scotia, in 1975.

"She told me how she was getting letters and flowers and it was exciting for her," says Carrie Rafuse. She says the inmate — nicknamed Mac — glossed over his crime, telling Jane that the murders "were accidental and he was just a kid at the time."

Jane was upset when she learned the truth, but the legal system had already put an end to the relationship, as she outlined in a September 1984 letter to Annette Bushen, one of her former nursing course classmates.

"I haven't been in contact with him since I got out of jail," she wrote. "One of the stipulations of my release is that I have no contact with any cons or ex-cons as long as I was on parole or probation. Well my parole ended on August 14th, but my probation doesn't end until August 1986.

"So I wrote Mac back in April and told him I couldn't write or have any contact with him anymore, and I haven't. I think that was one of the hardest things I ever had to do. He wrote me back one last time and wished me all the best. So that is the story of the lady and the con."

Jane could have contacted Mac after August 1986, but when she learned the murders were particularly cold-blooded and not, as he intimated, the result of an impulsive act born of panic, she wanted nothing to do with him.

"As soon as she learned what he was really like — boom — that was it," says Carrie. "She was really shocked when she found out."

The letter to Annette Bushen was written from Ontario, where Jane was staying with one of her sisters. In it she also said she was bored and homesick, even though she had found work two weeks previously.

"I got myself a steady job and I started on the 10th," she wrote. "I work permanent nights at an old folks home. It works out with Darren, as I am home in time to get him up and off to school. I sleep all day and have the evenings with him and then he is well in bed before I got to work — so he doesn't even realize I'm even gone."

Jane told her friend that Darren had no kids his own age to play with and that she had been enquiring about a nursing job in the Halifax area. She also talked about a male friend from Bangs Falls whom she had been dating between her trials. He had been calling and writing to her in Ontario.

"I miss him and I want to be with him," said Jane. "Yet I get scared when I think of getting seriously involved with a man. It was all right when I was seeing him before because I didn't think there was any future for us."

Within a month of writing that letter, Jane was offered a job at the Halifax County Regional Rehabilitation Centre, in Cole Harbour, and she and Darren returned to Nova Scotia. Annette Bushen, who had been hired by the centre three months earlier, says Jane never once talked about the man she had been dating in Bangs Falls. "It seems when Jane got close to any male person, she got scared, and you can't blame her."

But soon after Jane started working at the rehab centre, she met fellow-worker Ken Ackles, an orderly, who was immediately attracted to her. Jane was living in her apartment on Cole Harbour Road when Ackles took a job as superintendent of a low-rise apartment complex on nearby Merricmac Drive. He invited Jane to move in with him, and she accepted. Allen Whynot, her oldest son, decided to get his own apartment with friends in Halifax, but Darren and Jamie went with their mother.

"Ken was quite a bit older than Jane," says Carrie Rafuse. "But he was pleasant and very kind to her."

In a letter to a friend, Jane described Ackles as "a really nice guy. He is older (55), but we have been seeing quite a bit of each other. We get along well and I am comfortable with him."

Seven months later, in August 1985, Jane wrote to the same friend: "For me there are only two things that are permanent — my parents and my sons. Other than that, anything can change. I like Ken very much and I respect him, but I don't honestly know if I could say I love him."

Five weeks later she wrote: "I do not want anyone to feel that they need me, and Ken does give me that feeling. His is more a need to possess and that bothers me. I have told him, yet he keeps on. I think that maybe what I am after is a form of companionship. Whatever, each event in our life is a learning experience and as long as we learn and grow, it is well worth it. I think too, that perhaps love isn't the big deal that it is cracked up to be."

Allen said Ken Ackles "really loved Mom. But she didn't feel ready or he was a lot older, I don't know what it was."

Eventually, Jane moved into her own apartment in the same building and she and Ackles stopped dating.

Carrie Rafuse believes Jane found Ken "too smothering" at a time when she needed space. "He was all over her. He would say, 'If you need a car, let me buy you one,' or, 'Let me buy you a ring.' That just wasn't Jane. She wasn't impressed with that stuff. I think it was too mushy-mushy for her. She liked Ken, but he wasn't really significant in her life."

About a year after Jane left Ken, she was devastated to learn that he died suddenly while in hospital for an operation.

◆ ◆ ◆

Jane had a childhood friend, Valery Cromwell, whom she met in 1957 at Camp Gagetown, New Brunswick, when the army transferred their fathers there. Both girls were nine at the time and they became inseparable. Jane considered Valery's home an oasis because, unlike her own home and those of many of the military families around them, there was no excessive drinking, arguing, or violence.

Both families were eventually posted to West Germany and, in 1964, to Winnipeg. In early 1965 Jane moved to the Maritimes to live with her grandparents. It was there she became pregnant at sixteen and married Milford "Milfie" Whynot, her first husband.

Valery, who now lives in Toronto, said that in the years after Jane left Winnipeg she visited her in Nova Scotia "from time to time, until 1976 when she was breaking up with Milfie. I met Billy that year but I only saw him for a few minutes and I didn't really have an opinion of him, except that he was a big man."

After that, Valery lost contact with Jane. Six years later, in 1982, she read about Billy Stafford's death. "I was reading the paper and I said, *I know this person*, and I phoned home right away and I found Jane's mother and she gave me her number. Then I went home and saw her. We were really happy to see each other, but she didn't say a lot about Billy's death."

Jane was still living with Ken Ackles when Valery came to visit her in 1984. "He was much older than Jane. I think he was more of a father figure to her." When Valery returned for a visit the next year, Jane had been on her own for several months.

Valery's family was originally from Weymouth, Nova Scotia, on the Bay of Fundy side of the province. One of the cousins she grew up with, James Tynes, was living in the Halifax area when she came to visit Jane in 1985.

"Valery called me and I went out to see her at Jane's place on Merricmac," recalls Tynes, a heavy-equipment operator from Lawrencetown, a few miles from Dartmouth. He was a father of four, separated from his wife in 1978 and divorced in 1981.

"Now don't you be a stranger when Valery goes back to

Toronto," Jane said as he was leaving after their first meeting. After Valery returned to Toronto, Jane called Tynes.

"She said she had a couple of tickets to the hockey game and she asked me to go with her," he says. "We went to the game and after that we started dating." It was a relationship that would last, off and on, for more than four years. He moved in with Jane and Darren at the Merricmac apartment and later to a rented townhouse on nearby Arklow Drive.

"Jane was a beautiful person with a great sense of humour," says Tynes. "We didn't do a whole lot because she was working nights. Once in a while we'd go down and visit her parents. Mostly, though, we liked going for walks in the woods. She loved the woods. She knew a lot about animals. She studied them and she told me a lot about their habits."

When they had quiet time together, Tynes says he and Jane would often "just get a bottle of wine, listen to music, and carry on. We did a lot of that. We would talk for hours about real deep things."

Jane's relationship with Tynes was deeper and more romantic than her relationship with Ken Ackles and she was feeling good about herself. She was even able to kick her long-time smoking habit on New Year's Day 1986. "I was then smoking at least two large packs a day," Jane said in a letter. "I asked Darren what he wanted for Christmas and he looked at me with his big brown eyes and said, 'Mom, the best thing you can give me is to quit smoking. If you keep smoking you'll die and I want you to be my mommy forever.' So you see, that's what it took to break my smoking habit."

Tynes says he and Jane never argued, but the major problem in their relationship was that "she never really trusted that I loved her. She wouldn't confide in me. I would leave for a while and then we'd get back together again and laugh about how crazy it was. But I felt there was so much I didn't know about her."

Carrie Rafuse says she felt uncomfortable around James Tynes. "I didn't know him that well, but he just didn't seem very warm. I know that Jane did tell me that he felt she wasn't sharing everything with him and that she wasn't close enough to him. Maybe he resented me because I was close to her and she wouldn't let him get close to her. Or maybe I just misunderstood him. Other friends of Jane have told me he was a really nice guy."

In addition to Jane's secretiveness, Tynes was troubled by the number of speeches she was making. "I didn't want her to do anymore of those talks. I felt it brought back too many memories. About a week before every talk, she would break out with a cold sore — from stress. I asked her not to do it anymore. She did stop for a while, but people kept calling and she got back into it.

"She was doing a whole lot more than I knew about. I told her I felt almost like an outsider. I wanted us to be best friends. I wanted her to be able to come and talk to me about anything — any problem."

Tynes and Jane separated for good in early 1990. "After we broke up, she sent me letters, made me music tapes, and left cards and notes on my door. She said at different times she wanted us to get back together, but I felt it probably wouldn't work." He worried that she was helping other battered women to heal but not taking the time necessary to heal herself.

Tynes's view was shared by Victoria Jones, a nurse who retired from the rehabilitation centre and went to live with Jane in January of 1989. The two women had become friends at the rehab centre and Jane was sad to see her retire at the age of sixty-two and move to Montreal to live with one of her two sons.

"I figured I was going to Montreal to live for good but it didn't work out," says Jones. "Jane and I kept in touch while I was there and I phoned her one day and she said, 'Why don't you come and stay with me?' So I did."

Like Tynes, she urged Jane to quit speaking out because it was making her relive her life with Billy over and over. "My husband was an alcoholic who usually drank until he passed out and was nasty and hateful when he was sober," Jones told Jane. "After he choked on his own vomit and died, people said I should go to Al-Anon because the scars remain for the family and blah, blah, blah . . . . I says no, my problem is dead and buried now and that's where it's going to stay. I mean, what's the good of resurrecting all the misery?"

Jones says she wanted Jane to adopt a lower profile because so many people were hounding her, even total strangers. One of them, an abused woman who lived nearby, came to Jane's door for help. After the woman left, Jones told Jane, "You had to cope with what happened to you, let them cope with what's happening to them. They know there's shelters for women to go to now — so let them go."

There were periods when Jane didn't want to speak to anyone, and Jones would tell callers Jane was out. "I saw that a lot of them didn't get to her. But a lot of them did."

FRIEND

I have a friend who is a pen pal
she's a beautiful, special gal
her name is Jane
and she helps me get through the pain

She understands and cares how I feel
and this, I know, helps me to heal
there are but few who understand me
but the real person inside she sees

I don't have to hide
with Jane on my side
sometimes I still cry
but I no longer live a lie

— "Sara", 1991

VII
• • •
FRIENDS
IN NEED

JANE HURSHMAN AND VALERY CROMWELL celebrated the 1987 New Year in Bermuda. It was a trip they had planned for more than two years. "It was to celebrate my freedom — to mark the beginning of a new year and a new life for Jane Hurshman," said Jane.

Before they left, she visited Donna Smith, who had been admitted to the detoxification centre at the Nova Scotia Hospital, a psychiatric care facility in Dartmouth.

Jane was worried about her friend, and while she was in Bermuda James Tynes visited Donna regularly at the detox centre. It took about two weeks for Donna to break her Valium addiction. She was back in Bryony House shortly after Jane returned from her vacation.

In late January 1987, the transition house placed Donna and her children in its Second Stage program, which provided her with an apartment in a secure building in Dartmouth. The building included six apartments with heavy-duty locks, and police responded promptly to any calls for help.

Robert continued to stalk and harass Donna, and she was also embroiled in divorce and visitation-rights court proceedings with him, while simultaneously seeking treatment for her daughter.

"I had fifteen different people telling me what I could or could not do," she says. "There were therapists, Children's Aid people, doctors, lawyers, counsellors . . . I kept saying, 'Leave me alone, I can't take it anymore.'"

One day in February, Donna was to drop Mary and Bobby off at a supermarket where their father would pick them up for a two-hour visit, from 6 to 8 P.M. She always had someone accompany her when she was meeting Robert, but on this day, no one was available. The experience traumatized her.

"I shouldn't have taken the kids over by myself," she says. "I don't even remember coming home."

When she returned to her basement apartment, Donna locked the door and swallowed eighty sleeping pills. "I don't remember taking anything. I think I must have dissociated. I was told later that my family doctor called and she could tell something was strange. She must have called Jane because I remember talking on the phone and Jane saying, 'Don't go anywhere.'"

Jane rushed over to Donna's apartment with James Tynes. "I had to break down her door to get in there," he says. They found Donna unconscious. When Jane took Donna's pulse, she realized there was no time to call an ambulance. They carried her to their car and rushed her to Dartmouth General Hospital.

"Jane stayed with me the whole night," says Donna. "I remember seeing my doctor there. I guess I became terrified of her and the only person I would listen to was Jane. All I remember is Jane talking to me while they tried to pump my stomach out."

"Why did you stop me?" she asked Jane.

"I care about you and I don't want you dying on me," Jane replied.

By the summer of 1988, Donna and her children had their own apartment, not associated with Bryony House. Jane had grown close to the children and did what she could to help.

"My kids grew up with Jane," says Donna. "Mary had a lot of temper tantrums and she took one when we were over at Jane's one day. I'll never forget it. Jane held her for over an hour until she calmed down. If you didn't hold her, she would go right out of it and hurt herself or others. She has attacked babysitters, teachers, and other children.

"That day at Jane's, Mary was being held and she was ripping at the oilcloth table cover with her teeth. She was spitting and trying to kick out — it was pure, pure anger. But Jane just held her and rocked her in her arms until she finally calmed down. I explained to Mary that Jane loved her and that's why she was holding her — so she wouldn't hurt herself." The frequency and intensity of Mary's rages gradually diminished.

"The kids just loved Jane," says Donna. "And we saw a lot of her."

Donna's divorce from her husband became final in March of 1990. Two months later she learned that Bobby too had been sexually abused by his father. Despite the allegations of abuse, Robert forced another court hearing as he sought access to the children. Donna feared an unsympathetic judge would grant further visiting rights.

That fear, coupled with Robert's propensity for violence, convinced Jane that Donna and her children should go underground. An underground network for women and children seeking to escape their abusers does exist in Canada, but it is secret and seldom acknowledged. There are no figures on how many women and children are in hiding within the network, but the number is very small.

It is difficult to gain access to the underground network because most mainstream women's shelters are not involved in it. Jane knew of the existence of the network and, because of her connections, she easily paved the way for Donna and her children to go into hiding.

Initially, Donna cooperated, but after getting rid of her apartment and most of her furniture, she changed her mind. "What they didn't tell me is you lose all your identity when you go underground. They cut and dyed my hair, changed my name, and gave me sunglasses." The children's looks were also altered and their names were changed.

"The kids would have had no birth certificates and we would have to move from one safe house to another for at least a year," says Donna. "I wouldn't be able to work, and the children wouldn't be in school. And I had to worry about Bobby's chronic respiratory problem. If I ever had to take him to a hospital, we'd get caught right away."

She and the children spent several days in hiding on the South Shore as they made their preparations. They were to take a train to Calgary. "The tickets were bought for me," says Donna. "They were in my hand, but I decided not to go. I decided I was going to stay and fight — I'd had it."

Counsellors preparing Donna and her children to go underground understood when she changed her mind, but Jane was angry. "I called Jane to tell her, and she was very, very upset with me. She couldn't see why I changed my mind. She thought somebody had influenced me and that I didn't have a mind of my own. The others couldn't believe it when I told them Jane was really, really mad. I can understand it. She did a lot of the preparation, and then to see me back out . . ."

Donna and the children returned to Dartmouth the day before the court hearing. Despite evidence of sexual abuse, the family court judge allowed Robert supervised access to the children. Donna was stunned by his verdict. "When I heard that, I wished to God I had gone to Calgary," she says.

Donna did not hear from Jane for a month, and Jane would not return her phone calls. "Then one day," says Donna, "Jane walked in out of the blue. She said 'I'm back' and gave me a great big hug."

Their friendship endured, and when Donna and a friend started a crisis line to help other battered women, Jane was one of the first to volunteer her time to the project.

◆ ◆ ◆

James Tynes was still living with Jane when she offered to help out with Donna's crisis line. He was not pleased. "They started this hotline to help other women, but they needed help themselves," he says.

Jane's friend from work, Annette Bushen, says Jane tried to recruit her, but she turned her down. "I said, 'Jane, I'm not strong enough.' I couldn't listen to stories of abuse over and over and over again. I don't know how she could do it. Every time she talked to someone, her own memories had to flash back."

Tynes says Jane told some of her friends that listening to the stories of abuse "was almost like living with Billy again."

Jane did cut back on her speaking schedule, but an event in 1989 had a profound effect on her, reversing that trend. That event was the shooting of fourteen women — all students of the Ecole Polytechnique at the University of Montreal — by Marc Lepine, on

December 6. Lepine went on the deadly rampage to express his hatred for women, and then took his own life.

Jane wept uncontrollably when she heard the reports of the massacre. "She would be driving along and suddenly burst into tears," says one friend.

"She really got into it after those women in Quebec got killed," says Tynes. "That really bothered her. I was still with her at the time but we broke up shortly after."

(The federal government has since declared December 6 a National Day of Remembrance and Action on Violence Against Women, and most provincial and municipal governments have followed suit.)

On the second anniversary of the massacre, Jane gave a stirring speech in which she attacked Queens County Council for initially refusing to recognize the tragedy by lowering the municipal flag to half-mast. The small community of Bangs Falls, where she had lived with Billy Stafford, is in Queens County.

Prior to reversing its stand, three days before the anniversary, the council said it was concerned about singling out one sector of society for special attention.

"I am a very real victim of domestic violence, and I come from Queens County," Jane told a gathering of two hundred in Halifax. "Queens County Councillor Charlie Cushion introduced the motion that the municipality not honour the day because, as he said, 'Once you start these things with one group, it's going to escalate and sooner or later they're all going to be coming to you for help with this or that.'" Jane said that attitude did nothing to discourage abuse and demonstrated how much work was yet to be done to educate the public about violence against women.

It wasn't the first time Jane had taken on Queens County Council. At a meeting in August of 1985, it voted against a $6,400 grant for a proposed transition house. One male councillor stated that such facilities become vacation spots for some women and entice them away from their homes and families. Another councillor, also male, said nowadays women bring on their own troubles and what some of them need "is a good kick in the backside."

Jane, in a letter published in the local newspaper, *The Advance*, countered with a reasoned, no-holds-barred response, deploring the comments of the two councillors. A month later the vote was reversed. One of the councillors retired from politics and the other was defeated in the next election. The women's shelter — Harbour House — was established in Bridgewater.

In her address marking the second anniversary of the Montreal massacre, Jane said that "being a woman shouldn't make any difference to whether you live or die, or what kind of life you lead. But, unfortunately, the headlines and the statistics show that it does."

The next day the Halifax *Daily News* ran a poignant photograph of a sombre young woman comforting Jane after her address. The woman was Darlene Darrington, and she was wearing a name tag with the letters S.O.S.A. — Survivor of Sexual Assault. She was one of at least seven victims of John Arthur O'Brien, dubbed "the motorcycle rapist."

In an interview in a small, quiet room at Ann Keith's Services for Sexual Assault Victims, Darrington described how her life had been shattered by the attack and how Jane Hurshman had inspired her to face the tragedy and begin speaking out.

Darrington was thirty years old, married, and the mother of an eleven-year-old son when O'Brien attacked her on the night of September 18, 1988, while she was out for a walk. "He was driving along on his motorcycle and he must have gone ahead of me and parked it. As I walked by, he jumped me from behind and dragged me into the woods."

O'Brien forced Darrington to perform oral sex, threatening to stab her if she didn't. "And if you go to the police, I'll kill you," he warned. "Don't forget, I know who you are and I'll come back and kill you."

Darrington began to scream hysterically after O'Brien left. A family friend heard her and found her in the woods. "He was the one who took me home and he called the police because I was afraid to."

Two male RCMP officers from the Halifax County detachment came to her house. It was an experience she wasn't prepared for. Beechville, where Darrington lives, is an integrated community of blacks and whites, and Darrington, who is white, has a black husband. "And one of the first things they asked me was, 'Was it a black man that assaulted you?' They didn't ask me to describe him — they asked if he was black. It really upset me."

At the police station the next day, Darrington again found it disturbing that she had to relate her story to two male officers instead of a female. "I had to go into full detail of the assault and then they wanted to know why I didn't give all the details the night before. I told them I was in shock and describing what he made me do was not something to blurt out to two male officers."

Darrington says the attack nearly destroyed her life. She quit her job as an evening cleaner at the Halifax Infirmary because she was afraid to be outside at night, and she turned to alcohol and tranquillizers. "It was my way of coping with the nightmares that I was having constantly. I kept reliving the attack over and over again."

O'Brien was eventually arrested, and seven victims testified against him. "I was very frightened when I saw him in the courtroom," says Darrington. "But I was also angry for what he had taken away from me. I was out on my own since the age of fifteen. I had worked all my life and I was very independent. He took all that away from me. And I'm still living in fear that he will come after me for revenge when he gets out."

O'Brien was sentenced to thirty-seven years; he lost an appeal of his conviction in November 1992. Under Canadian law he will likely serve no more than a third of that time.

Darrington is as angry at the parole board as she is at O'Brien. He had been convicted of forty-two crimes since the age of sixteen and was on parole for a previous sex crime during the year he was terrorizing women in Nova Scotia. "If it wasn't for the parole board letting him out, none of us would have been assaulted," says Darrington. "I'm very angry."

She credits Jane Hurshman for encouraging her to vent that anger publicly. "I heard Jane speak out and she really inspired me. She had so much courage and she gave me the strength to speak out."

Before Jane spoke on the 1991 anniversary of the Montreal massacre, she and Darrington talked together at the SSAV offices.

"Do you ever get used to speaking out in public?" Darrington asked.

"No," said Jane. "Every time I do, it brings back all the bad memories. You do it because you want to make a change — to stop the violence."

Darrington says it was Jane who made her realize she didn't have to stay at home and hide from the world. "She made me see I had nothing to feel ashamed or guilty about. Society tries to make you feel that way by saying, 'If you didn't wear a miniskirt or you weren't walking at night, this wouldn't have happened to you.' Well, that attitude is wrong and I have the right to be treated with respect."

The down side to speaking out for Darrington was that she lost some of her friends. "It's like they're ashamed and you should keep things like that quiet. They don't understand that we need to speak about it in order to get on with our healing."

SSAV has helped a lot with her healing, but it's largely a volunteer organization and Darrington strongly believes the government should be funding and operating such programs. (All levels of government say they would like to provide more funding but the money just isn't there. Critics contend that the lack of programs to help abused women result in far greater social and dollar costs in the long run.)

Darrington also decries the lack of services available for sexual assault victims, citing the example of the woman who was forced to travel seventy miles each way from Kentville, Nova Scotia, for once-a-week therapy at SSAV in Halifax. "There's nothing down there," she says. "There's nowhere else to go.

"And when the woman was taken to the hospital in Kentville, they didn't have any special team to deal with sexual assault. A male police officer was in the room as she was being examined, and a male doctor did the examination. You don't need any of this after a man has just sexually assaulted you. You need a woman who understands what you're going through. There are not enough female officers on our police forces. There should be more of them and they should be trained to deal with sexual assaults."

Ann Keith says that police, hospitals, and doctors in Halifax/Dartmouth have become increasingly sensitized to the plight and needs of sexually assaulted and battered women, but in most other Nova Scotia communities "it's hit and miss."

(The situation is not unique to Nova Scotia. Physical and sexual assault victims in most communities across the country voice similar complaints about their treatment. There is a lack of consistency in policing from province to province and city to city. Many police departments have strong policy directives for dealing with batterers, but, in practice, they are often ignored.

In Metropolitan Toronto, for example, a police directive has existed since 1982 instructing officers to lay charges when warranted and not leave it up to the victim. But by 1988, police laid charges in only fifty-eight per cent of the reported cases of domestic assault. By 1991 the number of reported assaults was 5,100 and the percentage of those charged had risen to sixty-five percent. That percentage was considered much too low and in September 1992, the police department announced a new policy of charging and disciplining officers who fail to lay charges when warranted.

Staff Sergeant Gary Dealy, co-ordinator of family violence prevention programs, said the new policy was drafted because some officers were still instructing women to lay their own charges through a justice of the peace.

The Canadian Panel on Violence Against Women, appointed by the federal government in August 1991, is expected to propose a National Action Plan in late 1993 to address policing, medical, and other concerns. Panel Co-chairs, Pat Freeman Marshall and Marthe Asselin Vaillancourt, predict the plan "will lay the foundation for a changed society, motivated by the acceptance on all levels of a policy of zero tolerance for violence against women."

The panel says that for police forces, the adoption of zero tolerance "will mean changes in practices and procedures throughout the force, from hiring and promotion practices to the development of comprehensive training programs on issues relating to wife assault and sexual assault."

Adoption of zero tolerance for hospitals will mean "adopting a complaint procedure that is safe and accessible for patients, and continuous monitoring of all hospital procedures to ensure that everything possible is being done to support women's safety.")

◆ ◆ ◆

Ann Keith says that besides being an inspiration, Jane Hurshman helped other women by speaking to them privately. "If a woman called who had been battered but not sexually abused, we would refer them to other agencies, but sometimes I would give Jane their number," she says. "I wouldn't follow up on it. That was up to Jane, if she felt like it or not. She helped a lot of women."

In 1991, SSAV presented Jane with an award and a certificate for being one of the organization's outstanding volunteers. They took her out to dinner and presented her with a silver chain.

Many women who didn't meet Jane in person read about her and wrote or called her. One of those was Sara (a pseudonym), a woman in her early twenties. She was the youngest of nine children in a small town about a hundred miles from Halifax. She admired Jane and collected articles about her in a scrapbook. Eventually she gathered the courage to write to Jane.

"I was suicidal and it was Jane who kept me going," says Sara, who has seen unimaginable tragedy and abuse in her life. From the age of six, after the death of her mother from a brain tumour, she was physically and sexually abused by her father, two brothers, a cousin, a brother-in-law, and an uncle.

Sara can never forget the first night she was forced to sleep with her father. "I was six, pretty near seven. Dad said he wanted to break me in and make me into a woman. He laid on top of me and had intercourse with me. I was crying from the pain. Then he started telling me I was a whore."

A few days later, Sara discovered her father having intercourse with her eight-year-old sister. "I then took it to be something every father does to his daughter. I didn't know it was wrong."

She was on drugs by the age of eight, began running away from home in her early teens, and married at sixteen to escape the abuse at home. But her husband also physically and sexually abused her, as did a man she lived with after that.

Sara returned to her husband in March 1987, and the two of them entered a detox program. Since then, the abuse has stopped and they are drug-free.

Sara has been seeing a psychiatrist since early 1990, hoping to find a way to heal and forgive. "Sometimes when I'm feeling depressed, I think of Jane or read her letters and it helps," she says. In one letter, Jane urged Sara to go back to school. "It can only help you," she wrote. "Don't ever give up and don't ever stop learning."

Jane also recommended that Sara consider helping others as a healing tool. "I have kept very busy, very involved, with women and women's issues — and I probably will always be," Jane wrote. "It is great to be able to help others."

Society can't you see
the pain don't show
but the hurt still grows
deep inside of me.

— *Jane Hurshman, from prison, 1984*

VIII
• • •
BEHIND
BARS

LIZ FORESTELL, ARMED WITH A master's degree in sociology and several years' experience fighting for the rights of the disabled and disenfranchised in the health and justice fields, was hired to run the Elizabeth Fry Society in Halifax in December 1989. She arrived with bulldog determination to improve the lot of women in prison.

Named after a nineteenth-century reformer of the English penal system, there are nineteen Elizabeth Fry societies across Canada, each of them autonomous. The Halifax organization had been in operation for ten years when Forestell was hired as its first executive director.

The society fights to improve conditions for women in prison, to provide recreational and educational programs, and therapy and counselling. The society also seeks to educate the public about the economic discrimination that leads to the non-violent crimes that women are jailed most for. Many incarcerated women were sexually or physically abused as children or adults, and Elizabeth Fry believes they continue to be humiliated and mistreated by the justice and prison systems which fail to understand the dynamics of abuse.

Forestell says that in Canada there are women — who, like Jane, killed their husbands after years of abuse — serving long prison terms and they should be released. "Women who are poor and are charged with serious crimes often get legal aid lawyers who don't put the time into the defence that they should because they're not paid enough."

Soon after arriving in Halifax, Forestell began hearing about Jane. "I knew her story, but I didn't know she was here until I heard about the work she was doing through contacts in the women's community.

"A woman at the Halifax Correctional Centre who had killed her husband was having a really hard time dealing with what was going on in there. She had been abused by her husband and she wanted to talk to someone. So I called Jane and asked her if she would see her. She went to the correctional centre and helped the woman out and gave her support."

Forestell and Jane talked a lot on the telephone after that, but they didn't meet face-to-face until 1991 when Forestell asked her to join Elizabeth Fry's board of directors. Jane agreed and she and Forestell became good friends.

"She was someone I admired and respected and felt a pretty strong connection with," says Forestell. "We worked on committees together and I got to know her quite well. She was very strong and brave, with a great sense of humour, but certainly there was a lot of pain there."

Forestell considers the appointment of Jane Hurshman to the Elizabeth Fry board one of the shrewdest moves she made as executive director. "She was encouraging and very, very supportive of me," she says. "I used her a lot to check my impressions, and if I was thinking about a program or a strategy, she was my touchstone. She was very bright and she saw through people — she knew the good ones from the bad ones."

In October 1991, Nova Scotia's government created the Solicitor General's Special Committee on Provincially Incarcerated Women. The committee was to study the needs of women behind bars in the province "with respect to institutional program services, nature of correctional facilities, and aftercare services." It was to also examine existing programs and past studies and make recommendations for long- and short-term changes.

Solicitor General Joel R. Matheson appointed the committee when he and others recognized that facilities and programs for jailed women in Nova Scotia were clearly inadequate and that government, prison officials, women's and community groups, and inmates themselves should consult and cooperate to overhaul the system.

Liz Forestell was appointed co-chairman and Jane Hurshman was named a member by Solicitor General Matheson. It was an assignment both women relished. Jane had served her sentence for killing Billy Stafford at the infamous Halifax Correctional Centre in nearby Lower Sackville. It was a men's prison with a women's unit that held up to twenty-four inmates in maximum-security conditions. Forestell had long advocated closing of the women's unit.

At the time of her appointment, Forestell said that most of the women held at the Correctional Centre were not a threat to society, with most of them serving time for shoplifting or petty fraud. (A 1992 study of crimes committed by women in Halifax showed that most offences were crimes of poverty and only a fraction involved violence. The study, conducted for Coverdale Court Work Services, found that poverty led women to steal such things as Christmas gifts and clothing for their children. Of the 4,373 charges laid against women in Halifax between 1984 and 1988, 42 percent were for theft under $1,000. The study found that violent crime, including murder, robbery and assault, accounted for only 8 percent of the charges laid against women, while about 67 percent were for crimes against property, such as theft and petty fraud.)

These women, Forestell said, "can be secure in the community in a different kind of setting — one that does not separate them from their families. We are looking at an institutional setting that is not appropriate, where there is not enough space, and where it is difficult to offer women programs."

All Nova Scotia women sentenced to jail terms of less than two years were automatically sent to the Correctional Centre, while those with longer sentences were sent to the archaic Prison for Women, in Kingston, Ontario. Slightly more than two hundred of the twelve thousand inmates in federal prisons across Canada are women. At the time the Halifax committee was appointed, the federal government had already announced that it would build a network of regional federal prisons, including one in Nova Scotia, to replace the Prison for Women.

Forestell says Jane Hurshman's contribution to the prison committee was as valuable as her work with the Elizabeth Fry board of directors. "She connected with people and pulled them together in a really interesting way. Jane would sit through the meetings very quietly — then, when she had something to say, she said it. She was never aggressive, but what she said made sense and it came from the heart and it came from knowledge, and she would fight for it.

"I can remember a woman on the committee from the corrections system saying things had changed at the Correctional Centre and this didn't go on anymore, and that didn't go on, and Jane just had enough. And she said, 'Listen, I was there six years ago, and it's still the same as it was then, so don't say it has improved, because it hasn't.' That was very important coming from Jane.

"She had an incredible power on that committee. Nobody could argue with her because she had been through it. I don't know if she realized how much power she had. Sometimes I think she did and she used it very strategically, very effectively, and for all the right reasons. She didn't use it in a manipulative way at all."

To carry out the mandate of the committee, Forestell, Jane, and others interviewed women incarcerated at the Correctional Centre. "That was the basis of our research," says Forestell, who coordinated the research and designed the interviews, insisting that the inmates not be cut off. "You don't go on to the next question until people are really finished. If it takes six hours, it doesn't matter. Let them tell you what they need to tell you."

Debbie Sangster, who served as researcher, recorder, and communications director for the committee, recalls her first meeting with Jane Hurshman. "I didn't know who she was, but when our eyes met there was this kind of kindred spirit feeling and when I walked away, I remember thinking, *What a lovely woman.* I felt she had a lot of stories to tell."

Sangster had herself been in an abusive marriage for six years before fleeing to Nova Scotia from Ontario with her two sons — one from a previous marriage — when her husband threatened to kill her. "It started getting worse shortly after our son was born. He wanted a daughter. Living with an abusive husband, year after year, wears down your self-esteem. I moved over a thousand miles away because I feared for my life."

Sangster says it was probably her background that caused her to feel empathy for Jane, but she was also impressed with her input on the prison committee. "Jane was a big contributor to that committee. She told me that when they went out to the Correctional Centre and everybody went down the hall, she stayed behind, and some of the women opened right up to her because they knew they could trust her."

In all, the committee interviewed thirty-three women. Twenty-six of them said that had been physically abused, nineteen of them as children or teenagers. Twenty-one had been sexually abused, sixteen as children or teenagers. Spouses or partners were a close second to other family members as the most frequent abusers.

"Typically, the women found little support in surviving the trauma," the committee reported in a summary of its findings. "They often found themselves going from abusive childhood situations into abusive relationships with partners and spouses. Programs, they found, were either not available or did not respond to their needs."

Twelve of the women interviewed had a history of self-mutilation. This was not surprising to the committee, which referred to a 1979 Ontario study that found that 86 percent of adolescent females in custody in that province had inflicted injuries on themselves. Another study suggested a link between self-injury and early sexual abuse.

"Women talk about self-injury as something that happens when they are in crisis, and say that it actually brings about some release from their pain," stated the committee summary. "Self-injury includes slashing, burning, and sometimes, breaking bones. Typically, correctional institutions respond to such actions in a punitive, rather than supportive manner, which may in fact exacerbate the crisis."

Most of the female inmates told Jane and the other committee interviewers that they had been treated badly by police during and after their arrests. "Complaints included lack of information; rough treatment; not being permitted to change clothing; being shackled and thrown into a police van while pregnant; refusal of treatment for injuries; refusal of phone calls; and verbal abuse."

Following is a sampling of some of the comments from the female inmates:

- "Most of the people I know who have been in jail have gone back. It really doesn't help locking them in a cell and not working with them."
- "I suffered every form of abuse for over thirty years, both as a child and as an adult, from my parents, relatives and partner."
- "When I was a baby, my mother tried to kill me with a BB gun. . . She told the cops she hoped they'd hang me."
- "They tied me to a tree and [used sticks on me], because I told them I didn't want to do it because they were my cousins. That night I went home and told my mother and she beat me. They would climb into my window at night and Mom would beat me for it."
- "A police officer grabbed me . . . and blackened my eye, left hand-prints on my throat, and marks on my ribs and arms."
- "I was interrogated in lockup for seven hours without being allowed to call my lawyer. I was not allowed any phone calls. Police said I was not being charged, but I was not allowed to leave or make calls."

Ann L. Jacobs, executive director of the Women's Prison Association and Home, in an April 9, 1992, letter to the *New York Times*, wrote that "we're learning that 80 percent of women in the system have been victims of child abuse, sexual abuse, or domestic violence. They need drug treatment, counselling, education and job training."

The solicitor general's special committee released its report, *Blueprint For Change*, in April 1992. It recommended that the women's unit at the Halifax Correctional Centre be phased out by 1995 and that "small, community residential facilities be established in the western, central, and eastern regions of Nova Scotia.

"At minimum, all facilities will include single bedrooms, bath, kitchen and dining areas, smoking and non-smoking common areas, exercise/game room, meeting/program room, workshop/craft area, and family room. Bedrooms must be designed to accommodate a study area. At least half of the bedrooms must be large enough to accommodate child sleeping or living in. Yard space must be large enough to accommodate a garden and recreation space suitable for children."

Other recommendations:

- Incarcerated women should have the same rights to health and medical care as members of the community at large, including rights to private consultation and examination, to choices about treatment, to refuse treatment, and to have access to female physicians and nursing staff.
- Prison staff should be trained to deal with manifestations of post-traumatic stress, including self-injury, substance abuse, flashbacks, panic attacks, and nightmares, all resulting from childhood trauma, sexual assault, and spousal battering.

Throughout the committee's discussions, the issue of women-only staff came up again and again. Citing a study that said the presence of men in positions of control over women who have been victimized "was a real barrier to healing," the committee recommended that only women be placed in charge of incarcerated females. "While it might provide an opportunity for women to see caring males in positions of authority, it perpetuated the inequality of relationships and contributed to women's view of themselves as submissive to male power," the committee's summary stated. "Before women survivors of abuse can deal effectively with the men in their world, and enter into healthy relationships based on mutual respect, they must have a safe environment in which to heal from trauma, and then face men on a more equal playing field."

The committee's workload was heavy and demanding. Often Jane attended meetings after long stretches on the night shift at the rehabilitation centre. Whenever she felt the load was too much, she would call Forestell.

"Look, I'm just too tired and I can't be there today," Jane would say. "I have to look after myself."

"I'm sure it was hard on her," Forestell says. "And I'm sure it wasn't without pain — to go back and look again at the kind of traumatic things that you've been through. But she said that it gave her back a lot and it was very fulfilling. It was close to Jane's heart because she had experienced many of the things those women had experienced."

DAMN WELL GOT ME

i don't hear the door — don't hear anything except
pounding in my chest and then i feel him behind me
he's drunk and he's got me — damn well got me
i'm never quick enough — i never saw the fist after
he spun me around or the ring or felt it cut —
never felt anything until the floor came up and crashed
into my head and it came crashing over and over —
whisky — all i could smell was whisky — i try to kick him
but he kicks back — so you don't kick — you don't punch
he kicks, he punches and the floor keeps crashing into my head
i don't feel it anymore so i yell 'why don't you kill me and
get it over with' — with a last kick saying 'you shouldn't
have' he leaves — just like that the room is empty
i run outside night clothes torn — can see my breath
in the night air — crunching snow — darkness
just like the thoughts in my head — inside me
i do not feel — i run — i look back — see no one —
just my footsteps silently following — when he does come
i hope he'll finish the job — finish me forever —
i keep running until i get to a safe place for the night
and then it hurts — it hurts

— *Linda Cooper Waters, February 1992*

· IX ·

BILLY

ANNETTE BUSHEN REMEMBERS that when she heard that Jane Hurshman was acquitted of murdering Billy Stafford in 1982 "I just gave a whoop of joy. I read what she had gone through, and her acquittal couldn't have been more fitting."

Bushen didn't know that within a few months she would be taking a Certified Nursing Assistant's course with Jane. And she and Jane happened to be in the same group that was sent to Queens General Hospital on Mondays and Tuesdays, as part of their training.

Bushen was living in Petite Riviere, and it was a long drive to get to Liverpool for their early-morning hospital assignments. While Bushen was explaining her problem to her instructor, Jane overheard and approached.

"I live a lot closer to the hospital than you," said Jane. "If you don't mind, you can come up to my place on Sunday afternoon and stay overnight Sunday and Monday. It's only fifteen minutes to the hospital. We'll use your car one week and mine the next."

Bushen was impressed with Jane's generosity and agreed immediately. "We got along like sisters right off the bat," she says. "But I still didn't realize who she was." Later that day, Jane took her aside.

"You don't know me, Annette, do you?" asked Jane.

"No I don't. Should I know you?"

"I'm Jane Stafford."

Bushen shrugged, not connecting the name to the trial and Billy Stafford.

"Do you remember a trial in Liverpool a while back?"

"Oh my God! You're *that* Jane Stafford."

Bushen told Jane about her reaction to the not-guilty verdict and expressed her dismay over the Crown's appeal and her upcoming retrial.

"I appreciate you feeling that way about me," said Jane.

"Well I sort of stand in your shoes — different size, same shoes," said Bushen, whose unhappy marriage was ending. "My circumstances are different, but I can certainly empathize with you."

The following Sunday, Bushen made her first trip to Jane's house in Bangs Falls, where she met Darren, who was then six. When they sat down for dinner in the evening, Bushen noticed the kitchen table was on an elevated platform.

"We're sitting on his throne," said Jane. "This is where Bill sat when he issued all his orders."

Bushen says it gave her an eerie feeling.

"There's something else I have to tell you," said Jane. "Strange things do happen here."

"What do you mean?"

"The main thing I want to tell you about is the doors."

(The outside back door to the house opened to a small porch used to store jackets and boots, and the inside door opened to the kitchen.)

"If at any time you're in the house and I'm not here, don't be alarmed if you hear the doors," said Jane. "The outer door will open. It will close. The inner door to the kitchen will open. It will close too, but nobody will be there and nobody will come in."

Bushen is not overly superstitious and she was sceptical, but on a subsequent visit, it happened just as Jane described it.

"She and I were having coffee one evening," she says. "Darren had gone to bed and we were talking when we heard a noise. I looked at her and she looked at me and we looked at the door. And honest to God, I would not lie, both doors opened and closed and nobody came in. There was no wind, nothing."

"That's what I meant," said Jane.

Bushen says she still gets chills up and down her spine just thinking about it.

On another visit, Bushen wore a flannel nightdress to bed one night. "It had a little lace tie on the front. I'm not one to get up in the night. I crawl in, pull the cover up over me, and that's it — I don't rustle around."

When she got up the next morning, Jane was feeding the fire in the living-room woodstove. She looked up when Bushen entered the room. "Were you up during the night, Annette?" she asked.

"No, why?"

"Look down," said Jane.

Bushen looked down to discover her nightdress was on backwards. "I was stunned," she says. "Both of us remember it being on properly when I went to bed. I had tied the lace. I mean I would have known — I would have felt it. I did not get up through the night and I did nothing but sleep as far as I know. But it was on backwards — the sleeves and all."

"Jane," she said. "Please don't tell anybody about this, they'll think we're both cracking up."

Bushen remembers Jane sitting deep in thought at the kitchen table and then turning to her. "You know, Annette," she said. "Bill Stafford will never be dead."

"I don't know how many times she told me that in the time I knew her," says Bushen. "But I thought, my God, the woman is right."

◆　◆　◆

James Tynes says he too remembers Jane being haunted by Billy Stafford. "When we were living together, she sometimes had bad dreams about Billy, and there was one period when she thought she was possessed by evil spirits. She wouldn't talk much about it.

"She said she had some little knick-knacks Billy had given her over the years when he came in from the ships. She thought they were bad omens and she got rid of them, and after a while the bad feelings went away and she never talked about it anymore." He says her bad dreams ended when she started seeing a psychiatrist.

◆　◆　◆

To those who understand the dynamics of the battered-wife syndrome, Billy's hold on Jane, even after his death, is not surprising.

Sleep deprivation and the interminable, repetitive emotional abuse, accentuated by unpredictable outbursts of physical violence and degrading sexual episodes, were a form of severe brainwashing that left Jane broken and confused.

After her release from prison in 1984 she told a friend that she believed her breaking point came after Billy shot at her while she was filling the woodstove, and threatened that if she ever left him he would kill off her family one by one.

"Never again did I see the slightest ray of hope," Jane said. "That episode left me purposeless. It left me with no choices — nothing to be, nothing to do, nothing to believe in. Nothing but emptiness and death. I didn't know how I was going to cope. Stafford had total control of everything in that house.

"There was no emotion left in me. I would crawl into bed, tired and worn out, and if I did sleep it was a fitful one. I was just as tired when morning came. Each day was a continuance of the day before. It was never-ending.

"The fear was overwhelming. The pure hate for me and Darren would spew out of his mouth without warning. All activity in the house was tense — hearts pounding, afraid to move, afraid to breathe."

In one of her speeches Jane said she didn't know if it was love for her children or her "sheer hatred for Stafford" that kept her survival instinct alive.

And in a letter to her friend Sara, Jane said it is very difficult for those who haven't been abused to understand what it does to a person. "Abuse in any form is so traumatic. And you spend the rest of your life trying to get over it."

In a return letter, Sara asked Jane if she had been able to forgive Billy Stafford.

"I'm not sure if it is forgiveness or understanding," replied Jane. "Probably some of both. For the last couple of years that we were together, I just hated him. I couldn't get beyond that hate, even after his death. When I started my nurse training and we got into psychiatric nursing, I had a fantastic instructor who taught me that Bill was a very sick man, and from there my hate began to change to understanding. And then I was able to put a label on it and put it away.

"It wasn't until 1990 that I went back to our old house where everything happened. It was something I had to do, because I felt part of me was trapped there. I had to go and get it and set it free. It was very difficult and very scary for me, but I went. I got what I went for — forgiveness. I wanted to forgive myself, and that's what I did.

"What Bill did will always have an effect on my life. Sometimes I am very resentful and hateful and unforgiving — but that is a natural part of healing. To forgive someone does not mean you have to be around them or love them. It just means you have settled something inside yourself and you are at peace with your decision."

It was in the summer of 1990 when Jane returned to Bangs Falls. Besides wrestling with the ghost of Billy Stafford, she was there to seek answers from her former neighbour, Margaret Joudrey, the woman who once treated her like a daughter but turned against her on the witness stand.

No one will ever know what Jane was thinking as the single-lane bridge crossing the Medway River came into view, and behind it, Margaret Joudrey's trailer and the small weathered barn, with its sagging roof. And then, on the gentle slope at the end of a long driveway, flanked by a low white board fence, the frame bungalow with its painful memories.

Did she see herself behind the wheel of Billy Stafford's half-ton truck, bouncing over the bridge with the weight of his decapitated body pressing against her and blood and brain tissue splattering on the dash and the windshield?

And when she looked at the house did she see images of Darren being force-fed or Billy's massive fist breaking her nose — as it did at least three times — and loosening her teeth? Did she remember the rifle butt that finished the job, forcing her to have her teeth removed and lying to her dentist that she'd been in a car accident?

When she stopped at Margaret Joudrey's trailer and stared up to the house, did she remember Billy's voice booming down at her and Darren: "I'm number one, and you look out for number one, and fuck everyone else!"

Or perhaps she was remembering the day she summoned the courage to tell Billy Stafford she was leaving him. He glared at her and his response was cold and measured.

"Well, old woman," he said, "there's the door and you can leave any time you please, but guaranteed, you will be back, and I will not have to come looking for you. You will come back on your own, and you will bring that bastard kid with you. Because old woman, I may not know where you are, but I do know where your family is. And I will kill them one at a time until you do come back. I will not be a third-time loser."

Jane was hurt by, and never fully understood, how Margaret Joudrey could have turned against her on the witness stand, portraying Billy as an overgrown loudmouth whom she didn't fear and who liked to argue with her. She said they were great friends.

But Roger Manthorne, the man she lived with at the time, said he feared Billy and that Joudrey was upset after Billy threatened to burn them out. When Joudrey's common-law husband, Stanley Joudrey, died, he didn't leave a will and so she was left without legal title to the property. Billy inadvertently learned that information and began haranguing her about it, as Manthorne attested at the trial.

Margaret Joudrey also contradicted Manthorne's testimony that she was crying as she hugged Jane the night she killed Billy.

Jane's oldest son, Allen, who lived in the Bangs Falls house for two years, says Joudrey saw Billy abuse his mother many times, and on the witness stand he testified that Joudrey "always had a gun laying on the table with a shell laying on the bed. . . . I asked her what she had it there for and she said, 'If that fool ever comes down here causing trouble, he won't be walking back.'" Joudrey admitted that she stopped talking to Jane because she blamed her for involving her in the court proceedings. "I never had no more to do with her . . . because I don't want to get in no more trouble. I'm in thick enough now."

The jury didn't believe Margaret Joudrey, and despite all the evidence, she continued to insist that Billy never laid a hand on Jane. "I never, ever, in my life seen Bill lay a hand on that woman, but a lot of times he should have," she said in a telephone interview in December 1992. (Joudrey died on March 25, 1993, two weeks after the tenth anniversary of Billy Stafford's death. She was in her late seventies.)

She said it was true that she was very close to Jane at one time. "She always called me Mom and she told me she thought more of me than her own mother. I thought of her as my daughter until she killed Bill, then I just turned the other way." That was a false statement. Joudrey consoled Jane after Billy was shot, and Roger Manthorne helped Allen Whynot break down the shotgun Jane used, before it was thrown into the river in three pieces. Jourdrey didn't stop talking to Jane until she was forced to testify at the preliminary hearing.

Joudrey said she didn't think it was right for Jane to speak out against domestic violence. "She'd go in front of all them women, and oh my God. I seen her on TV and she'd tell them women about abuse and all this shit, and it's hard to tell what kind of hell she made for them and their husbands by telling them the kind of stuff that she was telling them. It would just cause them more trouble at home."

At Jane's trial, Joudrey said it was her belief that the man should be the head of the household. And in the telephone interview she claimed she told Billy that he was going to have a hard time as long as he lived with Jane. "I told him Jane's got you down as low as she can get you. I said she can't put you down any lower. Everything Jane did, Billy got the blame for."

Jane and her lawyer, Alan Ferrier, theorized that Jourdrey turned on her because she thought that her dealings with the police and the courts over Billy's death would somehow result in the loss of the property she was living on. Jane was there to see if she could confirm the theory when she went to the door of Joudrey's trailer in the summer of 1990.

Joudrey's memory of that visit was that they sat at her kitchen table and "just talked ordinary talk. To tell the God's truth, after what she done to Billy, I didn't give a damn if I ever saw her. But I wouldn't turn her away from the door — I wouldn't."

Jane told Liz Forestell, of the Elizabeth Fry Society, that she went to Bangs Falls to talk to Margaret "as a kind of closure." She was always bothered by the things Margaret said, so she went out there. She said Margaret opened the door and they went inside and Jane said all those years just melted away and she felt like she had just gone out to the store for ten minutes. It was like nothing had changed.

"And she ended up saying to Margaret, 'I wanted to come and ask you why you did what you did, but it doesn't matter.' She just had to go back and look. And then she went away. She didn't want to talk to her. It was no longer important."

Forestell says there were occasions when she thought Jane looked very haunted. "I wouldn't describe it as a dark side, but I could certainly see the pain. Sometimes when Jane talked about what happened to her, her eyes got very big and round. It was a very profound kind of thing — very easy to see."

Because of her own pain in recalling specific experiences with Billy, Jane was able to articulate what other battered women were going through. "I guess that was one of the most important things she did for me," says Forestell.

Most of us carry different levels of trauma around with us, Forestell believes, and the challenge is to turn that into a strength rather than let it cripple you, "and I think Jane did that extraordinarily well."

Jane may have turned past trauma into strength but the past was always with her. "We would be talking about someone else's situation," says Forestell, "and Jane would say 'oh yeah, I remember that happening to me,' and I would say 'how horrible' or 'how did you survive that?' And I asked her a few times if she ever thought about it."

"It never leaves you," replied Jane.

To Vernon Oickle, a reporter and editor with *The Advance*, a Liverpool weekly newspaper, Jane said she was able to put Billy and the years of abuse "away on a shelf where they can no longer hurt me, although they do come back to haunt me on a regular basis."

She also told Oickle, who wrote a book about her, that she was not sorry that Billy was dead. "I've accepted the fact a long time ago that if he wasn't dead, then I would have been."

Oickle, in an interview, said he believes Jane *could* "take Billy and put him on a shelf and forget about him. But subconsciously, he was getting down off that shelf, I think.

"I don't know how you could ever put anything behind you that was that traumatic. Not only the abuse — I think she was also trying to deal with the fact that she did kill another human being."

Jane was also concerned about Billy's parents, particularly his father, Lamonte Stafford, who had comforted her after the police picked her up for questioning. And while Jane was in jail in the spring of 1984, she was upset when she read a letter from Lamonte that appeared in *The Advance* on March 21.

In the letter he accused "the ghouls" at CBC's 'the fifth estate' of "crucifying" his son and said that Jane's son Allen, and Ronald Wamboldt, who boarded with Jane and Billy, "lived at my son's getting free room and board. They came to my house two or three times a week and I made a number of trips to their home at Bangs Falls. For all the physical abuse they were supposed to have taken from my son, I never saw a mark on either of them.

"My son was on boats for years and he never had any trouble, to my knowledge. It is all very well to give statements in court and to the newspaper when the one person who could deny them is dead . . . . The many people who could have been called to testify on his behalf were never summoned by the Crown."

Jane told Oickle later that she wept after reading Lamonte's letter. "I couldn't get those feelings out of my mind about what I had done to Bill's father," she said. "I kept thinking about how his mother and father must have felt and I could understand how upset all of this must have made them. I didn't wish his family any harm and I regret any pain I may have caused them."

On March 23, 1984, Jane wrote a letter to Oickle from jail, explaining why she didn't want to be interviewed for an *Advance* article. "I read Lamonte's piece that was published this week and I wish no more hurt or bad feelings to him. He is a fine man and I respect him very much, but he has suffered dearly and I choose not to have any more printed, even if only for that reason. He is a man that has been good to me over the years and I just want to let my past rest now."

◆ ◆ ◆

Jane Hurshman also had a lot of difficulty dealing with the reality that she had been unable to protect Darren against Billy's abuse.

The despair she felt over it hit her as hard as any of Billy's punches when she escorted Donna Smith's two children for a four-visit with their father one Christmas. The court had allowed Robert Smith supervised access to Mary and Bobby, and Jane offered to accompany them to ease Donna's fears that they might be molested.

Robert knew who Jane was and the atmosphere was tense. She told Donna later that he had purchased a cup inscribed with the words: "World's Greatest Dad."

Jane saw a striking similarity in the way Robert and Billy controlled the gift-opening ritual. The children had to wait for their father for permission to open each gift and had to neatly fold and put away the wrapping paper before being allowed to open another.

It triggered memories of Christmas at the Bangs Falls house, where Darren was not even allowed to open his own presents. Billy would open them, pass them to Darren to inspect for a moment, and then place them under the tree. Darren would look at them longingly but he wasn't allowed to play with them. Jane once bought him a motorized toy that he liked a lot. The boy was heartbroken when Billy gave the toy to another child.

When Jane returned to Donna's apartment with Mary and Bobby, she was emotionally drained and said she could never accompany them again. "All the bad feelings from her time with Billy came back," says Donna. "We talked a lot about it."

Ann Keith, of SSAV, believes that when a woman is abused, it's akin to a lifelong sentence. "People who have not experienced violence don't understand the long-term psychological effects that abuse has on women. Flashbacks of the abuse can be triggered by something very minor — a smell, a touch . . . anything."

Every time that Jane spoke, Keith believes it brought back memories of Billy's abuse. "If you heard her speak, you might not get that impression. Especially as she became more polished in her later speeches. But I'm sure that's how she felt, and she did express that.

"If you've been abused, you can put on masks, you can be three or four people. You can be hurting and have the biggest smile on your face. You could be tearing up inside, but you are not going to let anybody know, because you have been conditioned that way all your life."

Night
A deathly time
Your serpent

swallowing souls silently
Leaving them hollow
as a cavern

Ghostly silent
devious creeper
inducing bodily desire

to melt into the earth
Slink into the shadows
Bastard

Brutal bastard
with a black heart
of stone

Silence
Death wish
Alive

in a state of desolation

— *Angela Cupido, 1987*

X
NIGHT CALLS

JANE HURSHMAN BEGAN CALLING Annette Bushen "Annie" when she overheard her scolding herself a few weeks after they became friends during their nursing course.

"I used to talk to myself," says Bushen. "If I did something stupid I'd say, 'Wake up, Annie.'"

"Are you sure there's not two of you?" asked Jane the first time she heard it.

"After that she always called me Annie," says Bushen.

She says Jane was well liked and respected at school. "People admired her for many reasons. For me, it was her resourcefulness and will-power.

"It amazed me how well she did in school while facing a second trial with the possibility of a prison term hanging over her head." Bushen once asked Jane how she could do so well under those circumstances.

"Annie," she replied, "my life depends on it. You need a way of making a living. I'm earning my life."

They had been at the school about six months when Jane went to court in Liverpool for her second trial, at which she was sentenced to six months in prison.

"If you missed three days in the nursing course you were gone — history," says Bushen. "I missed only one day the whole time I was there. That was the day I went to sit in that courtroom. Nursing was to be my livelihood, but that morning school didn't mean much."

Bushen, who was several years older than Jane, was accompanied by her eighteen-year-old daughter, the youngest of her three children. "There were a lot of people in Queens County against Jane and I wanted to be there to support her. I felt I didn't know Jane well enough to ask her if I could go — I just went."

Bushen didn't get to speak to Jane in the courtroom and she watched in tears on the sidewalk as the sheriff drove her off to jail. "I thought, *no, she doesn't deserve that.*" Jane continued her schooling while she was in prison and was released in plenty of time to graduate with Bushen and the rest of their class in June of 1984. The two women kept in touch, and after Jane's surprise return from Ontario, in October of that year, Bushen was delighted to find her working at the same rehabilitation centre where she had been working for several months.

Bushen felt anxious for Jane, wondering how the others at work would accept her. "I was scared for her because it was no secret who she was and what she had done." She mentioned her concern to Jane.

"Don't worry about it," said Jane. "Those who don't accept me as I am — well, it's their loss."

Bushen needn't have worried. Jane soon gained the respect and affection of both staff and patients. Because of her experience working at a home for the aged when she lived in Bangs Falls and her brief employment in a similar institution in Ontario, she was assigned to the geriatric section. She was to remain there, working the night shift, for the next six years.

In all that time, Bushen says, she never once heard anything derogatory about Jane, from staff or patients. She was gentle and compassionate with the elderly and a diligent worker.

Bushen says Jane was always neat and clean and was always in early for her shift, which began at 11:30 P.M.

After receiving patient reports from the outgoing shift, Jane's job was to check every patient on her floor, ensuring they had clean bed linen, pyjamas, and nightshirts. Those who were bedridden were repositioned to prevent bed sores. Most patients were asleep by one, but Jane checked on them every hour until about seven, when she would rouse them for breakfast before her shift change at seven-thirty.

Between one and seven, then, Jane had a lot of quiet time to herself. It was time that was never wasted. Between rounds, she wrote letters to friends, family, and abused women, like her pen pal Sara. She also spent a lot of time talking with them on the telephone. Like Jane, those who had been abused, had trouble sleeping at night.

She probably talked most to Donna Smith, who continues to have problems sleeping at night. "I'm up at all hours," she says. "Jane and I talked every night, and she kept telling me how much strength I had. Our situations were almost identical except that Robert was still alive. She knew nights were always bad for me. That's when everything comes back. Anything — a noise, a smell — and suddenly there's a flashback. It was the same for Jane because Billy never, never died — no matter what, he was still there."

◆ ◆ ◆

Nights could also be bad for Jane's youngest sister, Mona, who lived near Barrie, Ontario, with her husband, Ed Donnelly. The sisters were close, and Mona went to Nova Scotia to give Jane support during her nineteen-day murder trial. And Jane and Darren stayed with her in October for a time before and after her second trial. The sisters kept in touch by letter and telephone after that.

The night calls to Jane's workplace from Mona became more frequent after February 14, 1985, when her husband was shot by a disturbed young neighbour who came to the door of their rented cabin late one night. The bullet travelled upward through Ed's neck, exited through his cheek, and penetrated a kitchen cupboard, where police found it in a silverware drawer. Ed eventually recovered from his wound. Mona, a religious person, called it a miracle.

The gunman was initially charged with attempted murder, but a plea bargain reduced it to aggravated assault and he was sentenced to two years less a day which meant he would serve his time in a provincial prison rather than a federal penitentiary. No motive was ever established.

After the shooting incident, the Donnellys never entered the cabin without sending their dog in first, and Mona had trouble sleeping. "I have really restless nights and I hear every noise, inside or out," she told Jane. "Eddie was never an edgy person, but now if he hears a noise, he sits and stares."

She says that every time they entered the rented cabin, they relived the shooting incident, and so several months later they moved into a house which Ed had built two miles away. But the move didn't end the trauma for Mona. "Now I check two or three times to make sure my doors are locked. And I'm a light sleeper and I wake up at the slightest sound."

Mona, an employment counsellor for Simcoe County, in Ontario, says there were many nights when she couldn't sleep and she would call Jane at work to talk.

◆ ◆ ◆

Carrie Rafuse says that whenever she had a problem she would call Jane, usually in the middle of the night. "If the kids were driving me up the wall, boyfriend problems — anything — Jane was always there to cheer me up. If she was your friend, she was your friend, she was loyal to you. I never once in nine years had to say, 'Jane, would you please not tell anybody this.' You didn't have to say this to Jane. You could tell her your deepest secrets and you knew they were safe.

◆ ◆ ◆

Jo Sheridan, who lives in a small community near Vancouver, was flipping through the TV channels on the night of March 13, 1984, when on the screen she saw "a woman with huge, agonized eyes."

The eyes were Jane Hurshman's and she was being interviewed by Hana Gartner on CBC's 'the fifth estate' current affairs program. The segment was aired a month after Jane was sentenced for killing Billy Stafford.

"The eyes riveted me," says Sheridan, a financial aid adviser for university students. "I didn't know if it was a soap opera or what it was." The program had just started.

"Come and see this face," she called out to her daughter and son, both teenagers.

"The three of us sat absolutely thunderstruck on the couch," she said in an interview in early 1993. "Her eyes absolutely haunted me, and to this day they haunt me.

"I wept through most of the show and I stayed up all night, just tormented by this." She says she was so struck by Jane, she sat down and wrote to her, care of 'the fifth estate.'

"If I could have borne just a little of that pain, to alleviate it for you, I would have done it," she wrote. "You are a good woman. You had no choice (in killing Billy) in my opinion. There is something in your eyes and soul that has struck every chord in my heart and I need you to know that I — a complete stranger — care. I'm thinking positively and projecting lovely thoughts to you and I will never forget what I have seen. You're on the right track — go for it."

All of Jane's mail that came in to the CBC after the TV documentary was screened by her lawyer, and Sheridan was thankful her letter got through.

Jane wrote to her immediately, thanking her and saying, "Your approach and your attitude were exactly what I need at this time. You have no idea what you've done for me."

They wrote frequently after that, and Sheridan sent flowers on the day Jane was released from prison. They learned about each other and their families through the mail and through photos, voice tapes, and telephone calls.

Sheridan, who was born in Britain, laughs when she recalls Jane's reaction to her English accent whenever she called her from British Columbia. "She preferred to write, but if I phoned her and we chatted, she used to say to me, 'You sound just like the Queen.' We laughed about that many times."

Sheridan came to consider Jane one of her dearest friends, even though they were never to meet in person. "I knew a lot of her history and she knew a lot of mine — things that I'd never shared with anyone, very sensitive things," says Sheridan, who grew up in a "proper" home.

Sheridan came to Canada on her own as a teenager, and she believes her strict upbringing, "in which I had to eat everything on my plate," was responsible for the anorexia nervosa that led to her being hospitalized in Toronto in her mid-twenties.

"I wanted to be perfect, so I starved," she says. "Nobody knew that, including my family. Only Jane knew it and my children knew it. I didn't know what anorexia was until I was in my late twenties. I thought I was just dieting sensibly."

Now a single mother with her children in their early twenties, Sheridan says that while in Toronto she had "an abysmally horrible first marriage. I was married to a gorilla. He was young and I was young. I did, to a very limited degree, understand what it felt like to live with somebody you loathed and feared."

But she says there was no way she could compare what she went through to Jane's suffering. "A little bit of me now and then feels guilty that I shared with her not only my joys but my sorrows — and maybe I shouldn't have. Because of the distance, in some ironic and strange way, I could relate to her better than if I was sitting across the table from her. So I dumped all this whining stuff on her — right down to my daughter mouthing off at me, or a third flat tire in two weeks . . . But Jane responded so warmly and so freely to my trite prattlings that I think it was almost a refreshing change of pace for her."

Sheridan believes she and Jane were so compatible because their life experiences, backgrounds, and hopes and dreams were so vastly different. She once asked Jane what she would consider a dream vacation. Jane told her she would like to take a hiking trip, on her own, through a remote and rugged part of Alaska. Sheridan shuddered at the thought.

"I believe that Jane was my soul mate," says Sheridan. "I know she shared her soul with many others, but I think a portion of her soul was uniquely mine, and I treasure that more than words can say."

In 1988 and 1989, Sheridan sensed that the work Jane was doing for abused women, combined with her busy everyday schedule, was exacting too large an emotional toll. In numerous letters, she begged Jane to curtail her speaking engagements. "It's too much for you to handle," she wrote. "It's getting to you badly. I can tell."

For a time, she says, Jane tried to back off "to find her way," but she continued to be pulled back into speaking, "and there was a lot of agony coming through. I was writing and saying 'Stop it, don't do it anymore. Take a break. You owe it to yourself and your kids. Be selfish, Jane, be selfish.'"

Jane acknowledged that others had been giving her similar advice, but she felt obligated to continue because women continued to be battered and since she had the experience, she had to be their spokesperson.

"She believed she had to educate the public, get changes made, and be there for women who were suffering," says Sheridan. "She was on a mission, but she wasn't, in my opinion, a missionary. I realized then that this was, for sure, a most remarkable woman."

MIND DEAD

Coming apart piece by piece
the bones separate
but I don't feel a thing

The penis goes in
and the mind goes dead
except to hope it will soon end

But the end doesn't come
for again and again
the penis goes in . . .

And the mind goes dead
giving me time
so I don't have to attend

— Linda, 1992

XI
· · ·
TAKING
THINGS

BILLY STAFFORD WAS still alive when Jane was caught shoplifting in Bridgewater in March of 1981. She never told anyone of the stress she was under — stress she believed led to the incident. Her oldest son, Allen, then a teenager, had a brush with the law while Billy was at sea, and she was terrified Billy might find out about it when he returned. "I knew that if Bill found out he would have killed Allen," she wrote after Billy's death.

A couple of days before Billy's return, Jane went shopping in Bridgewater with her neighbours Margaret Joudrey and Roger Manthorne, Joudrey's live-in companion. They went to Zellers shopping plaza in Bridgewater, where, said Jane, "an awful feeling came over me, and I walked out of the store with a full shopping cart. Next thing I knew, the man from the store had me by the arm and I was being arrested for shoplifting."

Joudrey said she had often seen Jane steal but she never told anyone. Her version of the trip to Bridgewater was that they arrived about 9 P.M. and she and Manthorne had "coffee, a piece of pie, and a smoke" while waiting for Jane to do her shopping. When Jane failed to return after an hour, Joudrey sent Manthorne to get the keys from her so they could wait in the car.

"Ten o'clock passed, then eleven, and then eleven-thirty," said Joudrey. "All the cars around us was disappearing." She says Jane finally came out, pushing a shopping cart filled with merchandise.

"Where in the name of Christ is she going to put all that stuff?" Joudrey asked Manthorne.

But Jane didn't make it to the car. "She just got outside the door and they grabbed her there," said Joudrey. "They took her back inside and then it wasn't long before we seen two Mounties run in. I said, 'Oh boy, Roger, are we ever into it.'" Jane was still in the store when a policewoman approached the car.

"We got nothing to do with her," said Joudrey. "We're *with* her only." She says the police eventually came out with Jane, who was crying.

"Jane, my God almighty, woman. Are you in trouble again?" asked Joudrey. "What in the name of God did you do? This is my last trip with you. Never again."

She said the three of them were taken to the police station, where the car was searched. "And one of them said to me, 'Do you know, Margaret, she had enough money in her purse to buy that stuff three and four times over.' And he said there was stuff she stole that she would never make use of. He wondered what she would ever do with it.

"I told him some people was born stealing, and Jane stole all of her life — I could prove that."

Billy returned home the day before Jane went to court, and she was terrified that he would find out what she had done. She managed to keep it from him, and Joudrey went with her to the courthouse. The judge was lenient, sentencing Jane to fifty hours of community service and one-year probation.

"I never told anyone the real reason I was shoplifting was because I was so worried about what would happen to Allen if Bill found out that he was in trouble," wrote Jane later. "And with this happening, I had even more to worry about." Jane saw a psychiatrist at that time but could not tell her why she had to keep the shoplifting incident secret from Billy. She couldn't admit to a stranger that she was a battered wife, that Billy would beat her terribly if he knew she had been charged.

Being arrested for shoplifting wasn't something new for Jane. She had four convictions against her on the same charge in 1975 and she had stolen from stores many times without being caught.

◆ ◆ ◆

James Tynes believes he may have inadvertently discouraged Jane from speaking to him about her shoplifting problem when they were living together. "When we first started going together, we used to talk about everything for hours and hours, and one time I told her I didn't like thieves. I said it was wrong to steal and lie. Meantime, I didn't know it but she had already been caught a few times. So she probably thought I would think less of her if I knew about it. But I would have tried to help her — she wasn't a common thief."

It wasn't until the shoplifting charges appeared in the newspapers, and she feared going to jail, that Jane told Tynes about her problem.

"Let me help you," he offered. "If you feel the urge, we'll go shopping together, or give me a call when you get that feeling." She would agree, "but I think it was just to get me off her case."

Jane did tell Tynes about one incident after that, but she had already been caught. He went to the manager of the store.

"It's in the hands of the police," said the manager.

"So I went to the police and tried to get them to drop the charge," says Tynes. "But they said it was already in the computer." He went back to the manager and pleaded with him to drop the charges. The manager refused.

"To them, she was just a common thief," says Tynes.

◆ ◆ ◆

Donna Smith remembers being in a pet store with Jane when she saw her pick up a dog leash. "It was winter, just before Christmas, and she tucked it under her coat. I thought I was seeing things. She bought something else and paid for it, but she didn't pay for the leash. I was scared. I thought I would get caught too. She didn't say a thing about it.

"Later the same day, we went into a jewellery store, and I was looking at a nice necklace and earrings."

When they returned to the car Jane shifted her body in the seat until her back was to Donna.

"Wait a minute," said Jane. Donna could hear rustling.

"Then she turned and handed me a little red stocking."

"This is for you," said Jane. Inside was the necklace and the earrings, worth sixty or seventy dollars. Donna realized the rustling sound was Jane removing the price tags from the jewellery.

"Jane, no!" protested Donna. "It costs too much, take it back right now."

"It's your Christmas present," said Jane.

"When did you get a chance to buy them? I was in there with you."

"I told the woman to go and do it in the back. It was a surprise for you."

Donna suspected the jewellery was stolen but she could never bring herself to ask Jane and Jane never talked about it. They did, however, have conversations about shoplifting, and Jane once told Donna that it gave her a high to get away with shoplifting, although, sometimes she wasn't aware she was stealing.

"She said nobody ever listened to her," says Donna. "The shoplifting was a cry for help and she couldn't stop it."

◆　◆　◆

Ann Keith learned of Jane's problem with shoplifting around 1986, when a friend from the probation office tipped her off. "I called her and I said, 'Jane, we've got to talk.'" Jane went to Keith's house and they had tea at the kitchen table.

"Jane, you've been shoplifting, haven't you?" said Keith.

Jane nodded. "Yeah."

"Why didn't you come to me?"

Jane grinned and said, "Oh, I knew you'd come to me when you found out."

"Look, I don't want to go and visit you in jail," said Keith.

Jane avoided jail on that and a subsequent charge. When it happened again, she told Keith she had to get help because she had no control over the shoplifting. She said the psychiatrist she was seeing wasn't helping her.

"I want hypnosis," said Jane. "I have to stop it."

Resources for the type of treatment Jane needed were scarce in Halifax, but Keith knew that if anyone could help her it was John Curtis. Curtis has a string of credentials giving him standing as an expert in psychiatry in Canada and the United States. His specialties are multiple personality disorders, dissociative disorders, and hypnosis.

◆ ◆ ◆

On February 2, 1989, two months after Jane Hurshman started treatment with John Curtis, she was shopping at Towers Department Store, in the town of Bedford, just north of Halifax. She was wearing a winter jacket over a red and black sweater and pushing a shopping cart with her purse in the upper compartment. Beside the purse were two beige planter trays and a pair of blue jogging pants with matching top. In the lower part of the cart was an audio cassette holder.

In an aisle in the outdoors department, she slipped the planter trays into her purse and tucked the jogging suit under her sweater. Gabrielle MacAulay, the store's loss prevention investigator, saw her conceal the items. Jane paid for the cassette holder and walked toward the exit. MacAulay approached her as she was leaving.

"Excuse me, ma'am," she said, producing her identification. "You have some items concealed that you haven't paid for."

"Yes, I do have items that I didn't pay for," admitted Jane.

MacAulay arrested her, read her her legal rights, and asked her if she understood.

"I understand," Jane said softly.

Jane followed MacAulay to the store's office, where she called a lawyer and waited for the Bedford police to arrive. The total value of the items stolen was $37.96.

At the time of this latest arrest, Jane had at least seven convictions for shoplifting. At her trial for the Towers theft, in July 1989, Jane told defence lawyer Linda Tippett that she remembered taking the jogging suit but not the planter trays.

"Who was the track suit for?" asked Tippett.

"It would have fit Darren," Jane replied.

"Was it something Darren needed?"

"No, he didn't need it."

"Did you have any money in your purse that could have paid for those items?"

"Yes."

"When you took the items, did you look around to see who might have been there?"

Jane didn't respond for several seconds. "I don't know. I don't think so. I just . . . didn't think. I just did it."

"What was going through your mind at the time?" asked Tippett.

"That's difficult to say . . . Nothing, really."

Tippet went through Jane's record of convictions and asked her if she remembered when she started shoplifting.

"Not really," she replied. "A long time."

"And other than the times you've been caught, have you taken things on other occasions?"

"Yes."

"When did you start realizing that this was a serious problem?"

"Probably about a year ago or less," said Jane.

"What did you do about it, if anything?" asked Tippett.

"Well, I went to see one doctor and it didn't seem to be doing any good." She said she was seeing a new psychiatrist, Dr. John Curtis, once a week. Jane said she wanted to stop shoplifting, but couldn't help herself.

"How much do you want to stop doing it?" asked Tippett.

Jane thought for several seconds. "In terms of how much . . . well," she said hesitantly, "if I thought of the thing that I would not want to lose the most, it would probably be my eyesight and I would trade that."

Jane said she would continue to see Dr. Curtis for as long as it took to stop shoplifting.

During cross-examination, Crown counsel Bob McCarroll told Jane she must have realized long ago that she had a serious problem. Jane agreed that she did.

The defence called Dr. Curtis, who told the court that Ann Keith referred Jane to him because "she had no memory of her childhood" and hypnosis might be helpful in recalling childhood trauma.

"It was felt the childhood trauma probably had something to do with her severe depression, her mood swings, even her kleptomania," said Curtis. He defined a kleptomaniac as a person who steals articles they don't really need and are quite capable of paying for. "And often these individuals will describe that it was not something that they had plotted or planned but more something they found themselves doing or had completed.

"An awful lot of the people I see with this disorder do not ever remember stealing," said Curtis. "Jane's having no recollection at all of stealing the planter bottoms is typical of kleptomania and typical of having a form of dissociative disorder in which you are unaware of certain actions — or amnesic."

Curtis said Jane did not remember most of her first twelve years of life and had no memory "of other things as well."

"I was aware that kleptomania was a factor," he said, "but it wasn't the focus of what we were doing until February 2, when she arrived late for my appointment because she had been picked up at Towers."

According to Curtis, Jane led a lifetime of accepting tragedy and problems and had learned to tune them out and ignore them. "It goes back into her childhood and into her family upbringing."

Defence lawyer Linda Tippett asked the psychiatrist if he thought Jane was improving — changing.

"Yes, she certainly is," replied Curtis. He said inducing a trance-like state to recall Jane's childhood didn't work "because she was literally so totally out of touch with herself and her emotional memories that when she went into a trance she didn't really recall anything. So we had to institute a kind of therapy in which I've been literally teaching her about families and about herself and what happened to her."

Curtis described the family system that Jane came out of as a boarding house. "It was a family where there was no discussion of any emotional events whatsoever."

As Jane's treatment progressed, Curtis said, she was getting very much in touch with herself emotionally. Through hypnosis, they were able to recognize "various ego-states" within her personality. "These are parts of the person," he said. "And there are two ego-states in her which have to do with the shoplifting." One state, he said, was associated very much with sadness and had to do with her upbringing "and never having really been nurtured."

The other ego-state was associated with an event that happened in Jane's life when she was twelve and living with her family on a Canadian Army base in Germany. Curtis related how Jane was asked to babysit a family of three children for the weekend. The parents didn't tell her where they were going, and when she went to the refrigerator to prepare supper, there was no food. "And she went to the cupboard and there was nothing in the cupboard," said Curtis. "There was nothing to eat." Jane went home.

"Mother," she said. "I can't believe this, there's no food in the house for the kids for the weekend."

Curtis said Jane's mother said nothing. "She never commented on it," he said. "She never said this was a terrible thing. She gave her enough food for one meal and sent her back to the house and made it very plain she didn't want to hear from her for the rest of the weekend.

"It was very clear to Jane that she should do what her father had done in that household since she was born — as a cook in the army, he stole every bit of food they ever ate. And she went out and started shoplifting and that was the origin of this problem.

"It was a whole family system — it was something that you just do. And Jane, unfortunately, has within her a belief system that's saying, 'This is something that's all right to do.' She's dealing with that now, but she wasn't even aware of it three months ago."

Tippett asked Curtis what goes through the mind of a kleptomaniac as they are taking things.

"It's something they're quite unconscious of and it's not a predictable thing," replied Curtis. He said he once had a client who stole an item with an RCMP officer standing beside her.

Curtis said it was interesting that in the two previous months, as Jane became more in touch with her emotions, her urge to shoplift intensified rather than decreased. "Now she can start doing something about it, whereas before she could not," he said. "And when she has the urge she's extremely careful when she goes into a store."

The ego-state that tells Jane to shoplift is associated with a tremendous amount of anger, said Curtis. "Jane has spent a lifetime of having things done to her — horrible things — and has never really expressed anger. I think a lot of it is encapsulated in that ego-state and in others as well."

He said Jane was cooperative, bright, intuitive, and was working very hard at her therapy.

"Jane herself has no conscious intent or desire to steal," said Curtis. "Her everyday self is in fact a very fine, caring, honourable, honest person who would never steal or do anything like that, but she does have ego-states inside her that would do this — for very child-like and immature reasons."

Under cross-examination by McCarroll, Curtis said the reason Jane had a heightened urge to steal of late "has to do with the fact that she's getting better. Oddly enough, this ego-state inside her cannot tolerate her getting better. That may seem rather odd to you, but Billy, her husband, could not stand her doing well either. Her family — father — could not stand her doing well, and she was continually put down by these people. And this ego-state is modelled after those people. So here you have an ego-state that's going to get you in trouble if you do well."

In her summation to the judge, Tippett said Jane's was an unusual case, and when she stole items from the store she wasn't thinking like a rational person. "She's appeared before the court with a number of convictions and she's quite well aware that someone with a record like hers could very well be looking at a jail term."

Jane was not a hardened petty thief who needed harsher penalties to rehabilitate her, Tippett said. Rather, she was suffering from an illness that sometimes left her incapable of thinking like a rational person. "No one is trying to suggest that she's insane," said Tippett. "However, she does have an illness that at the time of this incident rendered her incapable of forming the type of intent needed to sustain a conviction. A kleptomaniac she is — a thief she is not."

Crown Counsel McCarroll agreed that the issue of insanity was not a factor. "What we have here is a competition of egos in this lady," he said. "Every one of us has competition of egos of one type or another. This lady has more of a battle on her hands than most of us, but that doesn't change the fact that she knows what she does. She knows she has a history of it. She's reckless in not taking precautions to prevent herself from losing the battle with her ego."

McCarroll said it was a matter of guilt or innocence, and he suggested Jane had a guilty mind.

Provincial Court Judge Patrick Curran reserved his judgement until the following week because of the extraordinary circumstances of the case. "I'm not aware of any instances of kleptomania being recognized as a defence to a charge such as this," he said. "But I think there's a very important question raised here by the evidence and arguments I heard today."

Six days later, Jane was back in court to hear Judge Curran's decision. "One could conclude from the evidence that Mrs. Hurshman had a reduced degree of responsibility for her actions because of the condition which affected her and that it is something to be taken into account on sentencing rather than when determining guilt or innocence.

"Apart from the evidence of the dissociative state, it's clear that Mrs. Hurshman did steal property of Towers on February 2, 1989, and consequently I find her guilty of that offence."

Jane stood as Judge Curran sentenced her. He said he accepted her reduced responsibility as outlined by Dr. Curtis and commended her for seeking help. He placed her on probation and instructed her to continue with therapy.

The judge also recommended that she take somebody with her when she went shopping — "somebody that you're not afraid to tell what the history has been and to be right there with you and make sure it doesn't happen."

He tempered his advice with a warning that if the shoplifting continued Jane would have to face the consequences. "Because, notwithstanding some measure of reduced responsibility, the time is going to come sooner or later when the courts are going to conclude the only way to stop this kind of thing is to put you in jail for some period of time — which would be most unfortunate, especially since it seems in every other way that you lead a praiseworthy kind of life."

◆ ◆ ◆

Victoria Jones remembers shopping at a mall with Jane in the summer of 1990, when she was living with her on Arklow Drive. Some

aspects of the scenario were strikingly similar to the incident with
Margaret Joudrey at the Bridgewater mall years before.

"I'm not much of a mall person," says Jones, "and I got tired, so
I told Jane I would sit on a bench and wait for her." An hour passed
and Jane didn't return. "I thought, *What's going on?* so I went in
and found her."

Jane said she was looking for strawberries and sent Jones in one
direction while she went into the bulk food section. A few minutes
later, as they were leaving the store, two security officers stopped
them. They accused Jane of theft.

"I don't have anything," protested Jane.

"Either you come with us or we'll send for the police."

Jane handed Jones the keys to the car.

"Wait for me in the car," she said. "I won't be long."

Jane came out a short time later and they drove home.

"She didn't say anything," says Jones, "but I imagine they
searched her and didn't find anything. They wouldn't have stopped
her unless they were sure. I think she must have got rid of whatever
it was she had when she sent me after the strawberries.

"She used to buy me all these presents and I had kind of an idea
where they were coming from, but you can't turn around to the
person and say, 'Where did this come from?'"

Jane was likely dissociating in the store, and when Jones
appeared it jarred her out of her trance, and she returned the stolen
item.

◆ ◆ ◆

There is no doubt that Jane felt embarrassed and ashamed about her
shoplifting. She didn't tell her counsellor, Ann Keith, about it until
Keith came to her. And until she began therapy with Dr. Curtis and
came to realize her shoplifting was a disorder, she kept it a secret
even from her closest friends.

After her arrest at Towers, but before her trial, Jane drove to
Bridgewater and revealed her secret to Carrie Rafuse.

"I have problems stealing and I want you to know, because
you're going to read about it in the newspaper," said Jane.

Her admission was enlightening to Carrie. "She never wanted to go shopping with me, never — ever. When she told me about her problem, it just clicked."

Carrie clearly remembers one of Jane's laughing refusals to accompany her on a shopping excursion.

"Oh, Carrie," Jane said, "that's the difference between us. You like the malls and you like shopping, but I don't — I hate it."

Now Carrie understood, and they hugged and cried. "She told me about her therapy with John Curtis and she said she was feeling great — and I could tell it was true. For a long time before that, she was there but she wasn't there. Now it was like my friend Jane was back, and I told her I thought the therapy was doing good for her."

Jane's sister Mona says Jane was really excited about her therapy. "She felt very good about seeing Dr. Curtis because she was finally doing something for herself. She wouldn't say a lot about the sessions but she said there was hypnosis involved. She said he gave her books to read and movies to watch and they'd talk about the dominant characters."

What Jane didn't tell Mona was that, through hypnosis, she eventually remembered being sexually assaulted, as a child, by someone close to the family — as Ann Keith had long suspected.

◆ ◆ ◆

Margaret Jourdrey was asked in a 1992 interview if Billy ever learned about the shoplifting incident in Bridgewater. "No!" she exclaimed. "And I felt so sorry for not telling him."

Joudrey's response and her version of the incident bring into question her portrayal of Billy Stafford at Jane's murder trial and lend credence to the findings of Dr. Curtis. If Billy were as harmless as Joudrey professed, why would Jane be so afraid to tell him about the shoplifting charge? And why would Joudrey help her keep it a secret?

Dr. Curtis, at Jane's trial in Bedford, talked about the dissociative behaviour of kleptomaniacs. Jane surely was dissociating when she walked out of the Bridgewater store with a cart full of merchandise she hadn't paid for. It was very late and she was one of the last customers, if not the last, to leave. Workers at the store were preparing to close and no doubt would have been watching her, waiting for her to go through check-out so they could leave.

◆ ◆ ◆

Through John Curtis, Jane began to better understand the root cause of her mood swings and her kleptomania, and she began to speak publicly about it. She was adamant that people aren't born to be victims.

"We are born to be what we are taught to be, and what we are conditioned to be," she said in one speech. "As a child, I grew up in a home with an alcoholic father and a mother who only had time for him. In our home, there was no communication, no positive encouragement, no parental involvement of any kind in my life or in the lives of my older brother or my two younger sisters.

"I watched my mother being verbally and physically abused. Mom withstood this abuse for years and years, always believing that someday things would get better. To this very day, my mom will not discuss her life or the abuse.

"I was very fearful of and obedient to my father, always trying to please him, and growing up believing that life should be — please everyone but yourself."

At the time she made that speech Jane had been seeing Dr. Curtis for just over a year. "I can honestly say that it is the best thing that I have ever done for myself," she said.

She said being a kleptomaniac was like being an alcoholic. "You can spend the rest of your life clean and sober, but you are always an alcoholic. There is always the chance that you will take that one drink, or for me that I will steal that one item."

◆ ◆ ◆

On June 9, 1991, less than a year after the conviction for the theft from Towers, Jane Hurshman was arrested for stealing greeting cards and a bottle of cologne from a Dartmouth pharmacy. She pleaded guilty and was fined $375. The next day the story was in the news. "Hurshman Fined For Theft" ran one headline.

The stories always brought up Jane's past and the fact that she killed Billy Stafford. She believed she was being treated unfairly because of who she was, and she decided to fight back. She wrote a scathing letter to a Halifax newspaper in which she said her name "still sells your papers after all these years. If everyone that got caught and sentenced for shoplifting got media coverage, there wouldn't be any room in your paper to print anything else.

"Shoplifting — kleptomania — is a disease, the same as alcoholism, compulsive overeating, anorexia or compulsive gambling." She said shoplifting was a crime "while the others you can do anywhere and there is no repercussion."

Shoplifting, Jane said, "brings shame and humiliation to me and my family." She said she was fortunate to have family and friends who supported her, and she urged the media to "put more effort into publishing information about the problem" instead of keeping her in the spotlight.

"I am a good, honest, hard-working, caring, and helpful person, and it would be nice to live my life without constant comments from the media," said Jane.

When people see the word *shoplifting*, they associate it with "a bad, untrustworthy person," she said. "I am neither, nor is anyone else who has the disease of kleptomania.

"It's because of all the shit and abuse that I have endured during my life that I continually have to fight and struggle every day to live. Just because the abuse is gone, and Stafford is dead, does not mean that everything is okay, or normal.

"Myself and others like me have no idea what *normal* is. I must spend the rest of my life learning — one day at a time. And when I mess up — as in shoplifting — it is because I cannot believe that I deserve to be happy, or that I am worthy of good things or good people around me."

The Halifax *Chronicle-Herald* assigned reporter Gail Lethbridge to interview Jane about her kleptomania. The story appeared less than a week after the account of her conviction and fine. In the article, Jane said kleptomania was "a symptom of the abuse that I suffered, probably from childhood" and to a larger degree from her years with Billy Stafford. She said she was speaking out so that other women with the same problem would know they were not alone. "I want it brought out in the open so that kleptomania is an issue that is talked about like alcoholism. It's a disease."

Lethbridge wrote that Jane couldn't explain what triggered her to shoplift, but a memory from her past or an act of violence, like the Montreal massacre, could "send her into a swirl of emotional confusion and pain. Most of the time she suppresses the urge but occasionally she finds herself stealing. Afterwards, the feelings are always the same — sharp disappointment in herself, and anger at her inability to shake the urge and forget the past."

The article included a post office box address for Jane, who said she wanted to start a support group for those suffering from kleptomania and other effects of abuse. It was after that appeal that Sara, who had been sexually and physically abused as a child and a young adult, first wrote to her.

"I know you steal and understand that it's humiliating for you," wrote Sara. "But I do something that's even more humiliating and shameful." She was an obsessive masturbator, which is not uncommon for women who were sexually abused as children. (Donna Smith's daughter, Mary, who was discovered masturbating at the age of three at Bryony House, continued the practice indiscriminately and had to undergo therapy.)

Jane responded to Sara praising her for recognizing her problem and trying to do something about it. They corresponded regularly after that.

Liz Forestell says Jane's attempt to form a support group illustrated "what I said about her being able to take things that happened to her and turn them into a strength."

Despite the therapy and the efforts to go public with her problem and its underlying cause, Jane was frustrated that the urge to steal was greater than ever.

"I just can't control it," she said in late 1991. "I am getting help from my doctors, but it isn't easy. It's a constant struggle for me."

She lost the struggle once again when she was arrested for shoplifting from an IGA store in Dartmouth in November 1991. She kept it a secret from her family and pleaded not guilty when she appeared in court in December. Her case was put over to March 4, 1992, when she was scheduled to appear in Courtroom No. 2 at 9:30 A.M.

XII

THOUGHTS
OF DEATH

SUICIDE WAS AN OPTION Jane Hurshman often considered during the abusive years with Billy Stafford. "I took to believing that only in death would I find peace," she said. "But Darren would be left in Bill's custody and I couldn't stand the thought of that. He was my strength, my gift from God, my whole instinct to survive."

After Billy's death, thoughts of suicide subsided, yet they were never far from the surface. Jane was more open about it with some of her friends than with others.

"Jane and I often talked about suicide," says Donna Smith. "If we ever decided to do it, I said I would help her and she said she would help me. Jane kept saying we were so much alike.

"We laughed about getting older and opening a nursing home together. We pictured ourselves sitting on the porch with our canes and knocking over whoever we wanted to knock over.

"But suicide was always there. We didn't call it suicide. We called it *escape*. You know, you can only take so much."

In the summer of 1988, Donna and her children were invited for a week's vacation in Cape Breton by a friend who lived there. The friend arranged to have someone drive Donna up from Halifax.

A day or two before they were to leave, Jane called Donna.

"I'm not going to be around when you get back," she said. "I can't take any more. I want to die." Donna did her best to talk Jane out of it and then called Ann Keith in tears.

"Ann, she's going to do it," she cried. "I know she is."

Donna didn't want to leave Jane, but her children were excited about the trip and their ride was already en route to pick them up.

Keith, who was still counselling Jane at the time, called her on a Sunday night under the pretext of changing the time of their session the next day. That session went routinely until Jane was preparing to leave.

"I'm really glad you called me last night," she said. "I was going to commit suicide, but you jarred me out of it." Jane told Keith she had put her papers in order and had written letters to her children, the rest of her family, and her friends.

"She had a syringe," says Keith, "and she said she was going to inject air into her ear. She was a nursing assistant and she had access to needles."

Jane once talked to her sister Mona about using a syringe. "Mona," she said, "if I ever wanted to die, I could do it real easy. All I'd have to do is get a needle, inject air into my veins, and I'd be gone just like that."

While Donna Smith was in Cape Breton, her daughter contracted chicken pox and they stayed two and a half weeks instead of one week. "I kept calling Jane and Ann but it wasn't until two or three days after I returned home that I thought Jane was over it."

◆　◆　◆

Jane's eldest son, Allen, didn't realize at that time that his mother's shoplifting was something she had no control over, and he felt badly when he came to understand it was an illness.

"He didn't understand the extent of Jane's hurt inside and how all that stuff could be brought back up and make her feel victimized all over again," says his aunt Mona. "He didn't want to see it anymore. He didn't want to hear about it. And it seemed like every time he turned around, something was in the paper and people would ask him about it. It was an embarrassment to Allen, and I know that would have hurt and upset Jane, but not to the extent that she would want to kill herself."

Ann Keith says the media attention, and the embarrassment it brought to the family, hurt Jane deeply. "Because she loved her family so much, the last thing she wanted to do was to bring disgrace on them. And she felt, personally, that she was letting her family down."

There is no doubt that Jane's inability to stop shoplifting, and the fallout that resulted whenever she was caught, pushed her to contemplate suicide. That was the case in 1988, when she was arrested for shoplifting twice within three months in Dartmouth.

On November 15 of that year, she was fined $200 on one charge, then was picked up on a second charge two and a half weeks later. It was then that James Tynes went to the police and the store involved, and sought, unsuccessfully, to have the charges dropped.

"I told her it didn't matter to me and that I was there for support," he says.

(Jane had started seeing Dr. John Curtis before the second arrest but didn't tell him about her problem or the incident. She told a friend it was too embarrassing for her.)

Jane was scheduled to appear in court in Dartmouth on January 10 and was to report to the police station the day before for mug shots and fingerprints.

On January 6, Jane was at home sleeping, after working the night shift at the rehab centre, when the telephone awakened her. The caller said he was a constable with the Dartmouth city police. Jane missed his name and he ignored her when she asked him to repeat it.

"Several times throughout his conversation, I asked him to tell me his name, but he just kept talking past me and over me," she said later.

The caller told her that the newspapers would be present when Jane appeared in court on the tenth, and that the Children's Aid would be notified "and they would see that the children were dealt with the way they should have been before."

"He said that the newspapers would carry my story," said Jane. "This would be the eighth time I appeared in the Dartmouth court and he said that I would be doing jail time and my kids would be taken away and I would be proven to be an unfit mother."

Jane couldn't get back to sleep, and that afternoon she decided to kill herself. She booked a room in a Dartmouth motel and went to work that night as usual. At 4 A.M., when her floor at the rehab centre was quiet, she sat down and prepared a suicide audio tape for Tynes.

"James, I want you to know, darling, you are forever in my heart and in my mind," she said, in a soft voice. "You've been a very special person in my life these last years and you've made up for all the unbearable years I've lived. You've been a lover, a friend, and a companion, and I have been more honest and straightforward to you than I have been with anyone.

"You are a beautiful, special, person and I don't want to bring you any more shame and humiliation than I already have. I've brought it to my children too and I still continue to do so. Allen knows I stole way back when. I don't know what Jamie knows. Darren knows I steal, and he's been quite worried about my going to court."

Jane said on the tape it was difficult for her to accept that she wouldn't be seeing him or her children and family again but her death wouldn't be a surprise to them.

She said that only Tynes and her sister Mona were to know that she was killing herself because of the shoplifting. She wanted her sons and the rest of the family to believe she took her life because she was dying from incurable cancer. She said suicide by a cancer victim would be "a hundred times more acceptable" than a suicide resulting from shoplifting.

"I don't know if you can agree to a lie — but I do hope you don't tell my kids or parents the truth, and I ask the same thing of Mona. What I have is the same as a cancer — it's incurable and it destroys. It eats away just like a cancer — it has been with me all my life and it has destroyed me a little at a time. And it begins to gnaw and chew anything that I come close to or love. . . .

"I just don't want to be here anymore. I know that's going to cause you to be sad and hurt, and the pain is going to be enormous."

Her voice became stronger and more authoritative when she talked about her remains. "I do not want to be buried in the ground. I want to be cremated and I definitely do not want to be put in any coffin. I want Mom to take my ashes and in the spring when she plants her flowers in her garden, I want her to sprinkle my ashes there. Then I will be at peace at last."

Jane thanked Tynes for trying to get the store manager and the police to drop charges against her. "You'll never know how much that meant to me. Nobody has ever defended me like that."

She asked Tynes to keep the news of her suicide from her children until they were all together at her parents' house. "Darren really is a very warm and loving, and extremely sensitive, child, so I'd like his hurt to be buffered by him being with family."

Jane said she hadn't been a good parent "as far as consistency and punishment" and she hoped Darren would go to Ottawa to live with her sister Sandy and that Jamie would go to Mona and Ed, in Barrie.

Allen and his girlfriend, Charlene, were planning to marry in September, and Jane hoped "that everything goes well in their life and that they are together forever."

Jane and Tynes had talked about getting married, and she had even bought a dress. Her voice was barely a whisper when she said two moments she had often visualized were the look in Tynes's eyes as she came down the aisle toward him, and the exchange of rings as they said "I do."

"We have so much love to share with each other, I know we'd have a good life together," she said.

There was a tinge of anger in Jane's voice when she talked about the Dartmouth police and the call she received on Friday. "There is no way, James, that I could ever be an unfit mother. Nobody loves their kids more than I do." Society might consider her unfit, she said, but society didn't know the whole story. She said she wouldn't give them the opportunity to declare her unfit or to take her children.

"So I decided Friday afternoon that of my options, suicide was the way to go. That's the solution I came up with, and right or wrong, that's my decision. With that decision, for the first time in my life, I felt an inner peace — knowing that it's soon going to be all over."

Jane asked Tynes to call the court or attend on January 10, "and tell them that I am dead and that I won't be bothering them anymore. Also, I'm supposed to go on the ninth to the Dartmouth police station for mug shots and fingerprints and I don't want these assholes coming to my door. Could you just kindly tell them I'm deceased now and I won't be in for mug shots and fingerprints —

which they already got from me less than two weeks ago."

On the tape, Jane played two of their favourite songs, which they had chosen to be played at their wedding, read a poem, and reminisced about some of their good times together.

"I do have your memory hard in my mind — you and my children and my family — and I'll die that way," she said. "James, I do know that there is a Heavenly Father and a Lord Jesus Christ, who is our mediator and redeemer. But I also believe that he works for some, and some he can't help, because I think they gave up on him and vice versa. I think that's the point I'm at in my life now.

"Once again I am hurting so many people, but this will be the last hurt — there'll be no more."

Jane's closing words were barely audible: "You have my endless love and I know I have yours and I have taken yours to my grave — I love you, James."

She told him she took an overdose of sleeping pills because "it just seemed to be the easiest way and the least painful — to lie down and go to sleep and have a sleep that will be forever.

"The inner peace is near, babe, and I ask your forgiveness."

She ended the recording with a short prayer: "Dear Heavenly Father, protect him and my children, ease their pain, and fill their hearts with love only . . ."

◆ ◆ ◆

The tape was delivered to Tynes by taxi shortly after seven-thirty Saturday morning, about the time Jane usually returned home from work. The driver told Tynes where he had picked up the tape.

Tynes listened to part of it and immediately called the police. Jane was close to death when they found her. Had they arrived even minutes later, she would probably have died.

She drifted in and out of consciousness for several days, and when she was well enough, she was sent to the Nova Scotia Hospital for psychiatric care.

On January 10, Tynes appeared in court in Dartmouth on Jane's behalf and explained the reason for her absence. The case was put over for several months.

Donna Smith called Jane at the hospital, during her recovery.

"She was really sad, but more embarrassed, at what she had done. She said she could only get so far in her therapy.

"The hardest part of therapy is that you have to relive everything. Sometimes you feel anger toward the therapist because you go home and keep thinking about it and they just move on to the next patient. You're like a number and you don't mean anything to them. There are times when you don't want to go because you don't want to talk about it. I know Jane often felt that way."

Two weeks after her release from the hospital, Jane told Carrie Rafuse about the suicide attempt.

"I felt so bad," says Carrie, "and I asked her why she didn't call me if she was depressed. What bothered me most is that I didn't detect that she was feeling that way. She must have been depressed for a couple of months, but I didn't notice it."

(About two weeks later, on February 2, 1989, Jane was caught stealing the jogging suit and planter trays at Towers. This time John Curtis found out because after being arrested, she was late for her appointment with him.)

In a speech a year after her suicide attempt, Jane said she tried to kill herself because she couldn't deal with her problems and wouldn't discuss them with anyone. "You have the same kind of feeling and thoughts that you have in an abusive situation," she said. "The feelings of hopelessness and helplessness and that you are weak and a failure. But mostly, it's a feeling of being incapable of being normal.

"Death appeared better to me than having to go to court for shoplifting and having to be harassed by the media. Worst of all was having everyone know my secret and being told that I was an unfit mother and having my sons taken away."

In that speech Jane made a rare admission that she had deep-seated problems that she had ignored because she had spent so much time helping others. "Just because I was out of my abusive situation and just because I had my family together, and just because I allowed everyone to believe all was fine, did not mean that was how it was. I still had not dealt with me, personally. I still had a gigantic secret problem — 'shoplifting' — a problem that was destroying me."

While she was recovering in the Nova Scotia Hospital, Jane told Carrie Rafuse she couldn't think of anything to live for.

"The kids would be better off without me," she told Carrie.

Jane began reading in the hospital, searching for answers. "She thought she might be manic depressive and she went to her doctor who put her on Lithium," says Carrie. "She was on it for a while and she said, 'Yes, I can see light at the end of the tunnel and I think I do feel better.' But it didn't work. She was trying to convince herself."

Tynes, who was living on and off with Jane during that period, said she had wide mood swings. "The Lithium was supposed to balance things out and she was doing some exercises and reading, but it wasn't doing any good."

Jane eventually gave up on the Lithium, and there was improvement when Dr. Curtis introduced her to hypnotherapy treatment.

"The depression wasn't gone away," said Tynes, "but she knew how to control it, and she understood herself a lot more. She seemed better to me."

Victoria Jones noticed the same mood swings when she went to live with Jane a year later, in January 1990. "She wouldn't say much. She was just quiet and she would go into her room and sleep a lot when things were bothering her."

In her job as a counsellor at the Harbour House shelter for battered women, Carrie Rafuse encounters a lot of suicidal women. "Eventually you learn to pick up little warnings, but you couldn't pick up the signs with Jane.

"I was speaking with this woman every two or three weeks and I never sensed any of this. After her bout at the Nova Scotia Hospital, I decided I would have to really watch her — to see if there were any clues."

Carrie's vigilance paid off and she began to notice that Jane became more angry and aggressive than usual when she was despondent. "She would be very preoccupied and a little sarcastic to me. Her fuse was a little shorter. When I noticed her like that, I'd really talk to her. It was a warning signal, but she wouldn't tell you much. You had to either dig it out or, if she was in the mood, she might just tell you what was bothering her. You might not find out until a month later but, in her own time, she would tell me."

XIII
∴
WEDDING
BELLS

ON SATURDAY, JULY 21, 1990, Jane Hurshman drove to Bridgewater to spend the evening with her friend Carrie Rafuse as the kick-off to a two-week vacation at her parents' place in nearby Danesville. Jane had been on her own since she and James Tynes stopped seeing each other several months earlier. The women decided to drive to Mahone Bay and have supper at the Mug and Anchor, a local pub.

"As usual with Carrie, we were late getting there and the grill was closing," Jane wrote in a letter a year later. "We stayed and sat outside and had a couple of drafts."

After their drinks, they returned to Bridgewater to have supper at the Topsail Tavern. A band was playing and after their meal they decided to have a drink in the bar.

Joel Corkum, a licensed mechanic working locally at Hebb's Cross Esso, was sitting at a table near the band with his friend Fred. Around ten, Joel spotted Jane and Carrie walk in. He knew Carrie but hadn't seen her in about fifteen years.

The place was crowded, and on his way to greet Carrie, Corkum accidentally bumped into Jane. "You have to go through a little corridor and I just about knocked her over," he recalls. There were no empty tables, and he invited the women to join him and Fred. They accepted and Carrie made the introductions. Joel was soft-spoken and, at thirty-three, eight years younger than Jane. She was smitten.

"When I looked into Joel's deep, gentle blue eyes, I knew it was destiny," Jane wrote later. "I came alive."

Carrie explained that she and Jane met at school and Jane was a certified nursing assistant.

"That's good," laughed Joel. "I'm a mechanic and I beat myself up a lot at work."

He asked Jane to dance and they stayed on the floor for a full set. "It was comfortable," he says. "I was attracted to her as soon as I seen her. It was like I knew her — yet I didn't."

Sometime after midnight the four of them went for coffee. Carrie says she noticed Jane and Joel were holding hands as they left the tavern.

"We drove over to Tim Horton Donuts for coffee," recalls Joel. "And Jane and I did a lot of talking."

Carrie offered Fred a lift home. "They won't notice," she said. When she returned, Jane and Joel were still talking.

Carrie decided to leave, and Jane went with Joel to the nearby trailer he was living in. They drank more coffee and talked and, after a while, Joel asked Jane if she would see him the next day. It was Sunday and he would be off work. Jane agreed.

Joel met Jane's parents when he came by to pick her up the next day. Then they went to Cherry Hill Beach, where they spent most of the day getting to know each other. Soon Jane was spending her nights in Joel's trailer.

About a week after they met, Joel went to see Jane at her parents' place. "She was sitting at the table with her back to the wall," he recalls. "She had sort of a funny look on her face."

"What did I do now?" he asked with a smile.

"Oh, you didn't do anything," she said. "Have you ever read *Life with Billy*?"

"Yeah, I read that," replied Joel.

"Well, I'm Jane of that book."

He shrugged. "So?"

"Do you want to know about it?"

"That was then — this is now. If you want to talk about it, I'll listen. But if you don't want to talk about it, I'm not going to ask. It doesn't matter to me what happened in your past."

Joel says Jane seemed relieved at his reaction. "I gather some people would have got right nosy — want to know everything about it. Or they would back right away. I didn't do either. I just liked her for who she was."

When Jane left for Cole Harbour at the end of her vacation, she gave Joel a key to her townhouse.

"She invited me up for the weekend a couple of weeks after she went back," he says. "In between, my phone bill was hurtin' bad because I called her every night."

Carrie Rafuse didn't see Jane for a few weeks after their night out. "The next time she came down, I could see she was like a little kid in love. You could see it in her face. She was ecstatic."

Carrie wondered if Jane knew about Joel's past. Carrie had known him casually for several years and he seemed harmless, but she had heard things about him.

When Joel was three, his father died, and he left home at sixteen. He got into trouble with the law, serving two six-month sentences on break-and-enter charges as a teenager and three months for dangerous driving in his early twenties.

He was twice-married and had three children. "I had one kid before I was married — when I was sixteen or seventeen. It was one of those *oops* things. And I had two more with my first wife." Joel doesn't see the two children from his marriage. "They were adopted out a long time ago," he says. The son born prior to his marriage is now seventeen. Joel didn't see much of him until Jane encouraged him to do so.

"He's being raised by his grandparents on his mother's side and they're not really fond of me," says Joel, who worked on the fishing boats before he became a mechanic. He had been on his own for about a year before he met Jane.

Jane didn't ask Carrie about Joel's past. "I hinted to her," Carrie says, "but I never, ever, forced my opinion on her or told her what I thought she should do." And Jane appeared so happy, Carrie didn't want to say anything that would break the spell.

Jane soon invited Joel to come to Cole Harbour to live with her, Jamie, Darren, and their two dogs. He found a job with a muffler shop in the Halifax area, and in early September 1990, moved in with them. By late fall of that year, they were engaged.

At the end of September, Jane went into hospital for a hysterectomy and was told not to return to work until the end of November. After her operation, she decided to take a short vacation to Jamaica with Annette Bushen and her daughter Charlene. Bushen describes it as their "vacation from hell."

Things started to go wrong in Toronto when their plane was delayed by mechanical problems. Once they were in the air, they noticed one of the other passengers, a Jamaican returning home after a visit to Canada, had three umbrellas with him.

"We thought, isn't that great — it's so hot, they must use the umbrellas for protection from the sun," says Bushen. "We didn't know it was the rainy season in Jamaica."

They arrived to discover their luggage was still back in Toronto. Only Charlene had thought to carry a shoulder bag with summer shorts and a top. Jane and Annette were wearing jeans, turtleneck sweaters, and jackets.

"It was muggy and we had a two-hour drive from the airport to the hotel," says Bushen. "We had our purses, our money, our cameras — and our enthusiasm, which didn't take long to die."

They learned the next day they would have to go without their luggage until late that night.

"Necessity being the mother of invention, Jane and I used hotel bath sheets as sarongs," says Bushen. "We wore them down to breakfast and then down the main street and into stores to shop. We got a lot of funny looks, but our essential areas were covered."

They were warned that the streets were dangerous after dark. "We spent our nights with our Jamaican rum, our Kahlúa, and our milk, out on the balcony," says Bushen. "We were dreaming about this island in the sun, but it rained four of the five days we were there. We didn't enjoy the weather and we didn't like being confined but we did a lot of laughing."

◆ ◆ ◆

On a Sunday afternoon in November, Jane and Joel drove to Bridgewater to visit his seventy-seven-year-old mother. At one point she took Jane aside.

"Joel's finally happy," she said. "I can let go."

"It didn't really make any sense to us at the time," says Joel. But his mother, who suffered from angina, died of a heart attack the following Tuesday.

In April of 1991, Jane and Joel jointly purchased a house just up the street in Arklow Drive. Joel was in debt and had declared personal bankruptcy, so Jane put up most of the down payment. Most of his pay went toward the mortgage from then on. The house was small, but it had a decent yard and "a lot of potential." Joel built a bedroom in the basement for fourteen-year-old Darren, and a wall of shelves for Jane's growing collection of books. He also set up, adjoining their bedroom, a cubby-hole with a desk as an office for Jane.

Jane shared her feelings about Joel with Sara. In August 1991, Jane sent her a signed copy of *Life With Billy* and a photograph of her and Joel. "He is a wonderful man," she said in an accompanying letter. "We bought a lovely home in April and we are going to get married. I am really looking forward to it all."

A month later she wrote: "I have been on my own with my sons for nearly ten years. I have gone out with guys in that time, but none really interested me until Joel — and we spend all of our free time together. He is my best friend, my lover, my companion, and soon to be my husband. We are good for each other."

Jane and Joel set October 10 as their wedding day. She asked her friend Carrie Rafuse to be her maid of honour. As the wedding approached, Carrie noticed Jane became more aggressive and agitated.

"I don't know if I can do this," Jane told her.

"Look," said Carrie, "if you want to change your mind, it's okay, even if you're walking down the aisle. I'll take care of it. I'll explain it to everybody." Her assurances relieved Jane's anxieties.

The ceremony was at St. John's Evangelical Lutheran Church, a quaint steepled church facing the water in Mahone Bay. Two ministers jointly conducted the wedding service, Rev. George Wawin, the regular pastor, and Rev. Margie Whynot, whom Jane had befriended in her work with battered women.

Whynot had been sexually abused as a child, was pregnant and married as a teenager, and was physically and sexually abused by her husband for seventeen years. She finally left, divorcing him in

1978. By 1980 she was attending Mount Allison University in New Brunswick and, later, the Atlantic School of Theology. In 1985 she was ordained as a minister in the United Church of Canada.

Whynot began speaking out on domestic violence, and she met Ann Keith of SSAV and Jane Hurshman, whom she had long admired. "When she shot and killed Billy Stafford, I found a soul mate, even though she didn't know it then," says Whynot. "Twice I had tried to kill my husband, both times in a moment of rage while I was being brutally beaten."

Whynot says her husband was stronger than she was and that saved him. "I had to live with the knowledge that I, a servant of God, had those feelings — that I wanted to kill. Then, Jane did it." When Jane was acquitted by a jury at her first trial, Whynot says she too felt acquitted — of the guilt over wanting to kill her husband. "She became my hero."

Her hero stood before her and Reverend Wawin on a sunny autumn afternoon and, before a small gathering of friends and family, was married to Joel Corkum.

Ann Keith says that after Jane repeated her vows "there was a big sigh of relief that could be heard throughout the church. It was as if she was saying, 'I've done it.'"

Joel says he was nervous and hoping he would be third-time lucky. "I didn't have a great batting average, and I was just a little leery, wondering if everything would work out."

Jane described her wedding and five-day honeymoon to her pen pal Sara:

> It was just beautiful how the sun came streaming through the lovely stained glass windows. The ceremony was very spiritual and very uplifting. I wrote out our vows and everything went well. After the ceremony we had a buffet lunch in the church rectory. It was very informal and very relaxed and easy. No booze!
>
> Both of my sisters came from Ontario — and my best friend since childhood [Valery Cromwell] also came home from Ontario. That was very special. After the ceremony we went down to mom and dad's for the evening and later drove home.
>
> In the morning, we got ready for our honeymoon. We drove to New Brunswick, to the ferry to Prince Edward Island and

went to a gorgeous cottage. It was an old-fashioned place right on the beach. It had a fully equipped kitchen, a dining room, living room with a fireplace, and a bathroom with a huge jacuzzi! WOW! It was a fantasy come true. We had a fantastic time.

When we left there, we went to Cape Breton and stayed at an old inn that was surrounded by mountains. It was just breathtakingly beautiful with all of its splendid color! WOW!

We left there and went to Sydney and the next day we left for home. It was one wonderful experience — a beautiful collection of memories.

What Jane didn't mention was that she and her new husband were not alone. She had invited Carrie and her boyfriend, Bob, to travel with them.

A short time before the wedding, Carrie told Jane that she and Bob were planning a trip to Prince Edward Island and Cape Breton.

"Well listen, Carrie," said Jane. "Would you mind if we went with you? We haven't planned a honeymoon or anything, so why don't you just wait till we get married and then we'll take off together."

Carrie was taken aback. She and Bob had never been away together and she found it somewhat unusual to be invited along on someone else's honeymoon. "I'd want to be alone on my honeymoon, but I thought, oh well — it might be fun."

Although Jane appeared happy after the wedding ceremony, some of her friends noticed that her eyes at times widened and bulged as if she was dissociating.

"Her eyes stuck right out," says Carrie, "but she got through it."

Ann Keith believes Jane was experiencing flashbacks. Whatever she was going through, everyone close to Jane agreed that in the days and weeks that followed, they had never seen her so happy.

"Her wrinkles even seemed to have vanished," says Carrie. "It was wonderful to see her like that and know she was truly happy inside."

On the first night in the cottage on Prince Edward Island, Jane and Carrie cooked dinner, turned out the lights, and lit several candles.

Carrie begins to weep and her voice cracks as she remembers

how happy Jane was that night. "The whole place was full of candles and we all sat around the table and Jane said, 'Just a minute I want to say a prayer.' She was so happy. For that week anyway, she was away from all her problems. We all held hands and she just thanked God for her friends and for her new life.

"I wondered about her marrying Joel, but I thought, if it's going to make her feel like this, then fine with me — great."

After the honeymoon, Jane and Joel resumed their daily routine, with Jane working nights at the rehab centre and sleeping during the day while Joel was at work. Jane continued to speak out against domestic violence and on many afternoons and early evenings attended meetings or met with battered women. Joel knew her work with women was important to her and did not try to discourage her.

"We managed to get together most evenings and on our days off," he says. "In the good weather we would take the dogs down to the beach and walk away out when the tide was low."

They doted on each other, and Joel often found love notes or cards from Jane. "I'd find them around the house — even in my lunch pail." He had to ask her to stop packing his lunches when his weight ballooned from 175 pounds to 210.

"I could hardly close my lunch pail, she put so much into it," says Joel. "Finally I told her to let me make my own lunches."

Ann Keith says Jane was "just beaming in the weeks after her marriage. I thought, *This is great.* She had her kids together, she had her work, she had her house — everything."

Jane's feelings toward Joel were summed up in the letter she wrote to him on the anniversary of their first meeting, at the tavern in Bridgewater: "Over this past year, we have grown and learned so much about each other.

"We change every day, yet our love keeps growing stronger and safer! We have no need to fight or argue, although quite often we differ in our opinions — which is great! There is nothing we cannot discuss openly and easily.

"There is no way that I could ever see me without you. I no longer take life for granted, and because of you, I have a very special appreciation of its beauty. Our love is very precious and it certainly will continue to be an amazing, cherished experience.

"I knew in my heart that we would be so good for each other. The emotions you stirred inside were overwhelming and when you kissed me, I knew it was for real — I would lay my life on the line for you anytime."

Carrie Rafuse says Jane looked ten years younger and to see her so happy "was like a sigh of relief for me. I thought, *My God, finally I don't have to worry about Jane anymore* — because I was worried that someday she was going to kill herself."

XIV
• • •
'TIS THE
SEASON

DESPITE THE CONTAGIOUS EXCITEMENT generated by her sons as Christmas approached, Jane Hurshman did not welcome the month of December 1991 with much enthusiasm. She had been caught shoplifting at an IGA store in Dartmouth in mid-November and once again the threat of jail was hanging over her. As usual, she was embarrassed and ashamed, and she hid the truth from her husband, sons, and the rest of her family. Her court hearing was scheduled for December 17.

That pending appearance, before yet another judge, was weighing heavy on her when, on November 26, Jane talked about death in a letter to her pen pal Sara, who was also suicidal.

"There are times when I feel like ending my life also," she wrote. "So I do understand where you are coming from. You do not have to be ashamed of your body — and you do not have to be ashamed of masturbation. Remember my problem? Shoplifting! Well I still do that also and I just hate myself for it. I don't have the control to stop and because of it, there is always the chance of losing my job; losing my family; losing my confidence and self-esteem; and of going to jail.

"The underlying factors are never-ending and I can't stop. When I think negative like that, I wish that I was dead! So you see, Sara, I do understand."

In early December, television and local and national newspapers carried a flood of stories in the run-up to the second anniversary of the Montreal massacre. Toronto writer Donna Laframboise wrote in the *Globe and Mail*: "Having been declared a national memorial day by Parliament, Dec. 6 will become, for many of us, a day to reflect not only on the deaths of those 14 young women, but on the 100-odd Canadian females who are murdered by their current or former spouses each year and on the tens of thousands more whose lives are ravaged by sexual and other assaults."

Halifax and Dartmouth women's groups planned to mark the event with a press conference and memorial service. Ann Keith was invited to speak, and she called Jane to see if she was interested in joining her on the podium.

"I'm so glad you called," said Jane. "I've been driving around for a week and I can't stop crying, thinking of those women. It brought everything back."

Keith went over to Jane's house.

"I need to do this," said Jane. "When you called, I understood that I had to speak on behalf of those murdered women."

"She told me it was hurting her — eating at her," says Keith. "So I just sat in her house and I didn't say a word and she just wrote and then she went and she spoke."

◆ ◆ ◆

Carrie Rafuse didn't know that Jane had again been arrested for shoplifting, but on a visit with her in November she thought Jane was on edge and "not quite as patient with Joel. He was going away a lot of weekends. Jane liked her privacy. She wanted to be alone, so she would send him down to her mother's. She told me she sent him down to work with her dad on the cars."

Jane had tried working days at the rehab centre for a time, but it didn't work out and she went back to nights. "She couldn't sleep at night because she was tormented by memories of Billy," says Carrie. "I noticed that she wasn't as happy as she was before. I wondered if the marriage was just like the book — *'There, I've accomplished that'* — it was over again."

In early December, when Jane and Carrie were visiting Jeff, a mutual friend who lived with his wife in Bridgewater, Carrie thought Jane was in an aggressive mood. Darren, Joel, and their two dogs were with her, and Carrie was with her boyfriend, Bob. "I remember thinking, *Why is Jane like this?*" says Carrie. "I thought it might be the stress of Christmas."

Jane hugged and kissed everyone before she left.

◆ ◆ ◆

Victoria Jones, who had continued to live with Jane until shortly before Jane's marriage in October 1991, said she left because she felt uncomfortable around Joel. "I never felt comfortable from the day the man moved in. He came up for the Labour Day holiday in 1990, and the week after that he moved in for good."

Like Carrie, Jones believes that Jane had become despondent, even before the wedding. "She used to go to her bed and sleep for long periods of time when she wasn't working, and that was always an indication that she was depressed. She wanted to get away from everybody."

Jones decided, once again, to return to Montreal to see her son. Shortly before she left, she thought Jane was feeling guilty over killing Billy Stafford. "Two or three times she said, 'Jonesy, I wish Bill hadn't had to die the way he did, but I couldn't see any other way because the police weren't going to do anything about him.'"

Jane was upset the day Jones left. "She wouldn't come home until after I'd gone," says Jones. "I was very fond of Jane and I hated to leave, but I couldn't live where I felt unwanted. I had to sit in my room all the time because I couldn't very well go out where Joel was. He made it obvious he didn't want me there and I think he realized that I could see things Jane couldn't see."

On December 16, the day before Jane's court appearance, her dread, anguish, and bitterness surfaced in a letter she wrote to Sara:

> I do wish that for people like us there was some type of cure —
> but I guess we have a cross to bear and it will be with us for a
> lifetime.
>
> Sara, I love Jesus, and I know that both He and Satan are
> very real. With me, I have a problem believing that I am worthy
> of Christ. You see, with my shoplifting, I can't see it ever stop-
> ping — so if I am continually going to sin, then my coming to
> Christ and asking, even begging, for His forgiveness, is a mock-

ery when I know I am going to do it again.

How do you get past that? Is there something that I am missing? I want nothing more than to not sin, yet I constantly do. I am just totally unworthy. I don't know if my torment will ever end — until I die. And there are times that I want to make that happen — one of those times being right now. I have to go to court again tomorrow and I would sooner be dead than go there.

I know in my heart that Jesus is the only reason why I am not dead — as it is definitely not from my lack of wanting and trying. It is a demon that I can't get rid of.

I love Joel and my family very much, but I'd rather be dead than to continually bring them shame and humiliation. I am in a very strong dilemma right now as to living or dying. I am not crazy — yet I know that I cannot continue like this. There is no help available that I haven't already tried — I am so tired.

Well I feel that I have cried on your shoulder long enough and I just had to let it all out to someone. I am glad that you are there to hear me.

Sara, I don't know how I can help you or others when I can't begin to help myself.

Joel knows my problem and is very understanding — in fact, everyone knows my problem because it is public knowledge.

Well Sara, I am going to close for now because if I don't, I will just rattle on and on — so 'til later my friend, you take care. My heart really aches for you. Bye for now — and you and yours have a very merry Christmas and a Happy New Year.

Sincerely
with my love
Jane xo xo xo

Jane was in a Dartmouth courtroom the next morning, intent on pleading guilty. With her was Kathleen Jennex, executive director of the Coverdale Court Work Services, an organization that gives advice to women facing charges. Jennex has been with Coverdale for ten years and has worked with women facing charges ranging from disturbing the peace to murder. She had accompanied Jane to court on several occasions. Jane had also begun therapy with Mary Haylock, an abuse counsellor associated with Coverdale.

"We were very supportive when she was going through the shoplifting charges," says Jennex, who was opposed to Jane pleading guilty on that day. "There was a possibility of her going to jail because of the number of convictions against her. I wanted her to plead not guilty just to get it put over.

"But she was determined that she was just going to plead guilty, and she kept saying she wasn't going to go to jail. I couldn't convince her to get a lawyer."

While they sat in the courtroom waiting for the case to be called, Jane watched lawyer Patrick Duncan defending another woman and was impressed. "I always feel good when Pat represents a woman," says Jennex. "He not only looks after their legal rights, he thinks of them as a whole person."

Finally, Jennex persuaded Jane to talk to Duncan. She spoke to him briefly outside the courtroom and agreed to allow him to represent her. The case was put over to March 4, 1992.

The law recently has recognized a state referred to as automatous, in which a person commits an offence while in a robot-like mode and does not exercise her or his own will.

"That defence is not used very often, but Pat Duncan felt Jane fell within that category," says Jennex. "That was the kind of state she was in when she took things, and he was going to use that as her defence.

"Jane had more hope, I think, in this case than she had at any other time that I had seen before."

◆ ◆ ◆

On the night Jane's case was put over, Carrie Rafuse came over for dinner. After they ate, Joel went out to work on one of the cars and Jane and Carrie had tea at the kitchen table. Jane was in an unusually talkative mood.

"I shut up because she hardly ever felt like this," says Carrie. "She told me she had been in one of her dark moods again but this time she couldn't seem to shake it."

Jane told her she'd been feeling like that for about a month. Carrie didn't know it, but it was exactly one month since Jane's latest arrest for shoplifting.

"Jane, did you steal again?" asked Carrie.

Jane lowered her head and nodded.

"Why don't you tell me about it?"

Reluctantly, Jane told her about being caught at the IGA. Her voice was very serious but matter-of-fact.

"Look, Carrie," she said, "I'm not going to live like this."

"Oh God, Jane, no! Don't think this way again."

Carrie says Jane became very stern and stared directly into her eyes.

"I won't kill myself," she said, "but I will not live like this and I will not put my family through this. I won't do this to Joel, or the kids, or my parents, anymore."

She told Carrie that Kathleen Jennex and others from Coverdale had been at the house earlier in the day to work out a strategy to keep her from going to jail on the latest shoplifting charge.

"I steal and I can't do anything about it," said Jane. "I can't stop it and nobody can help me. I've been to the best. I can't control it and eventually I'm going to end up in jail.

"Don't worry for now because it's okay. I'm talking to these women and they're working out a defence for me, and it looks good. But if that doesn't work out, I won't go to jail and I won't live like this — but I won't kill myself. I have to go back to court in March. I was going to wait until the New Year to tell you this, but I decided to tell you now. I plan to tell Joel and the kids and my family after the New Year.

"Carrie, I want you to know, I don't have a death wish. I'm not crazy. I'm just not going to live like this."

Jane told her she was obsessed with her problem. "Not a day goes by that I don't think about it. If there's something about kleptomania on the TV or radio, I'm right in there watching or listening in case there's anything helpful."

"If you're sent to jail but you say you're not going to jail, and you're not going to kill yourself — what are you going to do?" asked Carrie.

"You remember when I saw you and Bob at Jeff's a couple of weeks ago? I thought it would be the last time I ever saw the two of you. But it wasn't."

"Jane, what on earth are you talking about?" asked Carrie.

"Last weekend, I sent Joel and the kids down to Mom and Dad's and I hired somebody to shoot me."

The colour drained from Carrie's face. "I was in shock for a week," she says. "It was so bizarre. And here was Jane, a normal person, telling me this. She was very calm, very calm."

Jane said she had gone to meet the person in her car.

"Where did you go?" asked Carrie.

"We just went down a deserted road and he had a gun and we got out. He put the gun to my head and fired it, but it didn't go off." At this point, Carrie felt sick to her stomach.

"There was something wrong with the gun," continued Jane. "A piece was missing or something and it wouldn't go off. I left and went back home and cried all night."

"My God, Jane, who would you get to do this?"

"Carrie, they're a dime a dozen. You can get anybody off the street to do that."

Jane said the person who was to shoot her was going to have the gun repaired and make a second attempt the following day.

"I was ready to go," she said, "but he got picked up by the police on some charges and couldn't meet me."

Carrie was shaken and didn't know what to think. She thought the story might not be true and that Jane was crying out for help. "But knowing Jane, it could have been true. I never knew of her lying to me — ever. I wanted to believe it wasn't true." But she remembers Jane's eyes bulging when she mentioned the person pulling the trigger — as they did when she was having flashbacks of the horrors from her time with Billy Stafford.

Jane told her she was glad she hadn't died.

"Now I'm working on this defence and it looks really good," said Jane. "I'm going to see this through and see if it will work out."

Joel came in at that point.

"She changed just like that," says Carrie, snapping her fingers. "And there I was, just like a friggin' piece of limp spaghetti. I had no energy whatsoever and my friend who I loved . . ." Carrie begins to weep as she remembers that night.

Jane got up from the table and laughed with Joel as she poured him a cup of tea. "She was another person," says Carrie, "and I didn't even know if I could drive. I went home and I was sick to my stomach and I went right to bed."

Her mind raced as she tried to figure out what to do. She thought about calling the police. But what could they do? And what about Dr. Curtis? Jane was already in therapy with him and he couldn't be with her every minute of her life.

"That night I called Jeff," she says. "Because he was the only one I could trust. And he came over the next day and we talked about what we could do — we had to do something." Jane had assured her that she would be okay until the March court hearing. They would have to think of something before then.

Carrie decided to spend as much time as she could with Jane and watch her closely. "And I decided that when the time was right I would call John Curtis and her sister Mona. I knew of Ann [Keith] but I didn't know her last name. I would try to get her too. I'd have to be careful because Jane's very smart, but we would have to do something."

The week before Christmas, Joel arrived at Carrie's to pick up gifts for Jane's family that Carrie was keeping for her in her recreation room. Carrie decided Joel was the closest person to Jane at the time and, without alarming him, she wanted to warn him about Jane's emotional state.

"He didn't have a clue about any of it and I really felt bad for him," she says. "He's just married two months, he's happy, he thinks everything is fine."

Joel had loaded the gifts into his car and was standing by the door, ready to leave.

"Joel, I've got to talk to you about something," said Carrie. "I've known Jane for a long time and over the years she has times when she feels suicidal. How are you finding her now?"

"She's fine, just great," said Joel.

"Well, you know, Joel, when I was in last week, I sensed she was in one of those moods and I'm really worried. I want you to keep an eye on her."

She says Joel promised to call her if he noticed anything unusual in Jane's behaviour.

Carrie says she definitely used the word *suicide*, but Joel disputes that. "She asked me if Jane was all right and I said 'yeah.'

What she said to me didn't really mean anything. It just puzzled me as to why she asked. She said to me, 'I love Jane like a sister — you take care of her.' I said, 'Yeah, I'll take care of her.' It didn't really make any sense to me."

Carrie's anxieties lessened considerably when she saw Jane at Christmas and they made plans to get together for New Year's Eve. "Joel and Jane came down and Bob and I went with them to dinner at an inn in Mahone Bay. She was in a wonderful mood. We just laughed and talked about our fun times and it really assured me that she was okay. And I thought, *Thank God*."

◆ ◆ ◆

In the first week of December 1991, Donna Smith and Jane met for what had become an annual pre-Christmas Chinese dinner to exchange gifts and enjoy themselves. Ann Keith was usually with them, but Jane hadn't invited her this time.

There was a bad winter storm that night and Donna thought they might have to cancel but Jane insisted they meet.

"Jane was in a really good mood and she gave me a picture of her wedding in a little frame and I gave her a wind chime with five porcelain doves. My roommate had one, and every time Jane came to the apartment she said how much she loved it. So I got a set for her. Doves are a sign of freedom."

After they placed their food order, Jane leaned forward. "I have to ask you something," she said. "I need your help. There's this woman — I won't say who she is, but you know her, and she's very well known. Well, she's dying of cancer and she's really, really ill. She called me and said she would pay $2,000 for someone to shoot her and $1,000 for someone to remove the gun."

Donna was stunned and her heart was pounding. She thought for a moment that Jane might have been talking about their friend Carol Struik, but she had already died of cancer. Jane said she would shoot the woman in the head and she wanted Donna to remove the gun.

"Why do you need me?" asked Donna in a panic. "If you already have the gun, you don't need me."

"I really need you to do this for me, Donna. You know we've

always been together and we're so much alike."

"But why do you need me?"

Donna kept asking the question, but Jane ignored her and continued outlining details of what was to happen.

"It will happen next Friday night, the thirteenth," said Jane. "It's better to do it before Christmas, because at Christmas the woman's whole family would be together. And you have to take the gun because this woman wants to make it look like murder. It would be better for the family if it looked like murder instead of suicide.

"I'll pick you up at Tim Horton's about eight o'clock. Wear old clothes and bring a change of clothes with you." (On the night she shot Billy Stafford, Jane ordered her son Allen to get her a change of clothes, in a garbage bag, before she drove off with Billy's body in the truck.)

Jane told Donna they would drive to the West End Mall on Mumford Road in Halifax and go into Sears, where Donna would be paid $1,000 "right then and there." They would shop a bit, pick up a Sears shopping bag, and then meet the woman in a secluded area of the rear parking lot near the railway tracks.

Donna had a friend, Shelly (a pseudonym), living with her at the time and sharing the rent. "What about Shelley?" she asked Jane. "She'll know something's up if I leave wearing old clothes and come back wearing something else."

"You'll think of something," said Jane.

"Why would I need old clothes, anyway?"

"When you shoot someone in the head, blood goes everywhere."

"I could never, ever, do this," said Donna, now frantic. "Doesn't it bring back the memory of Billy for you?"

"I did it once before — I can do it again," said Jane. "I've been having trouble getting a gun. I don't have it yet, but I'll have it in a day or two. It won't have any serial number and they won't be able to trace it. Nothing will ever come back on you. You'll be depressed for a while, but that's normal."

"But why do you need me?" pleaded Donna. "If you're holding the gun, you can get rid of it yourself and leave me out of it."

"No," said Jane sharply. "This woman really needs our help.

Somebody has to remove the gun."

Jane told her she would be driving Joel's Ford Tempo and not her newer Mustang. "She said she would have a purse and a garbage bag in the back of the car. I was to wear gloves, and as soon as the woman was shot I was supposed to take the gun and put it in the purse." The gloves, the gun, the purse, and Donna's old clothes, by then presumably bloodied, were to be placed in the garbage bag, which in turn would go into the Sears shopping bag.

"I was supposed to walk out of the mall with the Sears bag, dump the garbage bag over a bridge, or into a bin, and go straight home," says Donna.

"I kept asking her 'Why do you need me?' but she wouldn't answer. She kept repeating, over and over, 'Donna we're so much alike and I really need your help.' I don't know how many times she said it. And I kept thinking, *I can't do that, I'm not like that. I couldn't hurt a flea.*"

Because of the storm, they were the only customers in the restaurant. Donna had no appetite when their food came. "It just sat there. I couldn't eat a thing. Jane ate her meal as if everything was normal."

"I just can't do it," reiterated Donna.

"Don't worry," said Jane. "Don't give me your answer tonight. I want you to think about it for a few days. But I want you to promise me that you will never, ever, say anything about this to anybody, no matter what happens. If you do, it will be your kids that will suffer."

Donna says Jane's expression was very serious. "I really don't know what she meant by that, but it was scary. That was the first time Jane had ever threatened me. I kept saying to myself, 'Why is she doing this?'"

Donna also had to promise not to talk about it with Jane over the telephone because she thought her line was tapped.

"We were at the restaurant for over an hour, and when I came home, I was really upset," says Donna. "I was in shock. My roommate, Shelley, knew immediately that something was really wrong, but I wasn't allowed to talk about it."

Donna was in a fragile emotional state at that stage in her life and she thought she would have a breakdown if she didn't share the secret burden Jane had imposed on her. "I kept thinking, *I can't believe this is real.* I had to tell."

Donna was crying incessantly, but through her tears she told Shelley. "I didn't come right out and tell her," she says. "I got her to ask me questions and eventually she got the story." Beforehand, she swore Shelley to secrecy.

Donna didn't hear from Jane for about a week, but they were to see each other at the SSAV Christmas party on Wednesday.

"I went through hell for a week," says Donna. "Whenever I fell asleep, I would dream of shooting that woman."

On the morning of the party, she gathered the courage to confront Jane. "I left it to the last minute and then I called her and told her I couldn't do it."

Jane was angry with her for discussing the matter over the telephone but even more angry at Donna's refusal to participate.

"You *have* to do it!" declared Jane.

"Jane, I can't. I couldn't live with myself knowing that I helped kill someone."

"And I thought I could count on you."

"Jane, I can't."

"I've got the gun and everything is planned and set up for Friday."

Donna insisted that she couldn't do it, and Jane became more angry and desperate. "Do you know anybody else who can do it?" she asked coldly.

"No, I don't," replied Donna. She says she'd never known Jane so angry. Jane told Donna she would meet her at the Christmas party and drive her home and they could discuss it further then.

"She didn't show up at the party. I was relieved because I was afraid if we met face-to-face I wouldn't be able to refuse," says Donna. "I still felt guilty about not going underground after all the work she did, and now I was letting her down again."

On December 18, the day after Jane pleaded not guilty at her court appearance, she called Donna. "I hadn't heard from her for a week."

Jane was friendly and they talked for a while. Nothing was mentioned about the plan to kill the woman until the end of their conversation.

"Oh, by the way," said Jane. "Don't worry about anything. What we talked about before was taken care of — out of province."

Jane never mentioned it again.

XV
THREATS AND DISCONTENT

JANE HURSHMAN LEARNED ABOUT Mary Jacquart through a nurse at the Halifax County Regional Rehabilitation Centre. Jane was looking for a tutor for her son Darren, and the nurse gave her Jacquart's name.

"Jane called me and we met and hit it off immediately," says Jacquart, a teacher who tutored after-hours. Jane had Darren with her, and when he began acting up, Jacquart, who was used to dealing with rowdy teenagers, told him to sit down and be quiet. The boy eyed her a moment and sat down.

"Oh, you're a school teacher," he said.

"Yes, I am, and you're being rude here."

Jane looked at Jacquart with surprise. "I've never really said that to him." She smiled. "But I guess it's time someone did."

Jacquart became Darren's regular tutor. "When he first came he was a real hard ticket," she says. "But he's a real likeable kid and we got along just fine. I tutored him in math, science, and other school work and I really enjoyed it."

Jacquart also got along with Jane, and they began confiding in each other. "We talked quite a bit about my life and her life," says Jacquart. "But she never got into it about Billy. I told her my father was an alcoholic, and he'd come into your bedroom before a major exam for teachers' college and tear up your essays...that sort of thing.

"It was important to Jane that Darren go to university. She

128

didn't want him in a construction job or menial work because she thought he would be frustrated and he would get into trouble."

In a letter to Jo Sheridan in British Columbia, Jane described the importance of Jacquart to Darren. "He just hates school and everything about it," she wrote. "He has a tutor whom he thinks is just wonderful and when he is with her for his two hours a week, he accomplishes more there than he does all week at school."

Arranging a tutor for Darren was another step in the healing process that Jane knew was so important for her and her son. And she had been seeing the Coverdale therapist, Mary Haylock, since August 1991, as her problems with kleptomania continued to distress her.

In addition to her affiliation with Coverdale, Haylock is a chaplain with the United Church. She calls herself a "crazy old lady" and says she is classified as "clergy without a pastoral charge. I always tell the women that they are my church and for me, that is a more profound ministry — wherever the people are, I am."

Jane first heard about Haylock when she was facing one of her shoplifting charges in Dartmouth. A Coverdale court worker told her they had a therapist on staff who might be able to provide support and therapy for her problem. Jane was sceptical but agreed to talk to her.

"I met her at McDonald's for a coffee to see if she wanted to work with this crazy old lady," says Haylock, who has been helping women for more than ten years, including three years at Coverdale. Jane liked her and began weekly therapy sessions.

Haylock, and others close to Jane, believe that she stopped seeing Dr. Curtis because the hypnotherapy was uncovering childhood events that perhaps she didn't want to face. Had she continued she may have come to better understand and control the kleptomania.

"I liked working with Jane," says Haylock. "She was a very intelligent, articulate woman who endured an incredible amount of pain and suffering. She had insight into her total recovery — her move away from violence. But she was not unaware of the fallout from the abuse for herself or her children."

Haylock says Jane gave too much, and she could sense the pain when Jane spoke out publicly. "It probably did help her at first," she says, "but by the time I was seeing her, I think it was taking its toll. She understood that her way out of the pain was to go through it. But what I have to question was this facing it again and again and again."

Society sometimes asks too much of people who've endured trauma, says Haylock. She says Jane found it difficult to turn people down and she responded to abused women "any time of the day or night — and that was something she did privately."

Haylock believes Jane was feeling tired by the winter of 1991–92 and "the time was soon approaching when she would feel that she could let it be."

Jane was also telling friends that she was increasingly nervous about her safety, given her high profile. Nova Scotia was not a safe place for women. More than a dozen women had been murdered there in the previous two years[*] and assaults against women were on the rise — 260 in Dartmouth alone in 1990.

While she was still living in the rented townhouse on Arklow Drive in Cole Harbour, Jane had her son Jamie carve her a three-foot hardwood walking stick, which doubled as a billy club. He carved a pattern on it and added a leather strap she could slip around her wrist.

"She was worried and she wanted a little protection when she went walking the dogs," says Jamie. "She kept it in the car. She thought somebody was after her, and I remember I followed her to work a couple of times because she was worried."

Jane apparently decided the hardwood stick wasn't enough and, in early December 1991, she asked Joel if he could get a permit for a handgun. She said she would also try to get a gun on her own — perhaps from a motorcycle gang — perhaps Hell's Angels. She thought they might get her a gun because of her background.

"She had been scared for a while and it was clear in my mind she wanted it for her own protection," says Joel. "It was going to be small enough so she could carry it in her purse when she was out. At other times it would be locked up and I would have a key and she would have a key."

---

[*] See Appendix 1.

He asked the police about getting a permit for a handgun and was told he would have to fill out an application and that his chances of getting a gun would be better if he belonged to a pistol club. Joel decided instead to check with people in the Bridgewater area "who I knew were into guns at one time or another and I really didn't care if it was legal or not. I found one, but the guy wouldn't sell it to me without the certificate you gotta get from the cops."

On Thursday, December 19, eight days after she told Donna Smith that she had acquired a gun, Jane showed Joel an old .38-calibre pistol with no serial number. It was in a clear Ziploc bag. Six bullets were in a smaller plastic bag. "Where'd you get that?" asked Joel.

"You don't want to know," replied Jane. "If you don't know, you can't say."

"Fine." Joel shrugged. He says now he was certain the gun wasn't registered, but never again did he ask about its origin. "It's possible she got it from Hell's Angels, but she didn't want me to know and I didn't push the issue."

Joel promised Jane he wouldn't say anything to anyone about the gun. She wrapped it up and put it and the ammunition in a box. The next day, the Friday before Christmas, Joel and Darren were to drive down to Jane's parents for the weekend. Before they left, Jane handed Joel the box.

"Take it down home and try it and see if it works right," she said.

Joel says Darren didn't know the gun was in the car. He dropped the boy at his grandparents and drove to a friend's place in Bridgewater. "It was all wrapped in a box and I knew my friend wouldn't ask about it." He planned to leave the gun there until he had a chance to test it, but Jane called him and told him to bring it with him when he returned on Sunday. On the drive back to Cole Harbour, Joel, on impulse, pulled the car off the road.

"There's something I want to show you," he said, to Darren. He removed the gun from the box and put the shells into it. "Your mom told me to try it out."

Joel lowered his window and was about to fire a shot when he spotted a police car approaching. "The cop car went by and they sort of spooked me, so I put the gun back in the box and brought it home."

Jane was furious with Joel for showing the gun to Darren. "But I can understand her point," he says. "She told me not to show it to anybody. She told Darren, 'You ever say anything to anybody and you're dead.'"

"I got this gun for another lady," Jane told them, "and you're not to say anything about it, because I might get into trouble for giving it to her."

Joel says that although he didn't fire the gun, "I basically checked it over and everything seemed to work properly."

Jane and Joel went into their bedroom, where he removed the shells from the gun. "We cleaned all the fingerprints off," he says. "All the shells, the gun — everything was totally wiped."

The handgun went back into the Ziploc bag and the bullets into the smaller bag. "I put them up in the attic," says Joel. A few days later, he asked Jane about the gun.

"I got rid of it," she said. "I gave it back."

Joel says he checked the attic later and it was gone. "I don't know if she was carrying it around with her or not. It wasn't where I put it, so I figured it was gone. I thought no more about it.

"Later she told me she was trying to find a sawed-off shotgun, something she could wrap some material around and keep on the seat. It would be right there beside her in the car if she needed it."

◆ ◆ ◆

The last public speech Jane Hurshman gave was the keynote address to a City of Dartmouth task force on violence against women, on November 29. She spoke in a sweltering room at the Dartmouth Library to an audience of about 150. It was the final public event before the task force members sat down to hammer out recommendations they hoped would curtail violence against women.

Ann Keith, who attended the meeting, described Jane's speech as strong and "to the point."

"Hello from all the years of pain that I and my son endured and all the pain of a bruised body and spirit," began Jane. "I want to make people aware of what can happen to them and their children and their dreams — only then will life have a meaning and the pain go away and the nightmare end.

"It has been almost ten years, and for me the healing is not complete. I cannot rewrite my past or forget it."

Jane said that through speaking, she was helping herself by giving purpose and meaning to her life, instead of living with the old fears.

"Fear and shame and failure are all emotions experienced by battered women," she said. "I was born in a time when people did not reveal their personal problems. Emotions were kept inside — a secret. We all keep up appearances, and it is all part of an early conditioning and very deep-rooted."

Reiterating her oft-repeated message, Jane said speaking out against violence is the taboo, not violence itself. "It can only continue if we remain silent."

She urged battered women to leave their abusive mates and to come forward and be heard. "The more that come forward, the sooner we can change society's attitudes," she said. "There is still a lot to do and a lot to be said and I expect to be around to do it."

Kathleen Jennex, of Coverdale, says it was shortly after that speech that a frightening message in a male voice was recorded on Coverdale's answering machine: "You tell that bitch Jane Hurshman that if she doesn't stop speaking out on violence against women, I'll shut her up permanently." She regrets that the threat was eventually taped over. But another message threatening to kill Jane came in to Coverdale in the first week of January. This time it was preserved, and later turned over to the RCMP.

"My co-worker Margaret Rodger is from Scotland, and we listened to the tape with the RCMP a couple of times," says Jennex. "Margaret's been over here for a long, long time and she picks up our dialects much faster than we would.

"She said the voice was South Shore, and it wasn't until she said that, that I listened. And there was no doubt in my mind, it was Bridgewater — down that way. To me, it was definitely a man's voice. We talked about the terminology he used. It's not the type of language a woman would use — the aggression and the tone of voice. No doubt in our minds, it was an older male with a South Shore accent."

◆ ◆ ◆

Coverdale wasn't the only place receiving threats. On New Year's Day 1992, Liz Forestell went into her office at the Elizabeth Fry Society and checked her answering machine for messages. She says a muffled male voice on the tape made a threat "and the tone of it was really frightening."

Forestell couldn't make out the name of the person it was directed to, but the message was clear: "You better tell [name garbled] to shut her mouth and stop all this talking about battered women. If she doesn't shut up, I'll shut her up."

"I listened to it and listened to it, and it scared me," says Forestell. Her brother, who works for CBC Radio in Toronto, arrived in Halifax to visit her the next day. "I got him to listen to the tape, thinking he would have a better ear, but he couldn't decipher the name either.

"Finally, I just brushed it off. People told me that women's groups got these kinds of threats all the time. I had never received one before, but we'd been getting a higher profile in the press with the announcement in December that a prison for women was going to be built in Truro. I'd been on the news and the committee on jailed women had been quite vocal."

On January 2, another telephone threat, similar to the one received at Coverdale, came in to the rehabilitation centre where Jane worked. Jane was off at the time, but another female staff member heard it.

On the same day, a call was recorded on Jane's answering machine at home. It was from Sgt. Gary Grant, the RCMP's media relations officer for Nova Scotia. He wished her and Joel a happy new year.

Jane wrote of the call in her daily journal: "Sort of strange phone call — would not have been unusual if he had called Joel."

Both Jane and Joel had known Grant for years before they met each other, and Grant once visited them at the Arklow Drive townhouse before they were married. But Joel too thought Grant's call was out of place. "Before that," he says, "Gary never called me unless I called him and he always called me at work."

Grant, who left the RCMP in August 1992, says there was nothing at all sinister about his call and the only thing unusual was Jane's reaction. "It was easy to know it was me," he says. "I mean, I left a message on the machine with my name on it. If it would have been Joel's voice on the machine, I would have left the message for him. I said, 'Look, Jane, it's just Gary calling, sorry I didn't catch you at home but happy new year, and if there's anything I can do, please give me a call, and say hi to Joel.' That was it."

Jane left a return message on Grant's answering machine. "She sounded strange and she asked me if my call was business or personal," he says.

Jane answered when Grant called back, and he says her voice was accusatory. "It put me on the defensive, and I said, 'Gee, Jane, I was calling merely to say hi and to see how things were going.' She sounded very different, very strange, I thought."

◆ ◆ ◆

Gary Grant knew Jane when she was living in Bangs Falls with Billy Stafford. Billy hated cops, and he hated Grant most of all. They first met in 1977, shortly after Grant was posted to the RCMP detachment in Liverpool. He carries more than 250 pounds on his six-foot, three-inch frame and wasn't intimidated by Billy.

"Two or three months after I got there, I stopped him to size him up," says Grant. "I was friendly, but even though I'd never met him, he was totally hostile. He was one of those guys you'd look into his eyes and see the hate, like he wanted to tear your face off.

"If he thought you were intimidated, he'd own you. He was helter-skelter. The people who lived out there couldn't really enjoy the place, knowing he was around. I used to stop him every two or three months. He knew the police were looking at him and we took verbal abuse every time."

Grant was in the Stafford house only once, when he and two officers were sent to search for illegal venison. While the other officers searched the house, Grant stood in the middle of the living room fielding a string of obscenities from Billy.

"His eyes bugged out," says Grant. "He was red as a beet and started frothing at the mouth. I thought *If he explodes, he's going to be totally awesome to deal with.* His spit was hitting me in the face. It was just flying all over. He was like a demon."

After Grant and the other officers left, Billy screamed to Jane: "One of these days I'll get that fucking Grant. I'll get him alone somewhere and I guarantee you, only one of us will be coming out alive."

It was during Grant's posting in Liverpool that he also had cursory contact with Joel Corkum — contact that proved useful to the RCMP. Joel, then in his late teens, had just been released from his second six-month prison stretch, for break and entry, and he provided tips to Grant that led to a couple of successful drug busts.

"There wouldn't have been no busts if I wouldn't have made the calls — I'll put it that way," says Joel. "They were a couple of good ones too."

About the time Grant was transferred from Liverpool to the drug squad in Bridgewater in 1980, Joel was released early from a three-month sentence for dangerous driving. He was living in Bridgewater with his first wife and he and Grant got to know each other better. Joel, once a casual drug user, was never a paid police informer, but he continued providing tips to Grant.

"I had seen too many people burn out pretty bad on drugs," says Joel. "I made up my mind, I wanted nothing more to do with drugs."

After heading the drug squad in Bridgewater for several years, Grant was transferred to the RCMP's Cole Harbour detachment and later ran the force's drug awareness program for the province of Nova Scotia. He did that for more than two years before being promoted to sergeant and moving to the Halifax drug squad and eventually to media relations.

With Grant based in Halifax and Joel living in Bridgewater, they didn't see much of each other for several years, but they happened to meet in a bank in 1988 or 1989 and Grant gave Joel his card. When Joel moved to Cole Harbour to live with Jane, he decided to call.

"You'll never guess who I'm going with," said Joel. "You remember Jane Hurshman?"

Grant thought for a moment, and then he remembered.

"Well, we're living together," said Joel.

Joel says Grant was "right happy" about him and Jane being together. After that conversation, Joel called him on occasion and Grant suggested they get together sometime. Grant had been reading about Jane and her work with battered women and he thought it would be nice to sit and talk with her on a "non-professional basis."

"I told Jane I had talked to Gary and I asked her if it would be all right if he came over," says Joel. "She never really answered, and then a couple of days later she said 'yeah, okay.'"

Grant visited them in late 1990. "I sat down and had a cup of tea with them, and that was it — I never had any contact with them after that."

Jane told Mary Jacquart she was "a bundle of nerves" the whole time Grant was there but she got through it. She didn't trust Grant or any other police officers. She told Joel and others she thought Grant or some other police officer was behind the threats.

Jane did not consider herself a common criminal and she resented the police, who were continually arresting her for shoplifting.

"Jane was a good example of why I argue with the police all the time," says Kathleen Jennex. "She should not have had to go to the police station for mug shots and fingerprints every time she committed a new offence. They knew who she was and they knew her address. And for a lot of women who have committed more than one offence, to put them through that is just degradation. Jane shouldn't have had to go through that."

It is possible that Jane did not relish Gary Grant's visit or telephone call because it would trigger flashbacks. But after thinking about it for two days, she likely decided that facing the pain — as she did by returning to Bangs Falls to visit Margaret Joudrey — would help her to heal.

In the late 1970s, when Grant was patrolling Liverpool and Queens County, the problem of criminal violence in the home was still in the shadows, and the establishment of shelters and transition houses was in its infancy. Spousal abuse was considered a joke by much of society, as evidenced by the gales of laughter and hooting on the part of many members of the House of Commons, in May 1982, when they were told that one in ten women in Canada are battered in their homes.

The positive fallout from that incident was the backlash that forced governments and the legal system to take the abuse epidemic seriously and to begin to do something about it. It was only then that federal and provincial attorneys general ordered police and Crown prosecutors to crack down on batterers.

The new attitude wasn't police policy when Gary Grant was having his run-ins with Billy Stafford. If Grant saw bruises on Jane in the numerous times he pulled Billy over, he doesn't remember them. And even if he had seen evidence of abuse, nothing would be done unless Jane filed a complaint — something she wasn't about to do.

"There's no question, the police handled wife battering a hell of a lot differently then," says Grant. "But, in retrospect, I think if I had known Billy was abusing her, I would have probably tried to talk her into doing something, because I wanted that sonofabitch so bad."

Grant has his own theory about Jane's negative feelings toward him. "I had been stopping Billy, and hassling his ass and trying to bust him for every goddamn thing from soup to nuts. Ninety percent of the time he would be infuriated when he left me. Then he probably went home and beat the shit out of Jane. Now I'm wondering if there wasn't some transfer of blame, from him to me, on her part — I pissed Billy off, therefore I caused her pain. I've thought a lot about that, and it really bothers me."

◆ ◆ ◆

Joel says Jane took the threats against her seriously, but initially she shrugged them off as she had in the past. "She said, 'Well, there are a lot of crackpots out there.' It just didn't sink in."

On Friday, January 3, the day after the threat at the rehab centre, Jane called Carrie Rafuse and said she and Joel wanted to come down to Bridgewater the next day to go to church with her and Bob. Carrie was surprised because Jane hadn't been to church for some time. "She always had a strong faith in God. Then she just stopped going to church. She never talked to me about it and we didn't discuss religion much after that. But I know she loved God."

It was guilt over shoplifting that prompted Jane to give up

church. In a letter to her friend Sara in December, she wrote: "I want to thank you for sharing the sinner's prayer with me — but I am having difficulty with prayer lately. I guess that Satan is too powerful, and when I turn to Christ, I feel too guilty and unworthy, so it's easier to just avoid it all."

After the service at the Seventh-Day Adventist church, the four of them went to Bob's apartment for lunch. "Jane seemed happy and I thought, *Great — she's okay*," says Carrie. During lunch, Jane told Carrie and Bob about the threats she had been receiving. "She seemed genuinely concerned," says Carrie.

The next day another death threat against Jane was recorded at her home. She wrote in her daily journal: "Threatening message for me on answering machine. Joel took tape out of machine so he could keep it."

Jane may have appeared happy after attending church with Carrie, but on January 5 she wrote to Sara: "Until I get rid of the demons inside, I will not be contacting any pastor, nor will I go to church. I have tried that before and I just kept on sinning. I had more guilt to carry around and it made me feel like a hypocrite. I believe in Jesus, I pray, and in general, I do live a good honest life, so I'll have to be judged on that and on what is in my heart."

In the letter, Jane mentioned that the next day she was planning on having a family photograph taken at Sears, and she promised to send Sara a copy. As Jane drove to the photo session in her 1987 Mustang, with Joel beside her and Darren and Jamie in the rear, the car began vibrating.

"It must be that damn muffler," said Jane.

"That's no muffler," said Joel. "Get this thing pulled over. If it ain't the drive shaft loose, it's a wheel." He got out of the car and discovered the lug nuts on both rear wheels had been loosened. "I put those wheels on the car in November and those nuts were torqued down to 100 foot-pounds — the manufacturer's specification. Somebody loosened those wheels, and if the wheel on the driver side would have fell off, that car would have swerved into traffic."

Joel tightened the nuts and they continued on to Sears, where they met Jane's son Allen and his wife, Charlene, and they all sat for the photo.

Later that day, Joel telephoned the RCMP at Cole Harbor and told them about the loosened wheels and the threats Jane had received. "What do you expect us to do?" said the officer who took the call.

"I know there's probably not a lot you can do right now," said Joel. "But I wanted you guys to know this is going on."

He says the incident with the loosened wheels scared him and Jane. "She believed somebody was out to get her. It was after that speech to the mayor's task force that all this started."

Jane's journal entry for January 6 said: "The four lug nuts on the back wheel were loose — very loose."

To ease Jane's anxiety, Joel began driving to the rehab centre on his way to work to warm up her car and clean off any ice or snow. "When she got off the night shift she could just jump in her car and take off," he says.

Three days after the incident with the lugs nuts, Jane opted out of a group therapy session at Coverdale with Mary Haylock, stating in her journal, "I need one-on-one therapy and not group."

Haylock says she was trying to get a support group together for abused women and she asked Jane to try it, "but I think it was just not a good time for her. And I had to stop doing groups anyway. It's too hard to be someone's one-on-one therapist and then be their group facilitator."

In a January 9 letter, Jane gave some advice to Sara, who was considering pressing charges against her father for abusing her as a child. "I know of a lady who took her father to court, for sexually abusing her thirty years earlier, and he was found of guilty. It really is your decision, Sara, and don't let your family, or anyone else, influence your decision. You do what is in your heart."

Sara had told Jane that her family was against her and was treating her hatefully. She said she wished she could run away and hide from all of them.

"I know what you mean," wrote Jane. "It would be so nice to live back in the woods somewhere, without people around. That's what I want to do when my last kid leaves home — move back to the country and just stay there.

"Everyone deserves a chance. No one is perfect and who is anyone to judge someone else."

In a later letter to Sara, she wrote: "There are things that have happened in your past that you may never remember — do not dwell on those. If they ever do come to memory, then you can deal with them — and if they don't, well then I do believe that Jesus has a reason for us not remembering, because in one of His many promises, He says 'I will never give you more than you can bear.'"

That statement was another indication that Jane may not have wanted to learn anything more about her childhood because she didn't believe she could bear it.

On January 17, Jane met with Patrick Duncan, the lawyer who was to represent her at her March 4 court appearance on the latest shoplifting charge. On that day, she also met with Liz Forestell and the prison reform committee.

"I had been called by a reporter, from one of the major TV networks, asking if Jane would appear on a national news show," says Forestell. "They wanted to talk about the committee and profile her. There was quite a bit of publicity when the committee was announced — you know, 'husband-killer on committee,' that type of thing.

"I had connected Jane with reporters before, and usually she was quite happy to be interviewed. But this time, it was odd because she said no — and there was no hesitation."

The next day, Jane wrote in her journal, "I did nothing except sleep all day — did a bit of housework and took the dogs for a walk."

Around noon on Sunday, January 19, Darren noticed an envelope on the windshield of Jane's car. Though it was addressed to Jane, he ripped it open and took it into the house. Jane had worked nights and was still asleep. Darren handed the envelope to Joel, who read the stencilled message inside.

"Hi bitch!" it said. "I want you to know I haven't forgotten."

Joel waited until Jane woke up, at two-thirty, and then gave it to her. "You must have really ruffled somebody's feathers with that speech you gave," he said.

Jane's journal entry for the nineteenth read: "Today a letter was found on the windshield on my car. I was at work last night and I drove the car home at 7:30 A.M. So the threatening letter was put there sometime between 7:30 A.M. and noon. Joel called the RCMP at 3 P.M. They returned his call at 4 P.M. They wanted to know what we expected them to do. They are useless!!"

She went on to write: "There is no real way to handle grief. It comes in waves and it will hit you when you least expect it. If anything should happen to me, don't sit and feel sorry for me or for yourselves — just take all of our special memories with you and have a wonderful life, like I would want you to."

Two days later, Jane wrote about the threats in a letter to Sara. "I guess that I just have to be on my guard and take whatever precautions that I feel are necessary. I hate not knowing who wants me to keep my mouth shut or he is going to shut it for me permanently! It is crazies like that who scare you!"

◆　◆　◆

Jane had been cool toward Donna Smith since the December 11 telephone call when Donna had told her she couldn't assist her with the plan to shoot a woman allegedly dying of cancer.

"For quite a while, I kept leaving messages on her answering machine," says Donna. "Or I'd get Jamie or Darren and they kept taking messages, but she didn't call me back. I tried calling her at work, but the switchboard had stopped calls going through. You had to leave your name and number and they would call you back. But she didn't call and I kept feeling I had let her down and she was upset."

Their friendship was resumed in late January, when Jane told Donna about the threats she was receiving. "She said she was really scared and that's why the answering machine was on a lot. And she said the RCMP told her they wouldn't do anything unless something happened."

Jane's forty-third birthday was on January 25, and her childhood friend Valery Cromwell called her from Toronto with birthday greetings. "She told me a few things about the threats," said Valery. "She said she didn't want to be paranoid, but she said somebody was after her and she didn't know who it was."

On January 30, when Jane took Darren for his weekly tutoring session, she asked Mary Jacquart if she and her husband, Paul, would take Darren in if anything happened to her. "She said she was getting these threats and she wasn't so much worried about herself as she was about Darren," says Jacquart. Jane had earlier overheard Darren and Jacquart joking about him coming to live with her and her family.

"Would you really let me live here?" asked Darren.

"Sure, if your mother gets fed up with you, you can come here," said Jacquart, laughing. Two weeks later, Jane asked her if she was serious.

"Sure," said Jacquart, "I would take him if something happened to you and that's what you wanted."

Until Jane mentioned the threats, Jacquart thought that Jane and Joel might not be getting along. Jane had told her she was driving on the highway one night and she thought she heard a rattle in the car. She said it made her think of the loosened lug nuts and she prayed that the car hadn't been tampered with again.

"I pulled the car over," she told Jacquart, "and I thought, *My God, if they get me, what will happen to Darren?* And Mary, I said a prayer and it was just like God spoke to me. And I thought of you and Paul, because you said you would take him. I had this great sense of relief, but then I worried that maybe you wouldn't want him."

"No, there's no problem," said Jacquart. "But the main thing for you to do is to get everything in order in case something does happen."

XVI

FOREBODING

"I HATE THIS MONTH," Jane Hurshman wrote and underlined in her daily journal on February 1, 1992. It was a month she associated with pain and tragedy, including the death of her pregnant cousin the year before. It was also in the month of February that Jane went to jail for killing Billy Stafford.

On February 4, another stencilled threat against Jane appeared, this time at the rehabilitation centre. It came in an interdepartmental envelope. This message read: "I told you to keep your mouth shut, or I would shut it permanently."

In her journal, Jane wrote simply: "It is scary."

On the ninth, Jane drove out to the Halifax Correctional Centre with Liz Forestell to conduct interviews with inmates for the prison reform committee. The television reporter who had asked for an interview with Jane had called Forestell again.

"Maybe she doesn't understand what we want to do," said the reporter.

"I'm not going to try to talk her into it," said Forestell.

"Well, will you just give her the information."

Forestell agreed that she would, and on the drive out to the correctional centre she broached it with Jane.

"No, I really don't want to do it right now," said Jane, "and I'll tell you why."

"You don't have to justify it to me," said Forestell.

"No, I don't mind. I'm trying to keep a low profile right now.

I've been getting some threats." Jane told Forestell about them.

"Jane, I got a call at the office on the first of January and I couldn't make out whose name it was," said Forestell.

"They seem to know everywhere I go and everything I do," said Jane. She told Forestell about the loose lug nuts on her car. She also said she would lend Forestell the taped message from her home so Forestell could compare it with with what she heard at the Elizabeth Fry office on New Year's Day.

"She said she was quite frightened by the threats," says Forestell. "She said she had gone to the police and she was nervous about it because she thought maybe the police were involved, and that's when Gary Grant's name came up. She told me he had called her and she felt very uncomfortable with it. The call came on the same day that a threatening message came in where she worked. She was freaked out and she was scared."

The next day, Forestell listened to the threat Jane had received at the house, and it was identical to the one that had come in to the Elizabeth Fry office. "All the variations were the same. That's when I knew it had been recorded and then played into the answering machine. When I made the connection, the situation scared me very much."

◆   ◆   ◆

Jane had accepted an invitation to address the Canadian Panel on Violence Against Women during its March 6 swing into Halifax as part of its $10-million cross-country study.

On February 13, she arrived at Mary Jacquart's with a will, which included a provision for Darren to live there if anything should happen to her. Jacquart signed the will as a witness and gave it back to Jane.

The next day, Valentine's Day, Jane drove down to Danesville to visit her parents. That night, she called Carrie Rafuse, who was at work at the Harbour House women's shelter in nearby Bridgewater.

"She didn't sound good at all," said Carrie. "She said she and Joel had celebrated Valentine's Day the week before."

"I hate Valentine's Day and I hate February," Jane told her.

They agreed to meet the next morning. After she hung up, Jane played Scrabble with her parents. The phone rang while they were playing and Jane answered it. She listened for a moment and hung up. She told her parents it was nothing important, but in her journal she wrote: "While at Mom's, I answered the phone while we were playing Scrabble and the man said, 'I just want you to know that I am always aware of where you are at.' It was about 10 P.M. I did not say anything to my family but I plan to tell Liz about it."

On the same day, Valery Cromwell received a short letter from Jane with a colour photo of the family taken at Sears the day the loose lug nuts were discovered. "She told me she was still getting the threats," said Valery, "and if whoever was after her got to her, they would make it look like suicide and her body would probably never be found because it would be out to sea."

Jane drove to Bridgewater from her parents' place to visit Carrie on the morning of February 15, arriving about nine-thirty. They talked and laughed and discussed the possibility of another trip to Prince Edward Island at the end of March. Carrie was still worried, though, and as Jane prepared to leave for Cole Harbour, Carrie asked if she could come into town for an overnight visit.

"Oh good!" said Jane. "I'd love that."

"I'll call you by seven tonight and let you know if I'm coming for sure," said Carrie. She thought about Jane all day and decided to make the drive in with a woman friend.

"Jane and Joel were in the living room having a drink when we got there about eight-thirty," says Carrie. "Jane looked great. She had her housecoat on and was all fresh and bathed and waiting to get dressed. I never saw her in such a good mood."

As they left the house for a local bar, Carrie asked about the threats. "We gotta do something about this," blurted Joel, "because the police won't do anything. I'm gonna look for a gun."

Carrie was stunned that he would talk about getting a gun after she had warned him, before Christmas, that Jane was in a fragile state.

"No, Jane," said Carrie. "Don't do that. Don't get a gun. What if you had to use it to protect yourself. You know what they would say — 'There she goes again.' They wouldn't believe you."

Billy Stafford.

Jane with her husband, Joel Corkum, on their honeymoon in October 1991.

Maurice and Gladys Hurshman at the kitchen table of their Danesville home.

(Right) Jane's middle son, Jamie Whynot (*left*), with his girlfriend Anita Bruce, and his brother Allen Whynot.

BRIAN VALLÉE

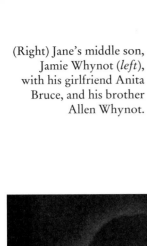

MONA DONNELLY

(Left) Jane's "pride and joy", her youngest son Darren.

BRIAN VALLÉE

Jane's oldest son Allen and his wife Charlene. Their daughter Haley Dawn, was born on Valentine's Day, 1993. She would have been Jane's first grandchild.

JO SHERIDAN

(Left) Jane's "pen friend", Jo Sheridan, from British Columbia, considered Jane "a most remarkable woman".

MONA DONNELLY

(Right) Jane, after her wedding in Mahone Bay, with her sisters Mona (*centre*), and Sandy.

VALERY CROMWELL

Jane and her childhood friend, Valery Cromwell, celebrate the 1987 New Year in Bermuda. "It was to celebrate my freedom…and a new life," said Jane.

(Right) Ann Keith, executive director of Services for Sexual Assault Victims, was counsellor and friend to Jane.

ANN KEITH

(Left) Liz Forestell, executive director of the Elizabeth Fry Society in Halifax, appointed Jane to her board of directors. Both women were appointed to a committee to study the needs of incarcerated women.

LIZ FORESTELL

ANNETTE BUSHEN

Jane with her friend, Annette Bushen, who worked with her at the Halifax County Regional Rehabilitation Centre.

(Left) Jane with Carrie Rafuse, one of her best friends.

CARRIE RAFUSE

(Right) Jane with James Tynes, whom she dated for more than four years.

JAMES TYNES

HALIFAX CHRONICLE-HERALD

Jane and Darlene Darrington, victim of the "motorcycle rapist", comfort each other at an event marking the second anniversary of the killing of fourteen women in Montreal.

(Right) The walls and furniture of the Arklow Drive house were spray-painted and the floors damaged with an axe during the August 2 break-in when Jane's ashes were stolen.

BRIAN VALLÉE

JOEL CORKUM

(Left) On August 2, 1992, Jane's ashes were stolen and the house on Arklow Drive was vandalized. Messages, including "Murderer" were spray painted on the walls and furniture.

Staff Sgt. Don Thomander, head of the Halifax Police Department's major crime section.

JOEL CORKUM

(Left) Retired RCMP Sgt. Gary Grant, the cop Billy Stafford hated the most.

GARY GRANT

(Right) Corporal Peter Astephen, the veteran Halifax police officer who led the investigation into Jane's death.

BRIAN VALLÉE

RCMP Sgt. Keith Crosland, who headed the investigation into the threats against Jane.

BRIAN VALLÉE

(Above) March 2, 1992 about 300 people lit candles at St. John's United Church in memory of Jane.

IN
REMEMBR
OF
JANE
THE PAIN HAS
TO STOP!
WE CAN BE
SILENT NO
LONGER
· A MAN WHO NEVER
KNEW YOU
(UNFORTUNATELY)

A tribute to Jane left in the parking lot where her body was found.

"We've got to do something," said Joel.

Carrie said Jane changed the subject. "We went out to a couple of bars and had a ball. We got feeling really good, except for Joel, who was driving and wasn't allowed to drink."

When they returned to the house, Carrie's friend from Bridgewater was tired and went to sleep in the guest room. "The three of us were at the table," recalls Carrie. "It was probably one o'clock and we started eating chocolate bars — Jane's favourite thing." Joel went to bed at two or three, leaving Carrie and Jane at the table. They were both in a talkative mood because of the drinks.

"Jane," said Carrie, "I've never, ever told you what I thought you should do — I've always gone along with what you want."

"I know that, Carrie, and I love you for it," said Jane.

Carrie begins to weep as she recounts their conversation.

"You're my friend and I've got to tell you how I feel," said Carrie. "I think you're making up those threats."

"No, I'm not," said Jane evenly.

"Okay, I believe you. I thought maybe you were still going to kill yourself and you were setting it up."

"No, I told you, I'm not going to do anything until after my court appearance on March 4," said Jane.

As they continued talking, the conversation drifted back to Billy Stafford. "It always came back to Billy when we talked late at night," says Carrie.

"When am I going to get over this?" asked Jane. "When is it going to go away?" Later they talked about abuse, and Jane told her she was going to stop speaking about it in public. Later still, they talked about Jane dying.

"I'm not going to do it," Jane reiterated. "And now that we're talking about this again, I've been meaning to tell you how sorry I am for telling what I told you that day. I just want you to know I would never hurt you and I know it upset you and put a lot on you. I'm sorry."

"Jane, you can tell me anything. *You've* always been here for me."

Jane assured her once again that she wasn't going to do anything drastic. "I was praying it was the truth," says Carrie. "Then we talked about the possibility of the trip to P.E.I. and she seemed fine."

Carrie became more inquisitive than she had ever dared in the past.

"Jane, do you know if you have a split personality?" she asked.

"No, I don't think so," replied Jane.

"I'm not saying you have. I'm just curious, because I know about three or four different Janes. Sometimes you get in a dark mood. And then you have a very aggressive, sarcastic mood. And sometimes, you're just Jane."

"John Curtis said what I've got is a dissociative disorder," said Jane. "I don't have times that I forget things."

"Is everything okay with you and Joel?" asked Carrie. "Are you happy?"

"Yes, everything's fine. I'm glad now that I had Christmas and it didn't happen, and I don't plan for it to happen. I'm going to wait until March when I have my court appearance — and it's looking very good."

"I was very worried about you, Jane."

"You don't have to worry."

Carrie says Jane was very convincing. "I told her I had thought of going to John Curtis, and Mona, and Ann. I thought she might react — but nothing. She wasn't threatened by that a bit."

"No, I'm really fine now," said Jane.

"Jane, I love you and I don't want anything to happen to you. I wish you would go back to John Curtis."

"He did all he can do," said Jane. "We reached a point and I can't get beyond that point — there's nothing else he can do."

"Jane, I think there's a lot here that I don't know about, and other people don't know about, and I think it's probably from a long time ago — maybe even before Billy. And with Billy, are there things I don't know about?"

"Yes," said Jane.

"Look," said Carrie, "have you been completely honest with John Curtis."

"Well . . . I haven't said everything."

"Why don't you go back to him. Just give it one more try, but be completely honest. Get it out, and you can break through and get help for the stealing."

"Nope," said Jane. "I'm not going back to him. He did what he could."

"But, Jane, people have therapy for years." Jane was adamant.

"I know she had very little memory of her first twelve years and I know that's what she didn't want to face," says Carrie. "That's why she stopped seeing John Curtis. It was very hard for her. Jane was in control of everything in her life — except the stealing."

The conversation returned to Billy Stafford.

"The only way for you to beat him is to live and be happy," said Carrie. Jane looked at her friend sharply.

"She didn't like it when I said that," says Carrie. "She didn't want to hear it. And then she said she was tired and she got up and went to bed. And I thought, *Oh God, everything is not all right.*"

Jane gave her a hearty hug before she left the next morning, but Carrie remained uneasy and knew she would have to do something soon. "But I thought everything would be okay up to the March 4 court date."

◆ ◆ ◆

Jane spent Monday, February 17, at an all-day meeting of the committee studying incarcerated women. Recommendations were formulated and readied for a draft report.

Over lunch, Jane told Liz Forestell about the threat she had received at her mother's house on Friday night. "She was really freaked out by that call. She thought maybe her phone was tapped because she had gone down there at the last minute, and nobody other than her family would have known that she was going."

Forestell said there had been problems with the telephones at the Elizabeth Fry offices since late January and she wondered if their phones might be tapped too. "The phones were malfunctioning and we were hearing strange sounds," she says. "It was weird. The lines weren't connecting properly and we'd get cut off on calls."

"This is too crazy, Jane," said Forestell. "You can't go on like this." She suggested mentioning the threats to a contact in the solicitor general's department. Jane agreed.

Forestell's contact thought the situation was serious and together they arranged a meeting with Nova Scotia Deputy Solicitor General Nadine Cooper-Mont.

◆ ◆ ◆

In the second week of February, Jane's sister Mona received a troubling letter from Jane in which she said there were some strange things happening and she was concerned.

Over the February 15 weekend, Mona called their sister Sandy, in Ottawa, to see if she had heard anything from Jane. "Sandy didn't know anything about it," says Mona. "Jane had contacted her to see if Darren could come up to Ottawa for the March break, but that was it. Sandy said, 'sure, let him come up,' and she was going to confirm it with Jane."

Mona was concerned over Jane's letter, and she telephoned her on Tuesday, February 18. Jane told her about the threats and said she planned to write them out in detail while she was at work in the early hours of the coming Saturday. She said she planned to send the letter to a friend (Brian Vallée) in Toronto, whom she trusted.

"Who do you think the threats are from?" asked Mona.

"You'll think I'm crazy," replied Jane, "but I think it's Gary Grant."

"Why do you feel that way?"

"Well, he called at the same time things started happening."

She explained how she and Grant exchanged messages on to each other's answering machines before their final conversation.

"It was his tone of voice," said Jane. "It was sort of mocking, like he wasn't sincere."

Mona says their conversation was brief and Jane didn't want to go into further detail because she planned to write it all down on the weekend.

◆ ◆ ◆

Wednesday, February 19, was to be a busy and difficult day for Jane. Difficult because it was the first anniversary of the death of her twenty-two-year-old cousin, Patricia Parnell, and her common-law husband, Phillip Nickerson, who was ten years older. Parnell,

Nickerson, and their unborn child had died instantly in a fiery highway crash. The deaths were on Jane's mind when, in the morning, she and Liz Forestell met with Deputy Solicitor General Nadine Cooper-Mont.

"Jane brought the threatening letters and tapes," remembers Forestell. "And she had written down everything that happened."

Cooper-Mont took the threats seriously and told Jane and Forestell that she knew a police officer "she would trust with her life." The officer was the RCMP's chief superintendent, Allen Burchill (now the force's assistant commissioner for Nova Scotia).

"I'll arrange for him to meet with you," Cooper-Mont told Jane. "He'll appoint an internal investigator. I know they've done this before and I trust this guy."

After the meeting Jane and Forestell went to a restaurant for breakfast, and Jane said she was satisfied that something was being done. "We talked for a couple of hours about all sorts of things," says Forestell. "Nadine called me later to say that Burchill would meet with us on Monday morning. I called Jane and she said that was fine."

After leaving Forestell, Jane went home and taped a lengthy message for Joel and her family. She began by saying she had just come from meeting Cooper-Mont: "And I was speaking to her in regards to what has been happening with me this last while, and the threats being made by phone and by note. Just in case anything does happen, I want you to know it's been reported to the top."

The taped message was to serve as an addendum to her will and it hinted strongly that she expected her death was imminent. She talked about financial matters that would need immediate attention, including the receipt of a paycheque that was expected "at any time."

On the tape, Jane also talked about her dead cousin. "This is the day, one year ago, that Patricia and Phillip and their unborn baby had their lives snatched away so quickly. Since that day, I've thought of a lot of things that had to be done. It doesn't make the pain any easier, to lose a loved one, especially one so young and vibrant and full of life. And I guess there's not been one day since their deaths that I haven't thought about that or them, and just how easily life can be taken away and how precious it is."

◆ ◆ ◆

Jane went to work Wednesday night, and sometime in the quiet morning hours she wrote at least two letters, one to Sara and the other to Jo Sheridan in British Columbia. The letter to Sheridan was upbeat when she talked about her family and job and her appointment to the special committee on incarcerated women. But the tone changed when she talked about the threats. Jane said it was "creepy" to think an unknown person wanted to hurt her and she didn't know why. But, she wrote, "life continues on anyway."

In the letter to Sara, Jane said of Billy Stafford: "He was a miserable S.O.B. who deserved what he got — but Sara — it is extremely hard for me to deal with. And I figure that is why I still shoplift — because I cannot forgive myself! No matter what, Bill was a human being. I am not sorry that he is dead, but I am sorry his life had to end the way it did — so violently!

"There are times I am angry over what he did — and all of its after-effects (I mean my shoplifting). By continuously doing that, I shame and humiliate my kids and family and hurt myself. It is my way of punishing myself for what I did — because of what he did to me."

Jane also mentioned her visit with Nadine Cooper-Mont and said, "Even though I do not have much faith in the system, I got enough courage to go beyond the RCMP, who aren't doing anything."

She said she still had doubts that people believe her when she tells them something. "That all comes from my time with Bill. So much damage gets done to persons from our backgrounds. I am not a liar — never have been. Nor do I exaggerate the truth — yet Bill always made me feel like a babbling idiot, and at times I still feel that way. But I was believed [by Cooper-Mont], although I don't know what is going to be done yet."

About her pending shoplifting charge, Jane wrote: "My case goes to court on March 4, but I don't have to go. My lawyer will go and he will get a new date, which will be as long away as possible so he can establish the defence he wants. When I know more about it,

I will explain it to you."

Finally, Jane confirmed in the letter that she agreed to the terms of a "suicide contract" contained in the book *Courage to Heal*, which Jane had sent to her. Sara says that under the terms of the contract, they would give each other at least three weeks' notice, by letter or telephone, if they planned to commit suicide. "That would give her three weeks to tell me why I shouldn't commit suicide," says Sara. "And it would be the same for me if she wanted to kill herself."

Jane wrote of the contract: "I take your word on what you wrote, and I shall pledge the same to you, okay?"

She also encouraged Sara to go back to school and then "go out there and help other abused people. You will be good at it, and it will be good for you. It still helps me and it always will."

On Thursday evening, Jane drove Darren to Mary Jacquart's and brought along a copy of her will, but it wasn't the one Jacquart had signed the week before. "My signature wasn't there, but Joel's was," Jacquart says.

Jane told Jacquart about her meeting with Nadine Cooper-Mont and she talked about the threats. "If they get me, it will be one of two things, Mary," said Jane. "They'll either never find my body, or they'll make it look like suicide."

Jacquart said that as they talked about the threats, Jane was sitting in a rocking chair and Darren was across from her in another chair.

"Mom," he said, "if anybody ever hurt you, I'd kill them."

"Darren!" said Jacquart.

"If they did get me, Darren, fight it and find out who did it, but be on the right side of the law," said Jane. "By you living here with Mary, I *know* she'll make you mind, I *know* she'll make you go to school, and I *know* she'll make you go to university. Darren, you be a lawyer, and you be a good one, and an honest one. Because if anything ever happens to me, I don't need a guilt trip of you killing someone."

Jacquart said Darren didn't mention killing again. Jane left about ten or ten-thirty, and Mary Jacquart never saw her again.

At work that night Jane wrote to her mother: "I am at work in the wee hours of the morning and I thought I would drop you a few lines to say that I picked out this material for you and I hope you like it. I feel it will really brighten up your living room and if you want, I have the week of March break off and I will come down and make them for you. Maybe a different style. They will look real nice with shears. I will make a couple of cushion covers and a doily or two. Well, I'll talk to you on Sunday. 'Til then, take care. Bye for now. Give Dad my love and I will see you on Tuesday the 25th for your doctor's appointment. I love you both. Janie."

XVII
• • •
MISSING

SHORTLY AFTER JANE HURSHMAN arrived home from the night shift on the morning of February 21, her son Allen Whynot drove up in his new half-ton truck. He was there to drive his brother Jamie to visit their father, Jane's first husband, who lived in Milton, near Liverpool.

Usually, Jamie had the use of Joel's 1985 Ford Tempo, because Joel had his own half-ton, and Jane had her Mustang. But Jane had warned him, a week or two before, that she needed the Tempo on this night because Joel was taking the Mustang to her parents' for the weekend to tune it up and change the oil.

She told her son that, before going to work, she needed the Tempo to drive to Halifax to see a battered woman who had called her for help.

"Why don't you use Joel's truck?" asked Jamie.

"Because I already told the lady what the car looks like, and if I go there with the truck, she won't recognize it," said Jane.

"Why don't you call her and describe the truck to her?"

"I can't phone her, because I don't have her number," said Jane.

Allen agreed to drive Jamie to Milton so he wouldn't have to take a bus. "Until I got there, Mom was going to take him over to the bus station," says Allen. "She had her housecoat on and I knew she was getting ready to sleep after working all night."

"Don't speed," Jane told him. "You don't want no tickets with that new truck."

155

Jamie gave his mother a hug and kiss while Allen stood by the door. "I was waiting for her to come over to me and hug me, but she didn't," said Allen. "She went into the living room and she didn't say good-bye to me. I should have told her I loved her, but I didn't. It was something I always did, even on the telephone — Like, 'I love you and I'll see you later.'"

◆   ◆   ◆

Jane was up by early afternoon, and Ann Keith telephoned about four o'clock. Other than at the November 29 speech, on behalf of the Dartmouth task force, and at the December 6 news conference marking the anniversary of the Montreal massacre, Keith had seen little of Jane since the October wedding. "She had Joel in her life and she seemed happy," recalls Keith.

She decided to call Jane after reading about plans to begin shooting a television movie based on *Life With Billy*. Jane was happy to hear from Keith but told her she couldn't say much.

"I've been getting threats and I think my phone might be tapped," said Jane.

"Oh-oh," said Keith. "Well, I won't say too much."

"I'd really like to see you," said Jane. "How about Monday?"

"Sure," said Keith. "Noon time and we'll go for lunch."

Keith says that was the only time Jane mentioned the threats to her.

Carrie Rafuse also called Jane at home on Thursday. "I had talked to her the day before and she didn't sound too bad — maybe a little flat, like the blahs," says Carrie. "I thought she was tired and busy, but nothing unusual. I told her I was thinking of coming in Friday, and she told me to come ahead. But my plans changed and I called her on Friday to say I couldn't make it. She understood and there was no problem."

◆   ◆   ◆

Joel left work a little early that day because a storm was on the way and it was already starting to snow. He wanted to get an early start on the drive to Jane's parents. Traffic would be heavy on Friday night and the storm would add to the congestion.

Jane had partially loaded the Mustang by the time Joel got home. He placed a couple more bags in the back seat along with Jane's dogs, Sasha and Oreo, and he was ready to go. He and Jane hugged and kissed and he told her he loved her.

"I'll call you when I get down there," he said.

"You don't have to. I'll call you tomorrow night," said Jane.

"No," said Joel, "you know I'll call you when I get there — I always do." Jane smiled and shrugged.

Shortly after six, Joel left for Danesville, about eighty miles away. He was to return on Sunday. Allen, meanwhile, had dropped Jamie off at their father's place in Milton and was home by four.

Jane had asked Darren if he wanted to go down with Joel to spend the weekend with his grandparents, but the boy declined. With Joel and Jamie away, Anita Bruce, Jamie's girlfriend, agreed to stay overnight at Jane's so Darren wouldn't be alone. She was there most of the day, and about 7 P.M., she saw Jane dial a number and speak briefly on the telephone, describing the Tempo to the woman she was apparently to meet in Halifax.

Anita also heard Jane say, "There's things I can't get into over the phone, because my line is tapped."

Jane had purchased and wrapped a birthday gift for Larry, one of the clients at the rehab centre, and when she got off the phone she told Anita and Darren that she planned to take the gift with her to work that night.

She put on a pair of Joel's jogging pants and, about seven-thirty, said she was going to the nearby Mic Mac Shopping Mall to pick up a cake for Larry. "Then I'm going to meet a lady in Halifax," she said. "I'll phone you from work at twelve o'clock. Leave the side door unlocked so I can get in in the morning."

Jane turned to them as she slipped on her jacket.

"You know what I did," she said. "I forgot my purse in the Mustang."

"Do you have any money?" asked Anita.

"Yeah, I have money, but I don't have anything else."

Jane telephoned her father in Danesville and told him about the purse.

"When Joel gets there, tell him to bring it into the house," she said. "There's nothing important that I really need."

"She kissed Darren and hugged him like she usually did," says Anita. "All she had was her jacket when she walked out."

The drive to Danesville usually took about an hour and a quarter, but Joel says it took him about two hours because of the snowstorm and heavy traffic. He arrived shortly after eight.

"Jane just called a little while ago," said Maurice Hurshman. "She left her purse in the car."

"I went back out to the car, and there it was in the back seat," says Joel. He took it into the house and called home. Anita answered.

"She left a little while ago," she said. "She's gone over to Mic Mac to buy a cake for Larry and she's going to meet a lady in Halifax."

"If she wants her purse," said Joel, "I can drive right back and get it to her. Tell her to call me when she gets in."

About 9 P.M. Anita and Darren were startled by a loud banging in the basement. They ran to the kitchen, thinking someone had broken into the house. Darren grabbed a knife from a drawer and they went to the basement.

"There was nothing there," says Anita. "We don't know what it was."

Later, as they sat at the kitchen table, the light in the hall went on and off. "We were nowhere near the switch and there was nobody else in the house," says Anita. "It was very weird. After that, we were scared and we took off."

She and Darren returned to the house just before midnight, the time Jane had said she would call them. But Jane didn't call.

Joel says he tried calling a couple of times to get Jane before she went to work, but there was no answer and he gave up about 11 P.M.

"She's probably at work," said Jane's mother, Gladys.

Joel was not overly concerned because Jane had met with battered women in the past and didn't always make it back to the house before she went to work. Also, she had told him not to bother calling that night and that she would call on Saturday. He went to bed.

◆ ◆ ◆

Mary Jacquart had told a friend who worked with Jane at the rehab centre that Jane had been receiving threats and was frightened by them. When Jane didn't show up for work on Friday night and she couldn't be reached at home, the Cole Harbour RCMP were notified.

The police showed up at Jacquart's house a short time later. "They tried to get me to say she was depressed," she says. "They said maybe she was dead or she ran away."

Jacquart had a family member who had been in and out of hospital for five years suffering from depression. "I know a depressed person when I see one," she told the police. "I've seen the mood swings, the games they play. Jane was not depressed — she was scared."

◆　◆　◆

Maurice and Gladys Hurshman were asleep when the telephone rang about 1:15 A.M. Maurice answered it.

"Hello, Gramp, it's Darren. Is Joel there?"

"Yes, he's in bed."

"Can you get him?"

"Well, he's asleep."

"This is very important, Gramp."

Hurshman hollered to Joel, who jumped to his feet and went to the phone.

"Mom never showed up for work and the police are here," said Darren.

"I'm on my way," said Joel.

Although the roads were bad from the winter storm, Joel says traffic was light at that hour in the morning and he made much better time on the return trip.

"I remembered Anita had said Jane was going to the Mic Mac Mall to get a cake," says Joel. "It was sort of on the way home so I stopped and looked around, but there was nothing there."

The police were gone by the time he arrived home. "I called her work and they said I'd best talk to the police," says Joel. "So I called the police, but they couldn't tell me nothing. I didn't know what to do. I didn't know if I should go and look for her or if I should stay at home and wait in case she called."

He decided to drive Jane's normal route to work, in case the car had slipped off the road, but there was no sign of her.

◆　◆　◆

The RCMP detachment of Cole Harbour is just blocks from Jane's Arklow Drive home. When officers there were alerted that she was missing, they treated it seriously because of the reported threats against her.

Sgt. Keith Crosland, a twenty-five-year veteran, was assigned to the investigation. Coincidentally, he knew Jane and Joel; Milford Whynot, her first husband; and had known Billy Stafford. A native of Prince Albert, Saskatchewan, Crosland was transferred to the east coast in 1968, shortly after joining the RCMP. His first posting was to Liverpool. Jane didn't know Billy at that time.

"I got to know Billy through my job as a policeman," says Crosland. "He was into some criminal activities at the time. It seems to me I met Jane in 1968 or '69, because I knew Milford. I got to know her better when I moved to Cole Harbor."

Crosland says that when Jane was reported missing, a bulletin describing her and the Ford Tempo was sent across the province through the police computer network, CPIC (Canadian Police Information Centre).

"In her case, she was receiving threats," says Crosland. "That's a little different twist as opposed to other missing persons, but in every case we put out reports as a matter of course. A lot of times it's for naught, because within twenty-four hours many missing persons are discovered or come back on their own. But you can't sit back and wait for that."

◆　◆　◆

Allen and Charlene had planned to go out Friday night, but Charlene felt a cold or flu coming on, and, instead, they went to bed early. Allen, a sound sleeper, says he was awakened by several phone calls, including one from a neighbour and two from callers who dialled the wrong number. He was sound asleep when the last call came, shortly after 1 A.M. It was Darren, but Allen was groggy and didn't recognize his voice. He thought it was a crank call.

"Were the police over there yet?" asked Darren.

"No," replied Allen.

"Well, come over right away."

"Okay, bye," said Allen, replacing the receiver.

"Who was that?" asked Charlene.

"I don't know. Something about the police and wondering if they were here."

Allen rolled over and went back to sleep. He and Charlene were awakened about seven, when Joel called.

"Your mother didn't go to work last night and she's nowhere to be found," he said.

"I'll be right over," said Allen.

When he got there he asked why he wasn't called in the night.

"I did call you," said Darren.

"Well, why didn't you tell me it was you?"

"I thought I did."

"I guess I was asleep. I'm sorry."

Allen says that while he was at the house on Saturday several calls came in that were "hang-ups — call and hang up, call and hang up. I answered four myself. The police said it was probably people who knew Mom was missing and they were concerned. But it hadn't been made public at that time and the number was unlisted."

Joel asked the police if the line was tapped, as Jane had suspected. The police checked it and said it wasn't. Allen said police then put a device on the phone that would record a caller's number so it could be traced. "As soon as the police did that, the calls stopped," he says.

◆   ◆   ◆

Joel called Ann Keith at 8:30 A.M. and asked if she'd seen Jane.

"No. I was talking to her at four o'clock yesterday and we were planning to meet for lunch on Monday," said Keith.

"Well, she didn't go to work last night and she hasn't come home."

Keith was at Jane's house by nine. Then she went over to the Cole Harbour RCMP detachment and gave a statement about her telephone conversation with Jane.

"I came back to Jane's and Carrie was there," says Keith. "I'd never met her before. She came in with Jeff and his wife, who were also friends of Jane."

Joel told Keith that Jane was supposed to see a battered woman in Halifax and the police were trying to determine the woman's identity.

Keith decided to look around the house and she came across Jane's office off the bedroom. Joel showed Keith Jane's diary and the black organizer in which she kept her accounts. On top were instructions to Joel to immediately close her accounts and put them into his name if anything happened to her.

"Until Jane went missing, I never, ever looked in that book," says Joel. "She had it all written what I was supposed to do." She instructed him not to turn any of her personal papers or writings over to the police. But Keith told Joel the police should see the diaries and organizer.

"I can't do that," said Joel. "I have to obey Jane's wishes. She said not to give the police anything in her handwriting."

"I'm sorry, Joel, but you have to give them to the RCMP."

Eventually Joel did turn them over to the police.

The RCMP at Cole Harbour were heading the investigation, but police in Halifax and Dartmouth were also looking for Jane.

◆ ◆ ◆

Allen saw the card and gift Jane had wrapped, and Joel explained who it was for. "Joel wanted me to take it over there because it was this guy's birthday that day," says Allen. "So I run it up on my way home because I wanted to take my time and drive the road Mom takes to work. It's a pretty dark road at night and it had been snowing, so I thought maybe she went off into the woods or something." But he saw nothing to indicate a car had left the road.

After dropping off the gift, Allen and Charlene drove around every parking lot and hotel in Dartmouth searching for the Ford Tempo. "I thought she had to be someplace close by," says Allen. "Because the tires on that car were all bald. Some of the belts were broken and steel was shootin' up through. She couldn't have gone far."

As the day wore on, Allen's anxiety grew. "This ain't good," he told Charlene. "If they do find Mom, she's gonna be tied up or choked to death. She wouldn't have just took off. She would have left a note and said, 'Look, I'm fed up, I'm gone.' But there was nothing."

◆ ◆ ◆

Liz Forestell was in her office at the Elizabeth Fry Society when an officer from the Cole Harbour RCMP telephoned around noon on Saturday.

"Is Jane Hurshman with you?" he asked.

"No," said Forestell. "Why are you asking?"

"She didn't show up for work last night. She's missing."

Forestell said her heart stopped, "and I had a sick feeling in my stomach that something really bad had happened to her."

"Do you have any idea where she might be?" asked the officer.

"No."

"Has she been depressed lately? Is she suicidal?"

"What are you talking about? Why would you say that? No! She's not suicidal."

"Well, she's missing and we always ask that."

"Don't you know that she's been getting threats for the last month?" asked Forestell.

"Yes, we know that, but we have to look at everything."

The officer asked Forestell if she knew anything about the meeting Jane was to attend on Monday with Chief Superintendent Allen Burchill of the RCMP. Forestell told him she knew about the meeting, but she began to feel uncomfortable when he asked her what they had talked about in the meeting with the deputy solicitor general.

"I'm not going to talk to you about this anymore," she said. "I can't answer any of your questions. I'd like you to call the chief superintendent and let him know this has happened. And if he calls me and tells me to, then I'll answer your questions."

After Forestell hung up, Jane's disappearance began to sink in. "I guess I knew deep down that she was dead, but I just couldn't deal with it," she says. "So I tried to reason out some other things — like maybe she had more threats and she decided to disappear for the weekend. I was terrified. I started thinking about getting a gun. I had never thought that in my life before. I had no idea what had happened to Jane. I had no idea what they would find. I had no idea if someone was after her for information and, by now, they knew that she had shared it with me. I didn't know what to think. I just felt terrified."

When she didn't hear from the officer, Forestell called the Cole Harbour detachment, seeking more information from him about Jane's disappearance. She asked him if he had called Burchill.

"No, lady," said the officer. "I can't just call up the chief superintendent."

Forestell then called Nadine Cooper-Mont, the deputy solicitor general, to tell her what had transpired and to ask Cooper-Mont if she, Forestell, could speak with Burchill. Cooper-Mont said she would arrange it.

Chief Superintendent Burchill called Forestell a short time later. "I want to know if you have someone doing this investigation of the threats," said Forestell. "I need to get all the information I have to someone — now — and I'm not giving it to some cop in Cole Harbour."

Burchill called her back in a few minutes with the name of an investigator, Sgt. Fred Fitzsimmons. "Do you want to meet him today?" asked Burchill.

"Yes," said Forestell.

Fitzsimmons called her about 6 P.M. They met, and she told him everything she knew from the time of the first threat.

"I told him at the beginning there was some stuff I wasn't comfortable putting on paper."

"Well, I have to have it down in statement form in order to begin my investigation," said Fitzsimmons.

"I'm not comfortable with my statement sitting there where anybody can see it."

"No, no, don't worry," said Fitzsimmons. "It's for my eyes only. I promise you. If you feel uncomfortable, I'll lock it up, but I have to have your statement."

Forestell agreed to give a statement on his promise that it would be locked up and not circulated.

"Fitzsimmons seemed like a fairly decent guy," says Forestell. "He was quite open with me and he took me with him to meet Joel. I had never met Joel before."

◆　◆　◆

Ann Keith made call after call from Jane's house to women who might know where she was or who might know the identity of the mystery woman she said she was to meet in Halifax. It was a dead end and eventually Keith went home. She decided to call Donna Smith so she wouldn't hear about Jane from the media first.

"Donna, I hate to tell you this, but Jane's missing," said Keith, briefly explaining what she knew.

"What was she wearing?" asked Donna.

"She had on Joel's dark-coloured jogging suit," said Keith, who thought it an odd question. "She was supposed to have gone to meet a woman in Halifax."

Donna says that as soon as she heard about the jogging suit, she knew Jane was dead. "Jane and I often went to meet other women who had been battered, and she always dressed nicely. She would never wear a jogging suit to go and meet a stranger."

Donna remembered the scenario Jane had laid out in December for killing the woman dying of cancer, and says she realized then that there was no other woman. Jane was talking about killing *herself*, and that was why she insisted that Donna be there to remove the gun.

Donna was stunned after the call from Keith, and she and her roommate, Shelley, went out about 7 P.M. to look for Jane. "We drove and drove," said Donna. "We went to all the malls and checked the lot behind Sears that she had talked about in December."

Donna also checked the parking lot of a particular hotel because Jane once told her that a simple way to overdose was to rent a room there under a false name and "go in and do it, and they wouldn't find your body until the next day."

Donna and Shelley returned home around eleven. Donna remembers, "I kept thinking, I've got to tell Ann what I know. I've got tot tell somebody, even if I get arrested." Minutes later Ann Keith called. "It was like she had ESP," says Donna.

Donna told Keith the full story, including her belief that Jane would never have dressed in a jogging suit to meet a woman she didn't know.

"We've got to go to the police right now," said Keith. "I'll call you right back."

Keith met an RCMP officer at a doughnut shop and told him the story. Then she telephoned Donna to tell her she would be over with the officer, who would take her statement.

"They came around midnight and I told him everything," says Donna. "Then the RCMP called me back around three o'clock in the morning to get my full name. I wasn't asleep — I couldn't."

◆ ◆ ◆

On Sunday morning, February 23, Joel says he discovered the audio tape Jane had recorded four days earlier as an addendum to her will. He says the tape was in the strongbox Jane kept under their bed. "We kept money in there," he says. "She and I were the only ones who had a key for it. I saw the tape and it said 'Last Will and Testament' on it."

He played the tape and showed it to Darren. "You don't have to listen to it if you don't want to," he said. He played some of it for the boy. "He heard the part about him and he cried a bit," says Joel. "Then he said, 'I got to leave,' and he went out."

Joel decided he would not tell the police about the tape.

XVIII
❖ ❖ ❖
DEATH

IT WAS SHORTLY AFTER 3 P.M. on Sunday, February 23, when Roy Kline notified the Halifax Police Department that a woman, apparently deceased, was in a car on the waterfront. Constables Bryan Naas and Colleen Kelly were in the marked cruiser that was dispatched to the scene.

It was clear and cold when they slid to a stop in the parking lot several yards from the 1985 Ford Tempo. From a distance, no one was visible in the car, parked at the end of the lot near the water.

Naas was a veteran officer who once worked for the Metropolitan Toronto Police Department. As he and Kelly approached the car, they noticed only one set of footprints — Roy Kline's — in the snow near the vehicle. Following his tracks, the officers drew closer and saw the woman slumped over. She was wearing an open multicoloured jacket over a black jogging suit. It was obvious to them that she was dead.

Peter Astephen, one of two corporals on the Halifax Police Department's fifteen-member major crime unit, was on call that weekend, and was at his in-laws' in Dartmouth for Sunday dinner when he was informed that a woman had been found dead in a car. He went immediately to the waterfront.

Astephen, of average height and weight, is dark and serious, his stiff black hair beginning to grey. He was into his twenty-fifth year in the Halifax department but was just forty-five, with a daughter in college and a son on the police force. He had been a plainclothes investigator for eighteen years, the first six on the drug squad. In the field, more often than not, he could be seen with a plastic-tipped Old Port Colt cigar clenched between his teeth.

By the time he arrived on the waterfront, Naas and Kelly had strung yellow police tape to cordon off a wide area around the Ford Tempo. Several other Halifax officers, some in uniform and some not, were already at the scene along with Dr. Kim McBride, from the medical examiner's office, and Sgt. Keith Crosland from the Cole Harbour RCMP detachment.

Crosland was in his Cole Harbour office, working on Jane's disappearance, when Halifax police notified him that they had found the missing woman and the car the RCMP had been searching for since Friday night. He arrived at the waterfront with Constable Angus Emberly.

"I remember it was very cold, with the wind coming off the water," says Crosland. "I talked to Peter Astephen for a few minutes at the scene and then stood back as he did his thing."

Corporal James Griffin, head of the Halifax department's identification (Ident) section, pulled up at the same time as Astephen. Griffin, also a twenty-five-year veteran, was enjoying Sunday afternoon at home when he was called to the scene. On-duty member of the Ident unit Wayne Fraser had already taken still photographs and video shots, and Dr. McBride had confirmed that the woman was dead. Naas, Kelly, and Dr. McBride used the same path to and from the vehicle, on the driver's side, to protect the scene as best they could.

Although senior officers were on the scene, including Staff Sgt. Mike Mahar, who outranked Astephen, there was an unwritten rule that as soon as the investigator arrived, he was in charge.

Astephen and Griffin surveyed the area around the car, and noticed icicles had formed from the car to the ground, behind the rear wheels. "That indicated that the car was there for some time," says Astephen. "It had snowed, melted some, and frozen again." He concluded later that the car had probably been there since Friday night.

Jane's body, he says, was "slumped toward the passenger's side from the driver's side, and that was the reason nobody spotted her earlier."

It had stopped snowing overnight and, says Astephen, "where the car was situated, with the sun and the glare, you'd almost have to walk right up to it and look in to see anything."

Vehicle tracks and footprints indicated that through the night other vehicles had parked as close as four or five feet on either side of the Ford Tempo. Astephen says, "It's common knowledge that prostitutes either meet their clients there or go down there with them." On Sunday mornings, discarded condoms and empty liquor and beer bottles can be found strewn on the ground. The fact that it had been snowing Friday and Saturday nights and that Jane's body was slumped over reduced the possibility of anyone spotting her, "especially," says Astephen, "when you consider the reason some of these people were down there."

Joel's car was a four-door, and only the front door on the passenger's side was locked when Naas and Kelly arrived. No purse or identification of any kind were found on Jane or in the car, but police knew who she was through the licence plate and because her face was familiar from her media profile as a spokesperson for battered women.

In the left pocket of her jacket, police found a sealed envelope. Inside was another of the stencilled threats, this one stating: "No more talk from you — Gotcha!"

Crosland had informed Astephen about the reported threats against Jane, and as Astephen went to the car suicide was the last thing on his mind. "We were treating it as a homicide investigation at that point, which is the way we treat any type of sudden death."

The body had not been moved in any way when Astephen approached from the driver's side and Griffin from the passenger's side.

"We did a visual check of the body first," says Astephen. "She was in the same position as when they found her — slouched over toward the passenger side." The keys were in the ignition. The officers noticed a folded flannel sheet, draped partially over Jane's lap, her right hand, and the seat.

On the floor was a paper cup partially filled with coffee. The cup was standing upright on the passenger's side beside three plastic grocery bags, one inside the other. Inside the bags was a large empty

Ziploc bag and a plastic sandwich bag containing three .38-calibre bullets. In the back seat was a loaf of bread and the boxed birthday cake Jane purchased at the Mic Mac Shopping Mall for Larry, the rehab centre client.

Astephen decided to move the body. "Jim Griffin was taking pictures and I began to carefully move her into a more upright position, back to where she would have been sitting," he says.

As the body was moved out of its slouched position, the officers noticed the barrel of a handgun. "It was on her lap and the sheet was sort of around and under it," says Astephen.

While holding Jane's body upright, Astephen looked for a gunshot wound and noticed a small hole through the black jogging top. "It wasn't much more than a pin-hole in the front," says Astephen. "I didn't notice it at first because it was so small."

The bullet had entered the centre of Jane's chest and travelled upward and to the right, exiting just below her right shoulder blade.

A small hole was visible in the back of the seat. A single deformed .38-calibre slug was later found lodged in the seat. The location of the hole matched that of the exit wound in Jane's back when she was in the upright position behind the steering wheel. No blood was visible on Jane's jacket or on the back of the seat.

"Once we verified there was a shot and we could see the hole in the seat, we took a closer look — with the doctor — as the body was placed on the stretcher," says Astephen. "Because it was so cold, the blood had coagulated quickly, but there was some blood visible on the inside of the jogging top."

Under police guard, a nondescript white van from Eastern Removal Service, a private company that transports bodies for the medical examiner, funeral homes, and others, delivered Jane's body to the morgue at the Victoria General Hospital in downtown Halifax.

Once the body was removed, the Ident men, Griffin and Wayne Fraser, carefully catalogued and removed the handgun, bullets, and other items found in the car. The car was then impounded and towed to the police garage to be screened inside and out for fingerprints, hair, and fibres. The gun, coffee cup, and other items would also be checked for prints and sent for forensic examination to the

RCMP's Crime Detection Laboratory in Halifax. Ballistics tests would be conducted to determine if the bullet found in the seat came from the handgun in the car.

After the car was towed, all of the police officers involved met at Astephen's office in the Halifax Police building to review the evidence and information gathered to date and to coordinate strategy for the investigation.

"We put our heads together to determine exactly what we were dealing with," says Astephen. "We basically decided to work on the investigation with the RCMP because they reported her missing and they were investigating the threats."

Crosland went into detail about the threats and other information the RCMP had gathered. "We were assisting Halifax police," he says, "because the body was found in their jurisdiction. My investigation initially pertained only to the threats. Then it became a missing person. Then it became a missing person found dead, but I was still dealing with the threats."

◆ ◆ ◆

About four-thirty Sunday afternoon, Joel Corkum says, he was sitting in the Arklow Drive home "watching every car that went by" when an RCMP cruiser with two officers pulled into the yard.

"I hadn't called them, and when they came I just sort of knew that they had found her and she was dead," says Joel. "I suspected right from scratch, she wasn't coming back."

"Mr. Corkum, we've found your wife and she is deceased," said one of the officers.

Darren was standing in the kitchen and Joel went to him.

"Darren, they found Mom and she's dead," he said, putting his arms around the teenager's shoulders. Darren pulled away, kicked a hole in the basement door, and went down to his room.

"Are there any guns in the house?" asked one officer.

"Yes," replied Joel.

"Can we take them as a safety precaution?"

"Yeah, sure, take them."

The police removed three shotguns and two rifles from the house.

◆ ◆ ◆

Ann Keith was at the house Sunday night and she noticed a remarkable change in Darren. She said the hurt and anger was gone and he had become animated and almost euphoric — perhaps a form of delayed shock.

"It was so peculiar," she says. "He was at one end of the table and Joel and I were sitting there. And Darren seemed up and elated and he was just talking and babbling away. He mentioned how Billy used to swat him. It was the first time I ever heard him talk about Billy."

Keith says Joel interrupted Darren at one point, and the boy said, "Shut up there, Joel, I'm talking."

"It was as if Darren was taking over the role of father and Joel was becoming the little kid," says Keith. "It was hard to explain. Joel was playing right into it."

And just before Darren went to bed, he approached Keith and told her he wouldn't be having any more nightmares.

"He told me about a dream he had in which he got out of bed and went into the kitchen, where he saw a man standing outside the window. He said the man had blond hair and he had a shotgun, which he cocked and fired at him. The time on the clock in his dream was 2:30 A.M."

Darren told Keith that with the blast of the shotgun "he woke up, and he went into the kitchen and looked at the clock. It was the same time as in his dream — 2:30 A.M."

Keith says she had never seen Darren show physical affection, but after he told her about the nightmare, "he came over and gave me a hug and said, 'I hope we see more of you,' and he went to bed. I couldn't believe it."

Keith describes what she experienced that evening as "bizarre" and says "I made sure I had my back to the wall."

◆ ◆ ◆

Wendy Annand was distraught when she learned that Jane was missing. "I talked to her just two nights before. She was going to be our special guest for International Women's Day and she was also planning a presentation to the Canadian Panel on Violence Against Women.

"I was beside myself, so I went to a friend of mine who is a psychic to see if she could track it. She felt Jane had been kidnapped and was being held on the waterfront, but had dissociated. It turned out she was very close with the geography."

Annand was about to drive to Halifax to search for Jane when Joel called and told her Jane was dead. "I was a wreck. She was one of my best friends, and to have her die that way just seemed so unbelievable and so unjust, after what she'd been through. You wanted her to be ninety years old and die surrounded by family."

Annand's psychic wasn't the only one thinking about the waterfront. Liz Forestell spent most of Sunday morning driving around Halifax harbour. "I'm not sure what drew me there," she says. "I had the licence plate number and I was looking for her car."

Early in the afternoon, she drove to the Dartmouth side of the harbour, picked up a hamburger, and sat facing Halifax from the Dartmouth Ferry Terminal parking lot. "I sat there looking over to the other side of the water and I kept thinking she was there somewhere."

Later in the afternoon she returned to the Elizabeth Fry offices in Halifax. "When I arrived there, I found footsteps in the snow going up to my window at the rear of the building and, from there, around to each of the windows in front. I wondered if Jane had been there or if someone was looking for me.

"It could have been anything, but I didn't feel very comfortable at the office, so I went home." About five o'clock Joel telephoned her and told her Jane was dead.

"I guess I knew it all along," says Forestell, "but I just couldn't believe it. I was sort of calm, but it just didn't seem possible. The whole time we were waiting, it seemed like weeks and weeks instead of a day. And I kept imagining what they would find and what had happened to her. I had some pretty awful images."

◆　◆　◆

The first news reports on radio and television in the Halifax area late Sunday afternoon said only that a woman had been found dead in a blue car at the waterfront. When Donna Smith heard the news, she had a strong feeling it was Jane. "They showed pictures of the car, and I ran in and taped it so we could see the car again," says Donna. "Then the RCMP called and said it was Jane's body."

As Donna hung up, a song that she and Jane liked was playing on the radio. "I broke down."

Her daughter, Mary, came into the living room. "Jane's dead, isn't she, Mommy?" she asked.

"Yes," sobbed Donna.

Donna said Bobby, then six years old, was the strongest. "I was crying so much and Mary was bawling, but Bobby didn't cry at all," says Donna.

"It's okay to cry, Mommy," said the boy, "because if you cry it means you care."

Donna says it was dark by then and Bobby went to the window and looked out. A single star was visible in the sky. "Mommy, look at that star," he said, motioning Donna to the window. "That's Jane looking over us."

As word spread that the dead woman was Jane, Donna was inundated with telephone calls. "We had so many calls because when anybody at Bryony House wanted to get in touch with Jane, they called me. It reached the point I was so upset I couldn't handle any more calls.

"It took the kids a while to get over it, especially Mary. They were so close to Jane and she always brought them something. I think she bought them every kid's movie going. Eventually, Mary came to realize Jane was at peace."

◆ ◆ ◆

Carrie Rafuse had called Jane at work at three on Saturday morning. "They said she didn't come in to work that night, and I wondered if I should call her house. It shocked me because Jane never missed work. I thought she was probably not feeling well and had stayed home and gone to bed."

Around 6 A.M. Joel called her to tell her Jane was missing.

"And I knew," says Carrie. "I just knew."

She says it's obvious to her that Jane planned her death. It wasn't only that she knew Jane was suicidal. "I knew Jane," she says, "and she would never, ever, leave her purse behind. And if she did, she'd go right after it — it's as simple as that. She wanted to leave her purse in the car. She wanted it to go somewhere else. And it didn't surprise me that she had the old car, because she probably wanted Jamie to have her new car."

◆ ◆ ◆

The morgue at the Victoria General Hospital complex includes a refrigerated body storage room, two modern autopsy suites, a lab for storage and examination of tissues, a small photo lab, two offices, and a change room and showers.

A bank of a dozen or so pull-out drawers, each with its own stainless-steel door, are built into the wall in the body storage room. Jane's body was put into one of the drawers. The door was closed behind her and a police officer secured it with a padlock.

Dr. Malcolm MacAulay, the province's acting chief medical examiner, was called at his home Sunday night and notified that police required an autopsy on Jane's body the next day. He informed the hospital and arranged for x-rays of the body to be taken in the morning before the autopsy. "I wanted to have the x-rays in my hand when I was searching for bullets," he says.

MacAulay was acting chief examiner in the absence of Dr. R. A. "Roland" Perry, was who was out of the province. MacAulay has taught pathology at Dalhousie University and Victoria General Hospital, since 1970. "My main role is to organize the training program for pathologists who are studying forensic work."

MacAulay is one of three doctors, two of them pathologists, who perform forensic autopsies at Victoria General for the medical examiner's office. Although Perry is the chief medical examiner and has considerable experience in the field, he is not a pathologist. MacAulay is the only one of the three who is both a medical examiner and a pathologist.

On Monday morning, February 24, the drawer containing Jane's body was unlocked and a portable machine from the hospital was brought into the morgue to take the x-rays MacAulay had requested. The body was then removed to a stainless-steel table in one of the two autopsy rooms across the hall from the body storage chamber.

MacAulay was dressed in full operating room garb, including surgical mask, gown and gloves, eye protection, and shoe covers, when he entered the room to begin the autopsy.

Ten years earlier, almost to the day, Roland Perry had conducted the autopsy on the body of Billy Stafford in the sub-basement of the same building. The building and morgue have since been renovated. "In the old days, there was a walk-in fridge," says Perry. "Now there are individual drawers. The police used to sit there all night. Now they lock the body in and take the key."

Perry didn't testify at Jane's trial because both the Crown and the defence accepted his report. "They sent Billy up here because initially there was a question of who did it," he says.

Billy was killed by a slug fired at close range from a Coey model 840 twelve-gauge shotgun. The slug was travelling at sixteen hundred feet per second as it left the muzzle of the gun — about twice the speed of the lighter .38-calibre bullet that killed Jane.

Perry says that when a gun is fired at close range, the damage inflicted results not only from the bullet or slug but also from the gas created when the gunpowder burns. "When it burns it goes from a solid to a gas," he says. "It's not just the bullet that comes out of the mouth of a weapon. There's also the burning gas. And the exploding effect of the expanding gases is what produces a lot of the damage — particularly with high-powdered rifles and shotguns.

"It can produce absolutely horrendous destruction. That was the case with Billy Stafford." In his 1982 autopsy report, Perry said Billy's skull bones were pulverized by the blast and there was "pulpification of most of the brain." A forensic witness at Jane's trial said Billy's skull literally exploded.

"I spent a lot of time trying to piece together the various parts, mainly to try to figure out where the entry wound was," says Perry.

In Jane's case, the bullet was much lighter and slower than the shotgun slug and the visible damage was considerably less — although enough to a result in almost instant death.

The autopsy on Jane lasted almost four hours. "A police autopsy takes a considerable length of time," MacAulay says. "That's because of all the photographs being taken and all the samples being taken and recorded.

"I have a series of diagrams that are preprinted, and I take notes, dictate, and I take photographs. It's a redundant system, so if you lose one, you've got the other as backup."

Photographers from the hospital and the Halifax Police Department's Ident section also took photographs during the autopsy. In addition, the police used a standard kit to check for gunpowder residue on Jane's hands.

"They use a brush similar to the type that picks up lint," says Peter Astephen. The collected samples were sent to the RCMP laboratory in Ottawa for analysis.

MacAulay's report stated the entrance wound in Jane's body was seven millimetres in diameter and that the bullet passed through the breast bone, the sac surrounding the heart (the pericardium), the right lung, and the ninth rib. The bullet barely grazed the heart, but it was close enough to tear a large hole in the wall of the right ventricle.

The exit wound in the right upper back was six millimetres in diameter, and MacAulay says the absence of blood on the seat or Jane's outer clothing was consistent with her "immediately falling over to one side." He says the exit wound was small and most of the blood drained into the right chest cavity.

Although the bullet pierced the back of Jane's jacket and the front and back of her jogging top, it did not go through the pink camisole she was wearing. At first glance it seemed odd that the camisole, which covered the wound at the front, had no hole in it. That there was no hole in the back was easy enough to explain — it was cut low and the bullet came out on an upward angle, missing the camisole.

And in front, MacAulay explains, the camisole had three buttons at the top, and the gun barrel was placed in the gap between the first and second buttons. "The camisole itself was not damaged by the bullet. But all the blow-back [soot] from the explosion was on the inside of the camisole."

Entrance wounds are designated distant, close, or contact. With a distant wound there is no powder residue on the target or victim, while there would be considerable residue if the wound was in the contact category. Contact wounds are further defined as loose contact or tight contact.

Jane's wound was described as loose contact because the jogging top was between the muzzle of the handgun and her chest. Police believe Jane loaded two bullets into the gun in case she was still conscious after firing the first shot.

Staff Sgt. Don Thomander, Astephen's immediate boss in the Halifax police force's major crime unit, says Jane could have lived for five or ten minutes after the shot was fired. "At that point, you could be in a semiconscious state, not even realizing what's going on."

MacAulay disagrees. "I think that was to big a hole for her to be alive that long."

◆　◆　◆

When Jane's youngest sister, Mona Donnelly, arrived in Cole Harbour on Monday from Barrie, Ontario, she was upset that no one from the family had been to identify or look at Jane's body.

"Why didn't you go over and look at the body?" she asked Jane's son Allen. "How do you even know it's your mom? You're allowed to see her."

"I don't want to," said Allen. "They know it's her." He says he didn't want to go into a cold morgue. Mona telephoned Peter Astephen and insisted on seeing her sister's body.

"Her body is under the control of the medical examiner," explained Astephen.

"I don't care, I want to see her," said Mona.

"Well, I don't think you can see her at this point, but if you really insist, I'll make inquiries."

Mona says she also asked Astephen why no one from the family was asked to identify the body. "He said that one of the officers identified her and they wanted to spare the family the pain. And I told him the family should have had the option of making that decision."

She says she waited and waited for Astephen to call back "and finally I called him."

"The autopsy has been completed," said Astephen. "They won't let you see her but they will give you a photograph if you want."

"I don't want no photograph," said Mona. "I want to see Jane and I want to see her now, and so does her mother, and so does her husband. I'm a pretty strong person and I want to see her."

Joel Corkum says he remembers Mona "climbing up one side of them and down the other. And finally I got to the point where I said I want to see my wife. I didn't see how they could possibly keep us out. If we didn't get to see her that night, I was going to the press. And there would have been hell to pay for that one."

Astephen agreed to call the medical examiner's office once again. This time, he was given the go-ahead to allow the family to view Jane's body at the pathology lab.

Dr. MacAulay says that, in the case of a suspicious death, family members are not allowed to see a body before an autopsy because, in their grief, they might do something that would interfere with or alter evidence.

"We usually hold the body until the next day, in case we want to go back to check something," he says. "It's a safety precaution."

Mona, Joel, and Jane's mother, Gladys Hurshman, met Astephen at the police station and went with him to the morgue. Jane's body was on a stretcher that had been wheeled into an alcove off a hallway.

"She was lying there with a white sheet over her and plastic bags on her feet," says Mona. "All I could really see was her face. And when I first saw her, I thought, *I've got to get her out of here.* She looked so lost and alone and innocent and I just didn't want to leave her there. Her face was so white and she looked like she was sleeping but her eyes were half open. I remember looking down and just thinking about her blue eyes. She had a little bit of purple around her mouth and her ears."

A woman from the medical examiner's office was standing near the body as Mona reached out and touched Jane's face. "If it's any consolation, she died almost immediately," said the woman in a very soft voice.

Gladys Hurshman seemed uneasy and wanted to leave. "Let's go, Mona, let's go," she repeated several times.

"I think maybe Mom was sorry she went in," says Mona. "But I wasn't. I would have liked to have been there by myself. I would have liked to have spent more time there with her."

◆ ◆ ◆

Dr. MacAulay, at the conclusion of the autopsy, felt certain Jane's death was a suicide, but he needed more information to make a definitive ruling.

"The attitude of the weapon and the attitude of the victim were compatible with her doing it herself," he says. "But somebody else could have rigged it. It's possible to stage a suicide. I mean, there's no magic to that."

The fact that the bullet did not go through the front of the camisole was one of the factors that pointed to suicide. If Jane felt one of the camisole buttons digging into her chest from the pressure of the revolver, MacAulay says the automatic response would be to shift the button aside with the muzzle before squeezing the trigger, "especially if you're sitting there deciding whether you're actually going to do this or not." He says if someone else shot Jane, it's extremely unlikely they would have been aware of the button beneath the jogging top, or would have bothered to push it aside.

MacAulay says there were no visible injuries on Jane's body other than a slight discoloration of her lower lip. In gunshot suicides it is not uncommon for people to bite their lower lip as they squeeze the trigger.

MacAulay believes it would have been improper for him to label Jane's death as a definite suicide while forensic results and investigation of the threats against her were still outstanding. "I had no doubt that it was suicide, but you need to know information about the person's state of mind," he says. "And so, before I became convinced, I needed to hear the information that the police gathered. Eventually, they had some fifty or sixty statements, most of which I went through."

MacAulay knew that because of Jane's public profile he would have to release a statement to the press.

◆ ◆ ◆

On Monday night most of Jane's family gathered in the living room of her home as Joel played the audio tape she had recorded two days before her disappearance. Present were her parents, her sister

Mona, her sons Darren, Jamie, and Allen and Allen's wife, Charlene.

Jane talked about her meeting with Liz Forestell and Nadine Cooper-Mont, the deputy solicitor general. "Just in case anything does happen, I want you to know it's been reported to the top," she said.

She then went into a detailed review of the financial aspects of her will and how her assets, including insurance policies, RRSPs, and pension benefits, would be divided among Joel and her sons. "Our home at 253 Arklow Drive will be paid off if I should happen to die or be killed," she said. "The house is to go in Joel and Jamie's name — and Darren's if it's legally allowed."

It was an emotional time as the family listened to her voice calmly and clearly talk about her feelings and list the things she wanted done in the event of her death. Her voice broke only when she talked about the possibility of her dogs being "put to sleep."

Jane said she wanted only her immediate family to view her body and that she be cremated in an inexpensive casket. She also said that Darren was to maintain close ties to his brothers, the rest of her family, and Joel if he went to live with Mary and Paul Jacquart.

On the tape Jane also read a letter she had written in November 1991 to "my precious loved ones, Joel, my sons, my parents, my sisters and brother and their families:

"Life has been good to me this past couple of years. I fell in love with a fantastic man and got married. A miracle. We bought a home and turned it into our castle, and all of this is more than I ever believed to be possible. Happiness has been overwhelming. There is a future. Life is good. I am safe and loved.

"I am writing this letter because I am positive that was exactly how Patricia Parnell and Phillip Nickerson felt just before life was so abruptly taken away. I have not been able to get them out of my mind, so I decided to write his letter to accompany my will. I want everything to be as clear as possible in the event of the inevitable — my death."

Jane told Joel to buy a new truck and let Jamie use her Mustang, and if the Arklow Drive house was sold and another house purchased, Joel was to put it in her sons' names as well as his own, and he was to list Jamie and Darren as beneficiaries of his life insurance and will. She also stressed the importance of education and urged Jamie and Darren to stay in school.

Mona says listening to her sister's voice was very difficult for her and Jane's sons. "I was crying," she says. "And at one point I even felt a little angry at Jane for not telling me what she was really feeling. You know, 'Why didn't you let me in on everything? You could have been here today if you would have reached out.' It was very emotional."

It was particularly emotional when Jane said she was at peace and addressed each of them individually:

Joel . . . I love you dearly and deeply. When the time is right, and you and the kids are settled, consider getting yourself a new partner. Get yourself a lady that is good, and caring, and loving, to you and to my kids.

To Al and Char, I want only the best for both of you and I ask your understanding and forgiveness for the shame and humiliation I have caused you. Remember the good times and live your lives to the fullest and carry my love in your hearts.

Jamie, I love you dearly. I am so very happy and proud that we have had the time and the opportunity to get to know how much alike we really are — so sensitive, caring, and loving.

Darren, my precious pride and joy, I love you. You and Jamie and Joel be good to each other, take care of each other, love and talk, and understand each other. Try to keep out of trouble and get your education. I will always know that I am alive in your heart and in your mind.

Mom and Dad, I am glad that we had these days and years to really get to know each other and I am thankful we are such a good family. I love you both so very much. Please take care of yourselves and of Joel and my sons.

Mona, Sandy, and Skipper [Jane's brother], I love you all very much and I am so proud to call you sisters and brother. I thank you all for all your support and love, and your caring and kindness. Now just show it to Joel and my sons as much as ever.

Jane included one more request. "And remember, should anything happen to me and the police come here, don't you allow them to take anything that's mine that I have written in, or written on, or any documents or papers."

XIX
• • •

QUESTIONS

ON TUESDAY, FEBRUARY 25, the day after the autopsy, Dr. Malcolm MacAulay made public his initial findings. He said Jane's death was consistent with suicide but he had not ruled out homicide. Halifax police also said Jane's death was probably suicide but that their investigation was continuing.

The news media reported both statements the next day and carried stories about the reported threats against Jane. Allen Burchill, the RCMP's chief superintendent, said that because Jane had served time in prison, she didn't think police would take the threats seriously. "It wasn't a case of faith in their [the RCMP's] competence," Burchill was quoted as saying.

Burchill told the media about the Monday meeting he had set up to discuss the threats with Jane and to tell her they *would* be taken seriously. "Unfortunately, I never got the chance to give her my assurances," he said.

The police investigation, meanwhile, was proceeding full tilt on several fronts. After interviewing Donna Smith and Carrie Rafuse, investigators began to feel strongly that Jane had intended to kill herself and make it appear a murder. They believed she paid someone to put the gun, the bullets, and the flannel sheet into the plastic bags and remove them from the car. But the person failed to follow through with the plan.

"We were still treating it as a very suspicious death," says Peter Astephen, "mostly because of the threats. You just couldn't treat it

183

as a suicide, even though, by that point, every indication made it look like suicide.

"With all the normal checks you make, there was nothing to indicate a homicide. Her clothing wasn't ruffled and nothing was disturbed on her person. There were no signs of a scuffle. The coffee cup was upright and nothing was disturbed in the vehicle whatsoever. As an experienced investigator, seeing the gun there, for sure it jumps out at you that it looks like a suicide."

Astephen and other investigators determined that Jane was last seen shortly before 8 P.M., on Friday, February 21, at the Mic Mac Shopping Mall, where she purchased the birthday cake. The coffee cup found in the car was from Perks Coffee, about three blocks from the parking lot where Jane's body was found.

Given times and locations, it's assumed the coffee was purchased sometime after Jane left the Mic Mac Mall. She seldom drank coffee, and police were unable to determine if she or someone else picked it up from Perks.

"There were several naval ships in from different countries," says Astephen. "They were extremely busy at Perks and there were so many people in and out of there that night, they couldn't remember seeing her."

He says police did not analyze the contents of the coffee cup "because there was no reason to. It looked and smelled like coffee, so I'm pretty sure it was coffee."

Dr. Roland Perry, the chief medical examiner, says no drugs or alcohol were found in Jane's system and there was no reason to check for caffeine.

No clear fingerprints were found on the coffee cup or the handgun — a military issue .38-calibre Smith and Wesson, manufactured, without a serial number, in the late 1930s or early '40s. The letters R.A.F. (Royal Air Force) were inscribed on the gun, and police said the model was widely issued within the Canadian military in World War II. Astephen's boss, Staff Sgt. Don Thomander, says "there's probably a lot of them around. It wasn't really an uncommon type of gun."

Jane did not have a permit to own or carry a handgun and, in initial discussions with the Cole Harbour RCMP, Joel did not mention that she had obtained a revolver. Eventually, a man from the Bridgewater area informed police that Joel had been looking for a handgun. Ten days after Jane was reported missing, Joel and Darren were brought in for intensive, separate, questioning, and it was then that police learned that Jane had obtained a gun.

"We bent over backward trying to find the owner of the gun," says Thomander. "It was quite obvious she was able to get the gun — maybe through an illegal operator or drug dealer. There's no way those people are going to come forward. There's no way on God's earth that we had any means of being able to trace the gun because there's probably quite a few in existence."

Astephen says that although police never showed Joel the gun found in the car with Jane, he gave police an exact description of it, including the *R.A.F.* inscription. He also described the bags the bullets and the gun were in.

Thomander says the flannel sheet around the gun was used by Jane to protect her hands from gunpowder residue, to muffle the shot, and to hide the resulting flash. "It was dark and there were people coming and going, and she didn't want to take a chance." He says it was the sheet that kept the gun from falling to the floor as Jane slumped to one side.

Astephen says forensic evidence subsequently revealed powder residue on the flannel sheet and on "the webs of both hands between the thumb and forefinger. In a close area like that, it wouldn't be uncommon for residue to be in lots of places, but the chances of it getting on both hands, in areas consistent with the hands being around the gun, I think would be almost impossible. Griffin, from Ident, and I feel that her thumbs were hooked through the trigger."

MacAulay says that because the handgun was held so close to Jane's chest, some of the residue from the blow-back would come from the muzzle when the shot was fired, but most of it would come from "the break between the cylinder and the barrel."

MacAulay also believes it was suicide, because "a killer shooting for the body, logically, would shoot twice — at least."

◆ ◆ ◆

As part of the investigation into Jane's death, the police attempted to track down the man Jane claimed to have hired to shoot her in the head. In her story to Carrie Rafuse, she said that after the gun misfired on the first attempt, the man was to try a second time, but in the meantime police picked him up on an unrelated charge.

"There was one way of finding out whether that was true, and that would be to find the guy," says Sgt. Keith Crosland, of the Cole Harbour RCMP. "And there's no ifs, ands, or buts — we have not found the guy." He says police checked arrest records around the dates Jane had indicated to Carrie. "Nothing came of it. It was a nice lead that dead-ended. The other side of the coin is, even if you did come up with the guy, virtually all you're getting is a little more information that's going to corroborate the suicide theory.

"I felt from the start that we would find her and we would find that she committed suicide."

The suicide theory was further buttressed in the minds of the police when they learned Jane had often talked about suicide and that she had already attempted to kill herself.

Some of her friends and associates thought she spent so much time helping other women that she didn't allow herself to heal. She was also worried about how her sons would turn out. But overshadowing all of that was Jane's continuing battle with kleptomania. She found it humiliating and hurtful to her and her family. It had brought on the 1989 suicide attempt, and the problem had worsened since then.

She was facing a court hearing on March 4, less than two weeks from the day she disappeared, and she hadn't told her family about it. Her lawyer would have had the case put over, probably for several weeks, even months, but there was the fear that the media would see her name on the court docket and play up the story as it had in the past.

And two days later after that, Jane was to address the Canadian Panel on Violence Against Women when it stopped in Halifax on its cross-country tour. The thought of public humiliation and embarrassment one day, and a public appearance before the panel the next, might have been too much for her.

◆　◆　◆

The news of Jane's death — the threats against her, the suicide speculation, the possibility of homicide — unleashed a tide of fear, anger, and confusion among many women in Nova Scotia and Atlantic Canada, where she had such a high profile.

Darlene Darrington, one of the victims of the so-called motorcycle rapist, at first didn't know that Jane had been missing. "I was home watching the late news when I heard it. It was like part of me was lost. It was very frightening because they didn't know, at the time, whether it was murder or suicide.

"I really believe that Jane committed suicide, and if that's what she needed to do to end her pain and suffering, I can understand it. My suicidal feelings still come and go today. After what happened to me, I wanted to commit suicide, and a lot of the women in the group that we have felt the same way. You do begin to get on with your life, but there's always something that brings it back — sometimes worse than others."

Darrington was troubled by the media coverage of Jane's death, particularly the focus on her problem with kleptomania. "It upset me that they said all these negative things about her instead of talking about all the positive things she did. The kleptomania was a result of her abuse. We do things to try to cope with what we're going through and we all do different things — I turned to drugs and alcohol. Other women do other things. Society doesn't understand that. As victims, we do understand."

Darrington wishes she had spoken out sooner about her own pain because she feels "we all used Jane in a way. She spoke out for everybody and we just sat back and let her do all the fighting for us. I'm just so thankful I got to meet her because she was such a special person."

◆　◆　◆

Jane's childhood friend Valery Cromwell had called her mother in Nova Scotia from Toronto on Sunday morning, February 23. "She told me she saw on the news that Jane was missing. My blood went cold and I said, 'Well, somebody's got her.' That was my first instinct. I remembered her saying they'd probably never find her body because it would be out to sea."

Her mother called back in the afternoon to tell her Jane had been found dead.

"I still say she didn't commit suicide," says Valery. "I feel somebody out there had something to do with it, and whoever it is they are not going to the grave with their secret. They must confess before they die."

◆   ◆   ◆

Valery's cousin James Tynes says he wasn't really surprised to learn Jane was dead. "I felt real bad about it. I didn't feel surprise or shock, but I called her parents to find out for sure. I was in Ontario from May until November of 1991 and when I returned I had the strongest urge to call her. And I did try her at work, but they weren't accepting any personal calls at that time. It was such a strong urge — to see how she was doing."

One of Tynes's sisters died of a heart attack in September 1991, and Jane had sent him a sympathy card. "I sent her a thank-you card and I put a little note in it," he says. "I had heard she was being charged for shoplifting again and I asked her if she wanted to share with me, or if I could help in any way, but I never heard back from her. I was thinking later, maybe it was the wrong thing to do, because she felt so ashamed that she couldn't stop.

"I was sad when I heard she died and I guess I always will be. I get that strong feeling that she can't be dead — it's hard to explain."

Tynes believes shoplifting "really played on Jane's mind, and the fact that she was going to court would have been hard for her. She said she'd never go back to jail again. She said that a couple of times — 'No matter what, I'll never go back to jail.'"

What Tynes cannot understand is how Joel would have gone along with Jane getting a gun when he knew how distressed she was about her shoplifting. "I think I know Jane as well as anybody and probably better than most," he says. "And I know she wouldn't want a gun to protect herself. She could never kill anybody, after Billy. She would be so passive — she would go into a shell, and become this little girl, to block out the pain or suffering. I know that.

"If she wanted a gun, I would know she wouldn't want it for protection. She would want it to kill herself."

Tynes replayed the suicide tape Jane sent him in 1989 and says he found it very difficult to listen to. "I knew Jane needed help and I loved her. I don't think I'll ever love again. I felt really loved by Jane. I was never loved like that by anybody."

Tynes's voice cracks when he talks about the difficulties that led to their separation. "Maybe I should have been there. Maybe she was in love with this guy Joel, but when we separated, she did everything to get us back together. But I just felt it wouldn't work. So maybe she just went out and met this guy on the rebound or out of spite. Things happened so fast — goodness — that wasn't Jane.

"I could have stuck by her more than I did. I think about it a lot. If I would have stayed . . ."

◆ ◆ ◆

Margaret Joudrey, alone in her trailer below the house where Jane had lived with Billy Stafford in Bangs Falls, heard on the news that a woman had been found dead in a car on the Halifax waterfront.

"They didn't give no name," she said. "And I said, 'For godsakes, that makes it bad. Why don't they tell us the name?' Then later they told the name, and I said, 'Hallelujah!' I said there's one damn piece of trash gone. That's the way I felt. I'm happy that she's dead.

"I said if she goes to heaven, none of us has got to worry. I guess we'll all go there. Yes sir, if that woman lands in heaven, we ain't got nothin' to worry about. We can do mostly anything and get away with it."

Joudrey said Jane did not commit suicide. "She was making too much money on her damn lies, so why would she kill herself? She got well paid for what she done." (Other than occasional travel expenses, most of the work Jane did for women's groups and others was voluntary.)

The police asked Joudrey if she had a copy of *Life With Billy* in her house. "I told them I wouldn't put that book in no outside toilets. They said, 'You didn't think much of her?' And I said I did at first because we was together all the time, but after she killed Billy I didn't want a thing to do with her."

◆ ◆ ◆

Even in death, Jane had other detractors in Queens Country, many of them still bristling over her attacks on the local council over its initial refusal to mark the anniversary of the murder of fourteen women in Montreal with a special day of mourning.

Vernon Oickle, of the Liverpool *Advance*, says there were people in Queens County who resented her speaking out and "didn't realize that maybe she had to speak out, or that she had a message to deliver."

Oickle says that people might think Queens County would be more open to dealing with the problems of spousal abuse because of Jane "and the attention we had because of the trial, but I don't think that's the case." Instead, he says, some locals saw Jane "as perhaps taking advantage of her situation, and if she had just gone on with her life, and didn't speak out or participate in *Life with Billy* — that type of thing — they might have been more forgiving.

"Sadly, there's still some people who say that she got what she deserved, that she could have left Billy, that sort of thing. I don't think any amount of speaking out or public education is going to help those people unless they should happen to experience violence themselves.

"Certainly, there was also some remorse for Jane. People who appreciated what she'd gone through and what she had given of herself."

He says there were others in the county who felt that Jane got away with murder. "They resent the fact that she killed someone and didn't really pay the price — she didn't spend a lot of time in jail. They do admit that maybe there was some abuse but, despite that, she still killed someone, and in their eyes she got away with it. They felt she should have been dealt with more harshly by the law."

◆ ◆ ◆

Donna Smith believes Jane killed herself and she thinks she had planned it for some time. "Once she married Joel, she felt she could die knowing somebody would look after Darren. I think she had it in her mind to kill herself before she was married.

"Jane and I were always open about suicide. She just couldn't take it anymore. She had court coming up again, and that panel on violence against women. There's no way she could handle that.

"I don't condemn what she did. Some people think I should be angry with her for what she put me through, but I'm not mad at her. They don't know what she went through."

Donna says that if she had agreed to go along with Jane's plan she would be dead too. "I would have gone there with her, thinking that there was another woman. She would have sat in the car and killed herself in front of me. She would have expected me to remove the gun and everything, but if she did that I would have killed myself — automatically. There's no way I could have lived with that. It would have put everything on me."

Donna doesn't believe the story that Jane told to Carrie Rafuse. "We figured out the dates, and when she told Carrie about hiring somebody, it would have been me she was talking about."

◆　◆　◆

Jane's parents couldn't believe their daughter was dead. As the initial shock subsided, Maurice Hurshman thought back to the night she went missing, and he's convinced she died about three-thirty Saturday morning, February 22.

Joel had left their house about one-thirty, after the call from Darren informing him Jane was missing. About two hours later, Hurshman heard footsteps at the front door. "It was just the same as if someone walked right across the steps," he says. "I said, 'That's Joel coming back,' and I got up and came out and opened the door." No one was there, and the only footprints in the snow were those left by Joel when he went to his car two hours earlier.

"I heard it clear as that," says Hurshman. "It was like someone coming right to the door. Even the dogs started barking. But there was no one there. I think that's when she died. That's what's on my mind all the time."

Gladys and Maurice Hurshman say they don't believe Jane killed herself. They point to the letter she wrote to them while she was at work in the early morning hours of the Friday she disappeared. "She was supposed to come down here on the March break," says Maurice Hurshman. "And she made an appointment with the doctor for Gladys. She always took us to these places because I could never find them. And she said in her letter, 'I'll see you Tuesday,' for the doctor's appointment."

Hurshman says that although Jane didn't tell them about her latest shoplifting charge or the March 4 court appearance, "this problem of hers was all out in the open. She even put it in the media. She never talked about suicide to us. I can't see her doing this."

◆ ◆ ◆

Victoria Jones was devastated when she learned of Jane's death. "I was at a friend's and it came on the news they'd found a woman's body in a car in Halifax. They didn't give any name, and I thought, *The poor soul.* And the next day Charlene called me and she said you know that woman that they found in a car was Jane."

Jones, bored with retirement, was working for a private nursing agency when Jane called and invited her for dinner and an overnight visit on the weekend before her death. "I'd been working two or three twelve-hour shifts and I was really, really tired," says Jones.

"Could I take a rain cheque on it?" she asked Jane. "I don't feel ill exactly but I don't feel great."

"That's all right," said Jane. "We'll do it another day."

Jones believes the dinner and overnight stay was Jane's way of saying good-bye to her. "I had no inkling that she was going to die that week. When Charlene told me that Jane was dead, I felt dreadful — I felt guilty too. I hadn't a clue she was going to do it. I cried for a week. I was just sick. How do you know you'll never, ever, see a person again? I often think about Jane and what I might have done to prevent this.

"I told the Mountie who came here doing the investigation how bad I felt, and he said, 'My dear, people who have got it in their mind to commit suicide just one day go out and do it. It can't be prevented because they've got it in their mind they want to die.'"

◆ ◆ ◆

Jane's pen pal Sara made a rare telephone call to her the Sunday before she was found dead.

"Call me next Saturday night," said Jane. "Joel will be going down to Mom and Dad's and I can have a better talk with you then."

Joel answered when Sara called on Saturday night and told her Jane was missing.

"I was upset," says Sara. "I didn't know anything bad happened. I thought, *Oh — she left me stranded.*"

Her first reaction upon learning of her friend's death was that she too wanted to die. "If there was no hope for her, then there was no hope for me," she says. "I wanted to kill myself."

◆ ◆ ◆

Jane's other long-time pen pal, Jo Sheridan, in British Columbia, is unequivocal in her belief that Jane did not kill herself. "I am absolutely convinced she was murdered," she says. "There's not one shadow of doubt in my mind.

"I feel that she was snatched away and I didn't get to say good-bye and I never touched her hand because I never saw her.

"In the letter written to me the day before her death, she told me she was fearful of the threats. She was clearly afraid and she said someone out there wanted to hurt her.

"There was absolutely no way she would have made me so anguished and petrified as I was when I got that letter. If she was planning suicide, there's no way she would have done that just to put people off-track. She was not an unkind or cruel person in any way."

Sheridan says the police investigating Jane's death never contacted her.

◆ ◆ ◆

Alan Ferrier, the legal-aid lawyer who defended Jane when she was acquitted of first-degree murder in 1982, and at the subsequent trial after the Crown won an appeal, is now a defence lawyer in private practice, with offices in Bridgewater and Liverpool. He didn't see much of Jane after the 1984 appeal, when she was sentenced to six months in prison.

"About three or four years after it was all over, she was guest speaker at a criminology conference I was at," recalls Ferrier. "She got up there and her eyes were just like they were in the 'fifth estate' interview. And I thought, *Why does she keep this up?*"

Ferrier says he saw Jane once again, less than a year before her death, as he was leaving the court-house in Liverpool — the same court-house where she had stood trial for killing Billy Stafford. "I was coming from family court," he said. "It was a Thursday and I think it was in the spring. She was walking up the sidewalk from the tennis courts toward the court-house. She was rigid. It was like rigor mortis had set in. She hadn't changed.

"I was friendly and upbeat, but she was on an edge. I thought if there was anybody she could be relaxed with, it should have been me. You know — life is cool, I'm really feeling good about myself . . . I didn't get anything of that — just the same old Jane."

With his limited exposure to her, it may have seemed to Ferrier that Jane hadn't changed in the years since her trial, but friends and associates would strongly disagree. It was likely that Jane seemed rigid and distant because Ferrier's presence, near the courthouse where she had divulged, publicly, the atrocities she and her children had been subjected to, triggered powerful flashbacks.

And the abnormally widened eyes and distant stare that he witnessed at the criminology conference were the result of a similar dynamic as she relived the horrors she was speaking about.

Ferrier's observations give credence to Mary Haylock's view that it is probably helpful for abuse victims to face, understand, and talk about what they went through, but reliving it over and over again retards the healing process.

Ferrier believes Jane committed suicide, and her death did not surprise him. "I saw her as an ongoing victim," he says. "She never got off the treadmill."

He says her kleptomania was out of control and was a symptom of deeper problems. "It was overwhelming. Some people asked why she didn't come back to me when she was caught shoplifting. It was because she was so embarrassed and felt she had let me down. That's why she changed lawyers so often."

Before all the details of Jane's death were made public, a Bridgewater police officer asked Ferrier if he thought it was suicide or murder.

"I think she concocted the whole thing to make it look like murder," replied Ferrier.

"What makes you think that?" asked the officer.

"Well, I just knew Jane."

During their conversation, the police officer said that in addition to Jane's many convictions for shoplifting, there were many occasions when charges against her were withdrawn. He said that as part of one investigation police went to her Cole Harbour home with a warrant and discovered numerous items "with the tags still on them."

"Here I'm telling him how this suicide is all concocted and he's telling me how serious the kleptomania was," says Ferrier.

By Wednesday, February 26, a day or so after Ferrier's conversation with the police officer, word was leaked to the media that investigators were looking into the possibility that Jane may have manufactured the threats against herself to make her death look like murder.

Ferrier says that, beyond any financial considerations, Jane would want her death to look like murder because if it was suicide "she would have felt she was letting people down — more recently, the feminist groups she was involved with."

He says it just didn't make sense to him that anyone would have enough hate in them to kill Jane. "She spoke out, but she wasn't a threat to men who were battering their wives."

In an interview with Vernon Oickle of the Liverpool *Advance*, Ferrier said it was sad "that this kind of media circus surrounds her death as much as it surrounded her murder trial. Some people's lives are destined to be tragic, and she appeared to be one of those. It's sad she couldn't have lived her life with some sort of dignity without all this media hype."

◆ ◆ ◆

Joel Corkum says he didn't think Jane was suicidal "and she never talked to me about suicide, or killing herself and making it look like murder — never. She told me about attempting suicide before when she was with James Tynes, but she didn't elaborate on it and I didn't ask about it. I said, 'That was your past, it's got nothing to do with me. That was then, this is now.'

"I've been around women who were suicidal. I know what to

look for. She wasn't suicidal. To my mind, she was scared."

◆ ◆ ◆

Liz Forestell says Jane couldn't fake the fear she felt over the threats. Forestell's voice was to become one of the loudest in a chorus of Jane's friends and associates who were convinced she was murdered.

Staff Sgt. Don Thomander says the police kept women's groups "aware of what directions we were moving in. We don't train to gain anybody's approval, but we were very up-front with them. We sat down with them very openly, discussed the thing, and laid it on the line what we could give them."

He says Forestell has a right to say what she wants. "She took a stand very early in the investigation without having any knowledge or background whatsoever, and she has continued that to maintain her credibility."

Forestell says the police were trying to make her feel guilty. "They were basically saying, 'Well, it's suicide and we've got all kinds of proof and now the media is going to have a field day because you've got all this press interest.' But Jane was known all across the country, so the media would have made a circus out of it anyway. Who told the media Jane had shoplifting charges against her? I'm damn sure it wasn't me, and it wasn't any of her buddies."

Thomander admits that Jane's high profile was a factor in the investigation. "What pushes us and what made this a very, very deep investigation is the media more than anything," he says.

Forestell was concerned that the police were discounting the threats against Jane, which she believed were real. She was also angry that the statement she made to the RCMP about Jane's feelings about Gary Grant was not kept confidential.

"That made me feel a little nervous, and that had a lot to do with my decision to talk to the press," she says.

But Staff Sgt. Fred Fitzsimmons, who took the statement from Forestell, says he had no choice but to give her statement to investigators once Jane was found dead. "If somebody wants something kept secret and I give my word, then it's kept that way. But when somebody's dead, this stuff has to be brought out."

◆   ◆   ◆

Although Forestell was only repeating what Jane had told her, Gary Grant was upset. He was on vacation in Florida when he learned of Jane's death and says he was shocked and was unaware she had been receiving threats.

When he returned to Halifax, he says, he heard rumblings in police circles and "through jiggin' the reels, I got word that maybe someone was thinking I was making these phone calls. And I said, 'Wait a minute! What is going on?'"

"As soon as I heard, I went over to the Cole Harbour detachment and said to the investigator, Keith Crosland, 'Listen, let's have a chat here. What's going on?'"

"I told him exactly what had gone on with the phone calls between us and that was it. I said anything else you need, come and see me. They were doing their job and I was helping them. And I heard no more about it after that."

Grant says he had great sympathy and great respect for Jane and he believes she must have been out of control to accuse him of threatening her after an innocent phone call in which he identified himself.

"The whole thing is a bit bizarre," he says. "I think at the time her mind was probably not working as it should."

◆   ◆   ◆

Although the police were convinced that Jane had committed suicide, the investigation was continuing on several fronts. The stencilled threats and the envelopes they came in were sent to RCMP labs in Ottawa to check for fingerprints and to conduct DNA tests on the envelope seals. Keith Crosland's "gut feeling" was that the DNA tests would prove the envelopes had been sealed with Jane's saliva.

"From everything I've discovered so far, it looks pretty certain that Jane orchestrated this herself," he said. "And I guess all we can do is hope that things like the DNA testing can be conclusive so we can put this whole thing to rest."

Police concluded that the verbal threats against Jane were prerecorded and then played over the telephone. Cole Harbour RCMP removed a tape machine from Jane's house to determine if it was used to record the threats. They also wanted to determine if Jane had somehow distorted her voice and made the threats herself.

In addition, police continued to interview friends and associates of Jane, and they were waiting for further results from forensic tests on the sheet, the revolver, and Jane's hands. It would be almost a year before all of the results were in, with the DNA taking longest, because the case was not considered a priority.

During their questioning of Joel Corkum after Jane's body was found, police discovered more evidence to bolster their belief that Jane planned her suicide to look like murder. He told them that most of Jane's financial dealings were done through Ora Harkins, a financial planner with Investors Group, which has offices across Canada, including Dartmouth.

Joel said that a week or so before Jane disappeared, he saw her with $1,000 to $1,200 in cash that was never accounted for later. "I had my cheque and two cheques that she hadn't got around to cashing. She sent me out to cash them and I brought her home the money. She said she had to take it to Ora to dump on her RRSP to reduce her taxes or something. It was cash money, which I thought was a little odd, because she usually just wrote him a cheque. It made me think a bit — why cash this time?

"Ora did not receive any money. The bank accounts did not go up, and the money was nowhere to be found in the house. It's gone without a trace."

Police believe that Jane earmarked the money to pay someone to remove the gun, sheet and bullets from the car after she shot herself. The amount fits with the scenario Jane outlined to Donna Smith, who was to be paid $1,000 in cash for removing the gun after Jane shot the woman in the Sears parking lot.

"For a thousand dollars," says Staff Sgt. Thomander, "all that person had to do was to open that door, pick up the gun, and dispose of it. Disposing of the gun would be very, very simple. You could take it down to one of the piers, you could bury it . . . As long as nobody sees you, there's no problem. The only one that's going to know about it is you.

"A thousand dollars is a lot of money. There are people who will kill for a thousand dollars."

Thomander says police believe Jane planned her death for some time and had been seeking someone to pick up the gun at least since early December, when she approached Donna Smith.

"It took time to get the gun," he says, "and the other factor was to get someone to remove it. You can go to that car when there's nobody around, and there's no snow on the ground, and you can open that door, take that gun, and be back in your car and gone in ten seconds. But there was a snow squall that Friday night. So you've got snow on the ground and the potential of leaving behind footprints."

Thomander says there would have been a lot of traffic in and out of the lot Friday night, particularly near the street. "The person is not going to approach that car while there are people coming and going because the percentages of being spotted drop away from your favour," he says. "So now you're thinking, 'I've got to wait until all the patrons from the lounges are gone.' But with the snow, the person starts to panic, and the whole scenario goes down the tubes."

Keith Crosland envisions a similar scenario. "If you got paid $1,000 or $1,200 and you went out and removed the gun to make the scene look like a murder, you're altering the evidence, and that's obstruction," he says. "But if they get the money but they don't remove the gun, they haven't committed any offence. That person definitely isn't going to jump up and walk into the office and say 'guess what I did?' They're just sitting down there, drinking it up and having a good laugh."

Crosland was sceptical that Jane may have obtained the handgun from a member of Hell's Angels or a member of some other gang. "With these guys there's definitely a possibility, but if you wanted to go and get a gun, you could get a gun anywhere. We all know that."

◆　◆　◆

Police were further convinced that Jane wanted her death to look like murder when they looked into life insurance policies in her name. If she was murdered, the ten-month-old mortgage on her

Arklow Drive house would have been automatically paid off and various insurance policies could have paid out in excess of $300,000.

There are clauses, standard in the life insurance industry, that state that if a policy has been in effect less than two years, claims can be rejected if there are misrepresentations in the original application, or in the event of suicide. The suicide clause states: "If the insured commits suicide while sane or insane, within two years from the date of issue, the company will pay an amount equal only to an amount equal to the premiums paid since such date."

The two-year stipulation did not affect the life insurance policy at the Halifax County Regional Rehabilitation Centre, because Jane had worked there for more than six years. That policy paid out $54,000.

Other claims, totalling $246,000, were rejected because the policies had not been in effect for two years. The claims could have been rejected because of the suicide clause, but in fact the insurance company, Great West Life, rejected them on the grounds that there were substantial misrepresentations in Jane's application for insurance.

The "misrepresentation" was likely Jane's failure to disclose, as required, that she suffered from depression, which led to her 1989 suicide attempt.

If Jane had died two and a half weeks later, Great West may have paid out the full amount because the two-year deadline would have passed — the misrepresentation and suicide clauses would have expired.

If Jane's "misrepresentation" was deemed to be fraud, however, the company could still have refused to pay. An insurance industry representative says that if an insurance company had advance knowledge of Jane's depression and her 1989 suicide attempt, "the policy never would have been issued in the first place."

XX

• • •

REMEMBERING

FOLLOWING JANE'S WISHES, her family held a private viewing before she was cremated. Joel and Jane's sister Mona made the arrangements.

"It was very quiet and it was close to home," says Mona. "I picked Jane's clothes out and I went in to make sure she looked nice before the family came in. She looked mean and they had sort of a frown on her face. She was pale, so I put a little bit of colour on her cheeks. I moved her collar up a bit, but she still didn't look like herself."

Mona says the viewing was difficult for the family. "I didn't think my dad was going to make it through. He broke right down. And I don't think my mom could really let her feelings out because she was worried about my dad and afraid she would fall apart. When Darren was looking at Jane he thought he could almost see her heart beating."

Allen, Jane's oldest son, could see how difficult it was for his grandfather. "If she had died from a heart attack, or old age, or even a car accident, he could deal with that — but this was hard to accept."

Allen's wife, Charlene, could not bring herself to approach Jane's body at the funeral home. "I got as far as the door and looked in," she says. "I could see her up there but I had to turn around — I couldn't do it. I think you should remember people as they are when they're alive. I can still see her in my mind, and that night I

201

was tossing and turning."

Allen did approach his mother. "She was just lying there, and I told her I was sorry for everything that happened and I told her I loved her a lot. I wish she could have come to me and said, 'Look, I got a real problem' or whatever. But it didn't happen like that."

Jane was cremated and, on Friday, Joel picked up the urn with her ashes from the funeral home.

◆　◆　◆

The weather was crisp on the afternoon of Friday, February 28, when more than one hundred friends and relatives attended a funeral service for Jane at St. John's Evangelical Lutheran Church at Mahone Bay.

A framed picture of Jane and the urn containing her ashes were on a small table, flanked by candle stands, at the front of the church. It was the same church she and Joel Corkum were married in four months earlier. Rev. George Wawin and Rev. Margie Whynot, the same ministers who had officiated at her wedding, conducted the service.

Reverend Whynot said that Jane's spirit would live on through all the lives she had touched. "Ten years ago, we cheered her strong spirit when she took action to free herself and her children from a madman who was destroying them," she said. "And when she began to speak out in public about her experiences, she opened the door for many other victims to do the same — to break the conspiracy of silence that surrounded their lives.

"I will never forget the first time I shared a certain part of my own story of abuse in public. It was the most tense and draining experience you could ever imagine. Some amount of telling is healing. Some sharing is healthy, but her public audience kept calling on Jane . . . to talk, to share, to give — for the past eight or nine years. We kept her immersed in the past, with all its pain and ugliness, and she tried not to let us down. We *liked* that brave mask she wore in public.

"There are those who don't like the idea of her being depressed in the midst of her new-found happiness, when everything seemed to be falling into place for her.

"By making Jane our larger-than-life hero, we didn't give her the time or the space to stop and forget the past for a while. You see, by asking so much of her, we were able to avoid our own responsibility for speaking out to help make our society a better, safer place."

Reverend Whynot said Jane was a "strong feminist but . . . she was different from many of the feminists I have encountered. Jane did not show any prejudice against other victims who would not, or could not, follow in her large footsteps. She allowed us to go on at our own pace and in our own way — as long as we did something.

"She knew real pain and fear . . . and depression was part of her life. She also had her faults and weaknesses. . . . Nevertheless, she was my hero."

Reverend Whynot omitted part of her written address because she wanted her words to be "more positive and comforting to her family and to others." The omitted section stated that regardless of how Jane died, Billy Stafford "has reached out of his grave and finally claimed his victim. You see, if Jane died because someone wanted to silence her feminist voice, remember that she started speaking out in the first place because of his abuse.

"And if she died at her own hand because she was tired of living with the constant pain and had nothing left for herself because she gave so much for so long to others — then remember who was the cause of that pain.

"I can't presume to know the cause of her death, but I know she was tortured by a lot of things in her past and no one should stand in judgement of her, nor let it detract from the good she has done."

Mona Donnelly, speaking on behalf of the family, told the gathering Jane was a "woman with a mission" and her struggle to put an end to violence in society must be continued.

After the service, many of Jane's friends and associates offered their sympathy to family members in the church vestibule.

Valery Cromwell came from Toronto for the service, and her cousin James Tynes was also there.

Donna Smith's emotional state was fragile and she found it difficult to accept that all that was left of her friend were the ashes in the urn at the front of the church.

Smith had always had trouble sleeping at night because of the abuse she had endured, but with Jane gone from her life her insomnia worsened. "We used to talk at night all the time, and I miss her so much. I found myself calling her at work without realizing what I was doing. Then I would remember and hang up before anyone answered."

Jane's friend and co-worker Annette Bushen and her daughter, Charlene, also attended the Mahone Bay funeral service. "It was a last good-bye. If her death was suicide, it was because of deep despair, but it takes great courage to take what cannot be bought, borrowed, or stolen. Whether it was murder or suicide, we all lost. I know many tears were shed by people who loved and respected her. To many she was a hero.

"Jane had many problems throughout her life, but her problems are no more. We will live with our guilt of not having done more for her and we will never again see her beautiful face or hear her laughter. Jane has gone home. She cannot be hurt ever again. I hope that somewhere in a better place, she will know only happiness."

◆　◆　◆

Three days later, a candlelight vigil was held at St. John's United Church in Halifax. The church was packed for the half-hour of poetry, song, and testimonials. It was billed as a celebration of Jane's life, not the mourning of her death. Still, there were many tears among the family, friends, and strangers who gathered to honour her.

Several framed photographs of Jane, surrounded by candles and flowers, were set up on a table near the lectern at the front of the church. Among them were wedding and family pictures.

Once again, Mona Donnelly spoke on behalf of the family, which she said had "drawn close" since Jane's death. "We've committed ourselves to care for each other. I know it would please Jane.

"Jane was truly a symbol of hope to the abused people in our society. We want you to know that her death was not a defeat for them, but a rallying point. And we vow to continue this work to create the society which Jane so desperately wanted — where love, caring, and respect for one another surpass the evils of anger, hatred, and violence. We have to continue on . . . and carry her banner until all the pain stops."

One battered woman said that, like Jane, "I suffered my own nightmare. On Sunday, I decided to follow in Jane's footsteps by speaking out against violence." Others tearfully vowed to keep alive her memory and spirit by fighting the "evil force" — domestic violence.

"Our time with Jane was too brief, but she will continue to be an inspiration as we carry on," said Liz Forestell, who had helped organize the event.

"The vigil was really nice," she says. "About three hundred people showed up, and Joel and Mona stayed at the end and chattered with Jane's friends. We kept the press in the choir loft and didn't allow them access to the family. It was good for Mona to talk to people without being hounded like we were all week. This night was for Jane and her family and friends, and we just wanted to be left alone."

Darlene Darrington was supposed to speak, but she was too upset by Jane's death. She had spoken out twice before, both times in Jane's presence. In the address Darrington wrote out in advance, she planned to tell the gathering that for three years after she was assaulted, society made her feel guilty and ashamed. "I kept seeing Jane speaking out, and she made me realize I had no reason to feel guilty or ashamed," she wrote. "God did not put us on earth to be abused, but to be loved. Jane tried to make people understand that.

"Jane is the most courageous person I've ever met, and she will live as long as we keep speaking out."

◆ ◆ ◆

Gary Grant had returned from Florida in time for the candlelight vigil, which he attended, and it wasn't until a day or two later that he learned that Jane had expressed concerns about him.

During the previous week Mona had asked Joel if he thought Grant was involved in the threats.

"No," said Joel. "He's a friend of mine. I knew Gary long before I ever got involved with Jane. It might be another cop, but not Gary Grant."

In the late afternoon before the vigil, Grant called the house and asked for Joel, but he was out. Mona answered, and Grant said he was calling to offer his condolences. He said he would be attending the vigil that night.

Mona didn't get to speak with Grant at the vigil because so many of Jane's friends wanted to talk to her. However, Grant did offer his condolences to Joel.

◆ ◆ ◆

Three days after Jane's body was found, a simple memorial appeared in the snow in the parking lot near where her car was parked. It was a bouquet of flowers in a soft-drink bottle with an attached note: "In remembrance of Jane — the pain has to stop. We can be silent no longer." It was signed: "A man who never knew you (unfortunately.)"

From that poignant tribute to items and editorials in the local and national media, the public outpouring of grief was remarkable.

Judy Hughes, Nova Scotia's representative on the Canadian Panel on Violence Against Women, which Jane had been scheduled to address when it came to Halifax on March 6, spoke about Jane in an interview with the Halifax *Daily News*. "Her death makes the reality of violence against women so crystal clear to me," she said. "I just feel sick about it. She was so symbolic of the women coming to the panel. The fact that she's dead is very disheartening."

One editorial said that Jane "broke the silence and focused public attention on an issue once buried under private shame. Through women like her, we've learned the shame must not be borne by the victim, but by the men who commit the abuse and by a society that has done too little to face this problem."

Writing in her column in the *Daily News* on March 3, Joyce Deveau Kennedy said that "grace under pressure" and "courage under fire" are stock phrases applied to athletes and soldiers. "Yet this grace and this courage may mark [an abused woman] even more."

She cited Jane Hurshman as an example. "Used as a punching bag for years, unable to protect herself or her children against the assaults of her husband, driven to mutiny and murder, tried twice for her treason — i.e. attacking her superior — jailed and finally set free, she was never able to escape her servitude.

"Jane wanted to help other women like herself who had been victims of abuse. She wanted to be the true athlete, whose competition is really with self. She wanted to be the soldier who pulls others from the trenches and leads them back to safety." Instead, said Kennedy, Jane found a bullet through the heart. "When will we learn the grace of women like Jane Hurshman, to dance the dance of life even in the face of death? I don't know, but such women give me hope."

◆   ◆   ◆

Vernon Oickle, reporter and editor with the Liverpool *Advance*, spoke with Jane on the telephone two days before she was reported missing. He had interviewed her at his home in mid-September of 1991 for a lengthy article he planned to run on the tenth anniversary of Billy Stafford's death, in March 1992.

"Certainly when I spoke with her on the phone, I couldn't tell one way or another what her personal feelings were," he says.

Oickle says he was surprised to learn that others who had talked to Jane shortly before her death insisted she wasn't suicidal. "I wouldn't even begin to think I knew somebody that well. You can live with somebody for years and not really know them."

Initially, Oickle didn't think Jane committed suicide. "There are certainly still some questions out that aren't answered and I don't know if they ever will be. But I think every person, if pushed enough, is capable of killing himself or herself.

"I think the media provided the motive for suicide and I think the police should have done that. To me, that's when the investigation broke down — when the media came out first with the fact that she was to appear in court on the kleptomania charge. They provided the motive."

Oickle says he doesn't know if the pending charge was enough to drive Jane to suicide. "I know it bothered her a lot, but when I spoke to her in the fall, she seemed to think that she was dealing with it — that it was the result of the abuses she had suffered. I don't know if anybody will ever know if that was the reason — if she did commit suicide."

Oickle says when he interviewed Jane in the fall of 1991, "sometimes she was forceful and quick with her answers, while other times it was almost as if she was looking for that answer that she had given so many times before — almost as if it was rehearsed.

"Certainly, whenever she spoke publicly or spoke with the media, she came across as very strong, in charge of her life, and in command of her feelings. But since her death, I've come to realize that maybe that was just a front, that maybe she wasn't as in command as she tried to make me think she was.

"Sometimes the conversation would stop as if she was collecting her thoughts, or trying to pull some strength from inside herself and so on. That kind of body language didn't mean much at the time."

Jane told Oickle that she did not like being considered a celebrity. "That's a hard thing to live up to," she said. "It doesn't give you a chance to fall down once in a while. It's really not fair that people put you on a pedestal. Sometimes I feel like I am under a microscope . . . but you learn to cope with the attention and live with it."

◆ ◆ ◆

Three days after Jane's body was found, Jo Sheridan felt compelled to write down her feelings and send them to Joel.

She wrote, in part: "Jane was not a person who'd be crushed by past events and social stigmas. Quietly and bravely, she forged ahead, always writing to me of tomorrow, next week, next year; always resolutely making future plans.

"She spent hours writing of her volunteer work and the cause so dear to her heart — speaking out and being heard, so that other women could learn from her experiences and benefit from an improved, compassionate society. She wanted women to be strong and respected.

"Despite my pleas at times, she persisted in her work, exhausting herself while contending with her shyness and deep sense of privacy. It cost her so much, but nothing stopped Jane from caring, speaking out, and fighting for change.

"Her quiet resolve, noble spirit, and loving gentleness amazed and profoundly touched me. She was my best friend and I was so deeply proud of her.

"This remarkable, compassionate woman has been so cruelly and suddenly taken from us, but she made her mark — oh, how she made her mark. And it's indelible."

◆　◆　◆

Jane's death was doubly devastating for Maurice and Gladys Hurshman because they'd grown so close to their daughter, who loved visiting them because it provided the peace and quiet she so desperately craved.

She was down to visit them the weekend before she died. "She came down on a Thursday and we had a wonderful time," recalls her father.

The Hurshmans weren't aware of the extent of Jane's problem with shoplifting, nor did they realize the depth of her involvement in the fight to end violence against women and children. "When Jane came here, she never talked about that stuff," says Hurshman. "She came here to relax and that's what she done."

Hurshman has diabetes and does a lot of walking "to keep the sugar out of me." Jane often walked along with him. "We'd drive over to Mill Village, about five minutes out the old No. 3 highway, and walk from there," says Hurshman. "There was a big rock up there and sometimes we would sit there and talk and she would say what she was going to do when she retired."

It was Jane's favourite spot, and she talked about building a small home where she could look after the elderly. It was the same dream she and Donna Smith often talked about.

"She was going to try to get that piece of land up there and she showed me how she was going to have it all landscaped and have flowers growing," says Hurshman. "She planned to do that when she retired. She told me that many a time."

He says Jane often came to visit without Joel and she went shopping with her mother "or we'd go down to walk on the beach. I couldn't believe how many women she touched. I didn't realize this until after her death. I don't know where she found the time."

"She seemed so happy, I can't understand," says Gladys Hurshman.

XXI
• • •
CONTROVERSY

On June 8, 1992, three and a half months after Jane's death, the Halifax Police Department closed its file on the case, concluding, as they had believed all along, that she had killed herself. The announcement was made after the department received forensic results from RCMP laboratories in Ottawa. Chief medical examiner Dr. Roland Perry agreed with the finding.

Staff Sgt. Don Thomander said Jane died between 9 P.M. on Friday, February 21, and 9 A.M. February 22. He said the bullet that killed her came from the gun found on her lap in the car and that forensic tests confirmed residue from the shot was found on her hands and on the flannel sheet that was used to muffle the sound.

While Halifax police were closing their file, the Cole Harbour RCMP said they were continuing to investigate the threats reported against Jane and were still awaiting test results on the stencilled threats and the taped voice threats. The announcements brought immediate reaction from Jane's family and some of her friends and associates.

Maurice Hurshman said he would never believe his daughter killed herself, because she had too much to live for. He said that in light of the threats police should not have immediately assumed her death was a suicide.

And Mona Donnelly, in a telephone interview with the Liverpool *Advance*, said she was "very disappointed and saddened by the outcome of this investigation. You may be thinking that our

210

family does not want to admit that Jane took her own life. Jane is dead — nothing will bring her back, I know that. I wish that this was a clean-cut case, but it is not."

Liz Forestell was also sceptical of the police finding. "The police evidence doesn't convince me that it's suicide," she told the Halifax *Chronicle-Herald*. "I'm still of the opinion she was murdered. I'm not satisfied they investigated with an open mind.

"I think there was some sloppy stuff done, but I don't have any evidence on that. It's a real difficult position to be in."

Forestell says the fact that Jane had a gun doesn't prove a thing. "If I figured that somebody was following me around and knew where I was all the time, I might get a gun. She couldn't have one legally, so she got it through other means."

Even if she is wrong, Forestell says Jane's death is tragic and sad. "It makes it harder when there are so many questions around. "But it's tragic no matter how she died. Whether she committed suicide or was murdered, she died from the violence that she suffered and survived for a while. I think there are answers we'll never have. I think there are things we'll never know about it."

◆ ◆ ◆

But Thomander is convinced that Jane's death was a long-planned suicide she intended to look like murder. He points to the threats, coffee cup found in the car, and all the business she left unfinished — such as delivery of the cake and gift to the rehab centre, sewing of drapes for her mother, taking her parents to the doctor, meetings planned with Ann Keith and other associates, and her appointment with Burchill of the RCMP. "There's no doubt about it," he says. "It was part of the scenario — that she wouldn't follow through on all the details."

The plan fell apart because the person she depended on to remove the evidence — the gun, the bullets, and the blanket — didn't show up, says Thomander. "With no gun, we would have had a problem. It would have been harder to prove it was a suicide. But still, there are very distinct factors that are consistent with suicide, like the discoloration of the lower lip.

"If you look at one thing by itself it doesn't leave you with all that much leeway, but when you have a combination of things, it becomes clearer."

He says Jane was sitting straight back behind the steering wheel, and given the angle of the bullet, "for someone to shoot her they would have to be almost sitting in her lap. And there was no sign of a scuffle. Obviously, if someone tried to do it this way, they would have tipped that coffee over.

"And if there had been someone in that car, there would have been a footprint."

Some of Jane's family and others say that because it snowed both nights on the weekend Jane went missing, footprints made Friday night would have been obliterated by Saturday's snowfall. Thomander disputes that suggestion. He says that about an inch of snow fell Friday night and half an inch on Saturday.

"The snow melted to a certain degree on Saturday, but it would have been quite obvious if someone had been in that car," he says. "There was no indication of any exit whatsoever from that vehicle — from the driver's side or from the other side."

Halifax police inadvertently added to the murder/suicide debate by providing conflicting information to the media about which doors of the Ford Tempo were open and which were locked. After speaking with Thomander, Vern Oickle wrote in the Liverpool *Advance* on June 17, 1992: "One vitally important fact, uncovered during the investigation and confirmed by officers with the Halifax Police Department, casts a shadow of doubt upon the suicide theory.

"Mysteriously, the driver's door . . . was locked while the other three doors were not. Those who support the murder theory believe that door was locked to prevent [Jane] from escaping. There, they say, she was shot to death as she was trapped behind the car's steering wheel. The death scene was then arranged to make it look like a suicide."

Other reports from Halifax police said that the driver's door was open and all the other doors were locked.

In February, 1993, Peter Astephen checked the file and verified that only the front door on the passenger's side was locked. This was confirmed by Bryan Naas, one of the two officers who were first on the scene.

And Jane's son Jamie Whynot, who drove the Ford Tempo most of the time before his mother's death, says that the handle on that door was broken and it could not be opened from the inside.

That information explodes the theory outlined in Oickle's article. It means that if there was a killer in the front seat with Jane, he or she would have had to climb over the back seat or over Jane to get out of the car. Or, a killer could have opened her door and shot with the left hand from a crouch, since the bullet went slightly upward and slightly to the right through her chest. But if a killer did come at Jane from that side, why would she remain seated square in the normal driving position? And how did blow-back residue get on the web of skin between the thumbs and forefingers of both her hands? That the driver's door was open would also provide ease of access for someone reaching in to remove the gun and sheet from her lap, stuffing them into the plastic bags, and leaving.

Beyond the physical evidence, both Halifax police and the RCMP point to the scenario that Jane laid out to Donna Smith in early December. The details paralleled those of her death, including the old clothes, the older car, the handgun, the parking lot, and the plastic bags.

"Don't forget," says Thomander, "you have a lady repeating a story from another lady, so there are going to be some changes, but the changes were so slight — even down to a parking lot where there were a lot of comings and goings."

And on the day she disappeared, Jane told her son Jamie that she didn't know the telephone number of the woman she was supposed to visit in Halifax, and therefore she couldn't switch vehicles as he had requested. But later the same day, Jamie's girlfriend, Anita Bruce, saw Jane purportedly dial the woman's number and talk to her. Police believe that there was no woman and that Jane was pretending to call the woman as part of her plan to make her death look like murder.

Thomander says the investigation by Halifax police was thorough and that Peter Astephen is a "top-notch investigator who did a very excellent job. I have all the faith in the world in him."

Astephen says that "because of who she was and because of the threats" the investigation into Jane's death was probably more thorough than most. "I guess, as an investigator, you put extra pressure on yourself," he says. "You do that to make sure that you're doing the investigation as perfectly as it can be done."

Dr. Roland Perry says that police went to the "nth degree" investigating Jane's death, "whereas normally we would never go anywhere near this to satisfy ourselves. Everything was consistent with a self-inflicted wound and there was no question that the self-infliction was done with intent to commit suicide."

Perry says Jane's family and friends find it difficult to come to terms with her death because of the reported threats. "With any death, you could literally go on forever doing things until you come to the final decision, 'This is it, we're not going any further, we're more than satisfied.' We were satisfied ages ago, but because of the nature of the death, because of who the person was, you have to go further.

"This case is a little unusual because of the high profile of the deceased. If she had been Jane Nobody then there wouldn't have been much publicity."

Perry says he has seen "probably a thousand suicides" in his years as a medical examiner, and most — seventy-seven percent — are male. The most common method is by firearm. He says women are less likely to use guns, but those who do are more likely to shoot themselves in the chest than in the head. "Off the top of my head, I can remember just two," he says, "and both shot themselves in the chest."

Perry says he's talked to a lot of families who've lost a loved one to suicide. "It's natural and normal for people to deny that somebody could take their own life. That's very common with close family members, who find it difficult to deal with.

"There's the initial denial, followed by feelings of guilt and anger and then grief. It's like a broken record. I tell families we have enough trouble trying to understand ourselves, let alone trying to understand somebody else. We know everybody superficially, even our most intimate associates — our wives, husbands, children, parents even. There are many things I know I would never tell my wife and vice versa.

"People can accept, eventually, natural death, accidents, murder

— but suicides tend to be very difficult to accept because they're initiated by the individual and the guilt that then shows up with family members and friends is really quite spectacular. And of course you get the denial. This is what happened with Jane Hurshman, to a great degree, with some of the groups that worked with her."

Perry says Jane was "a very disturbed woman. She was put upon tremendously by women's organizations and other people to try to get her story across. She was under a tremendous amount of pressure, and to her credit, she hung in there.

"It doesn't surprise me at all that she got to the point where she figured, 'This is it, it's just too much for me.' And her brushes with the law were a reflection of the deep emotional problems she had to deal with. Living with a guy like that all those years, putting up with his abuse to her and to her kids, you mean to tell me that after he's dead, she's all of a sudden going to be perfectly normal? Impossible."

Perry says he would not have said, as Dr. Malcolm MacAulay did, that Jane's death looked like suicide but homicide couldn't be ruled out. "It was a statement by a person who had little experience in dealing with the news media. What he should have said is that the cause of death was gunshot wound and that no further information would be given until we were satisfied we had enough information."

MacAulay says he had considerable experience dealing with the media as head of pathology at Dalhousie University for twelve years. "I found it worked better to come out and be very direct with the press."

Furthermore, the statement he prepared after Jane's death was vetted by a lawyer who was press adviser in the attorney general's department. "I didn't just fling that thing out," says MacAulay. "I composed it and faxed him down a copy and then we discussed it over the phone and then it was released."

◆ ◆ ◆

MacAulay's statement that Jane's death was probably suicide did much to ease the fears of many women that a killer was out there ready to strike again. Jane's therapist, Mary Haylock, says that "as a woman, there was a part of me that hoped it was suicide — that we didn't have a crazy on the run, who might cause other deaths."

From the time Jane was reported missing, Haylock had a strong feeling Jane killed herself "and yet it was a bizarre place for her to be — on the docks in Halifax. Jane, the woman from rural Nova Scotia, who thought all the evil stuff happened in the city of Halifax. It's ironic that she ended up there in her death."

◆ ◆ ◆

Gary Grant says that when he first heard about Jane's death he didn't believe it was suicide. "I never saw that in the cards. She was a fighter, and it looked as if there was light at the end of the tunnel.

"In retrospect, knowing what happened in her life, all the abuse, then being put on a pedestal by a lot of groups that needed someone to carry the flag for them, worrying about how her children were going to turn out — maybe it was just too much.

"There was a tremendous amount of strain on that woman, and I hope that the women's groups can just accept the reality of what has taken place here.

"Maybe she was making a final statement — 'I've had enough, I can't deal with it anymore, and this is what I want to do.' But boy, I'll tell you, I still get the shudders when I think about her dying of a gunshot. Because Billy's death was so traumatic for her. And I know how she relived that horror over and over.

"That drive she took along River Road that night, with Billy's decapitated body against her, was unbelievable. And then to take her life in a vehicle with a gun . . . She must have had a flash of what that was. It was a hell of a way to go.

"I don't believe there was any residual guilt over killing Billy. I don't think she had any remorse. I think she did what she did because she believed there was no way out and she would have been long in the ground if she didn't kill him.

"No, I think it was the burdens placed on her, and her own inner burdens, and her fight to regain some sanity, that forced her over the edge."

Grant says Jane was a woman who "did not deserve this ending.

She could not carry the flag for everybody, and I think it may throw some caution into other groups that lean so heavily on people who have been down the road before. I think that's a caution that should be made clear — that we run the risk of damaging further those already damaged. I think that the women's groups — God love them — expected an awful lot of her. She was never healed herself, and that's a damn shame."

Grant is convinced that Jane's kleptomania was symptomatic of deeper emotional problems, and her fear of going back to prison, coupled with other stresses in her life, may have been the catalyst that lead to her death.

"There's a lot of women who've been in jail who would sooner die than go back," he says. "It leaves their self-esteem so low — I've seen it first-hand."

◆ ◆ ◆

Kathleen Jennex, of Coverdale Court Work Services, doesn't accept that Jane's pending court case, and the possibility of a jail term, pushed Jane to suicide. "The police were basically saying that was the reason she was over the edge. I don't believe that."

Because of the defence of automatism proposed by her new lawyer, Patrick Duncan, Jane "really had more hope, in terms of the court case, then at any other time I had seen," Jennex says.

She believes Jane was also feeling positive about her therapy with Mary Haylock. "But there is a possibility that Jane couldn't take it, and I can understand if she couldn't and that it was suicide. There's just no way that you can suffer that much abuse and it not affect you for the rest of your life — no matter how together you seem to be to the world. Sometimes it's when you're the most together that something like this happens — when you can see a light at the end of the tunnel."

Jennex says she was ambivalent about how much she asked Jane to do, "but I also had a really strong feeling that she would say no if she didn't want to do something. I didn't want to exploit her because she was generous. I know she felt she needed to do this kind of thing, but you can exploit people.

"Jane did a lot of work on the sidelines that no one ever knew about — going to see women who were in distress. She didn't want the limelight. She just wanted to do what she could do regardless of how much pain it caused her, and I know it caused her a lot, because she relived her own experiences every time she helped someone else. That's why I was careful about what I asked her to do."

Forestell was similarly careful. "I think she knew what she was capable of and she made it very clear to me that when it was too much she would let me know. She didn't have any problem saying no to the things she couldn't do. And there were times when she said, 'No, I just don't have time to do that.'"

◆ ◆ ◆

In the July/August 1992 edition of *New Maritimes* magazine, several of Jane's friends, including Forestell and Wendy Annand, wrote a seven-page cover-story entitled "Why Did Jane Hurshman Have to Die?" The byline for the article read: "By Some Angry Women."

Annand says the media coverage of Jane's death "upset me so much for months and months. That's why we finally wrote the article."

The article stated that the media dwelt on "why she must have killed herself" and seemed to ignore the fact "that many people are unconvinced that Jane's death was suicide.

"We are not only angry, we are afraid. The fact is, all women have experienced some kind of violence, whether they have been harassed, threatened, molested, battered or raped. That is why wherever we go, we hear women whispering among themselves, '*We know Jane didn't kill herself.*' From Yarmouth to Glace Bay, women (and some men, too) of every class and age — in offices, on street corners, on the phone, in coffee shops — are muttering and whispering. And what is the message that media coverage of Jane's death has given to battered women? It is that a woman who speaks up against wrong should expect death threats, and even death itself, as her just reward. Shut up or be shut up. The victim is blamed for her own death."

The women said they suspected the police investigation was not thorough and "there is a real possibility that there is a cold-blooded murderer on the loose who stalks women who speak out against violence against women."

They also wrote of the closeness of Jane's death to the tenth anniversary of Billy Stafford's death. "Both were shot. Both died in vehicles. It is too coincidental. It doesn't have the feel of a *'guilty suicide.'* It has the feel of a *'hit.'* Jane had survived too much in life to give it up when she was the happiest she had ever been."

◆ ◆ ◆

Ann Keith believes that Jane purposely avoided her in the weeks before her death because Keith might have sensed she was planning to kill herself. "The fact that she didn't tell me about the threats, or that she thought her phone was tapped, until the day before she disappeared makes me wonder," says Keith. "Maybe she didn't come to me because she was worried that she wouldn't be able to disguise what was going on. I might have picked up on it." (It was the telephone call from Keith that changed Jane's mind about committing suicide in the summer of 1988.)

Keith says Jane may also have been avoiding her because she didn't want her to know about her pending court case. "When I heard about court, I thought, *Oh my God!* Because I know what she went through the last time she had to go to court."

Keith says she too was careful about calling on Jane to help with abuse victims or to speak out. "I always said to her, 'Jane, if you feel that you don't want to do something, or if it's too heavy — don't do it.' Sometimes she said 'no,' and I said, 'Good for you.'

"On the other hand, I always felt that speaking out and helping others was her way to cleanse herself. Jane was always a very spiritual person and I don't think she ever got over the guilt of taking another human life."

Media coverage of Jane's death bothered Keith, and she publicly urged that Jane be left in peace and be treated with dignity. "You know, if we walked on water we might be able to respond to all the questions that only Jane could answer. You can't get inside somebody's head. And regardless of how she died, the important thing is the legacy that she left us."

Keith says the police, and Peter Astephen in particular, were open and cooperative with her and SSAV and other women's groups. She thought the investigation was thorough and she said so publicly in June of 1992, when the Halifax department announced it was closing the case.

Wendy Annand, as indicated in the *New Maritimes* article, espouses a contrary view. "I think she was murdered," she declares. "The fact that she was doing so much public speaking was always an indication that she was up. Jane knew when she was under a lot of stress and she would take time on her own — go into therapy or do whatever she needed to do.

"There were times when she withdrew for a year or two. Lately she'd been doing so much, and to me it was just another indication that she was feeling good. So I think some asshole's blown her away. That's what I think."

Jane's kleptomania is a non-issue, in Annand's view, because "everybody knew about it."

She says Jane's death "goes against all the theories of suicide. In war-time people don't kill themselves. When you're under great personal stress, it's the last thing you would consider.

"There's no way she would have done that to her family — to Darren in particular. I said to the police, 'Look, if she was going to kill herself, she would not do it in this horrendous manner.' Not the way she felt about guns and knowing the violence that everybody had already been through."

Annand said, before the Halifax police announced they were closing Jane's file, that "we can't bitch at the police — they're just trudging along as best they can. They're going to have to rip that car to shreds to find out what really happened."

She believes there will eventually be a public inquiry into Jane's death.

◆ ◆ ◆

At the time of Jane's death, Joel Corkum had lived with her for eighteen months and been married to her for four. If she was depressed, he says he didn't know it. And he doesn't believe she killed herself. "I don't think she could do it," he says. "And I know she wouldn't put us — the family — through this, because she was too loving, too caring. And especially Darren, because he was her pride and joy and a big part of her life."

Joel agrees that almost from the time they returned from their honeymoon, until her death, Jane was deeply involved in speeches, meetings, and in helping battered women one-on-one. (She had also been picked up for shoplifting in mid-November, appeared in court in December, and saw her case put over to March 4 — all of which he knew nothing about.) He says that once her work was completed on the committee on incarcerated women and after her March 6 appearance at the panel on violence against women, Jane planned to step out of the spotlight.

"I was getting a little concerned that she was doing too much," he says. "I said to her a couple of times that she should take some time for herself. I think she was finally ready to let that part of her life come to an end and spend more time with her family. We had plans to go away on a cruise to Alaska on our fifth anniversary and to do some other things like that — just the family."

Joel believes that the handgun Jane purchased and showed to him was the one that killed her, but he doesn't think she pulled the trigger. "There's two ways of looking at it," he says. "The money, a thousand or so, was nowhere to be found after I gave it to her. There was a gun, and the bags and bullets were there, but now, the next question — did she pay someone that money to come and pick up that gun and they didn't come, or did she pay somebody to pull the trigger and they panicked and threw the gun down?

"There were no fingerprints on the gun. The whole thing is too bizarre. Someone that's happy don't kill themselves and they don't go through the efforts of picking up a cake for a resident at work they think a lot of, and they don't have a gift sitting at home for him."

Joel knows and likes Keith Crosland. "He comes out to the garage to get work done on his car. We talk quite a bit. I knew he was a cop, but I didn't know where. So when I walked in there, I already knew him by first name. I don't trust cops as a rule, but I do trust Keith.

"Peter Astephen may be an excellent police officer, but I just don't think they looked hard enough. The only way I can get anything out of the police is if I corner them. If I never called them, they'd never call me. Everything was released to the press before I got it. I got nothing."

(Astephen says he tried to make the investigation as easy as he could on Joel and the family. "I went up to the house and answered their questions as much as I could.")

Joel said that if DNA tests by the RCMP proved that Jane's saliva was on the envelopes that contained the stencilled threats, "that would clear up quite a bit, but if it's not Jane's DNA, they've got a very big problem.

"If a reporter came up to me and asked, I'd be in shit, but I'd say 'police cover-up,'" says Joel. "I got nothing to substantiate that, only my gut. But I don't believe Jane committed suicide, and no one is going to make me believe that."

◆ ◆ ◆

Allen Whynot and Charlene concede that Jane may have committed suicide, but they believe a lot of questions remain unanswered.

Allen believes his mother didn't embrace him the last time he saw her at the house because he might have sensed her intentions.

"Allen often knew what she was thinking and it was the same for her," says Charlene. "They had something special together. He would read her a lot and if she planned to commit suicide, she might have been scared that he would look at her and tell what she was thinking."

"I didn't want it to be suicide," says Allen. "It's an awful thing to think about — that your mother shot herself, took her own life. I think about life and death all the time now."

He says he wishes now he had understood that kleptomania was an illness. "I figured if I stayed right away from her she might stop stealing, but I guess, in all honesty, it hurt her — did more harm than good."

Charlene was pregnant within three months of his mother's death, and Allen wishes it had happened before she died. "I could have told her, 'You're going to be a grandmother,' and she might have had a different outlook."

Allen says he wouldn't mind seeing a public inquiry "because I'd like to know what happened to my mother. I honestly believe that somebody was there with her. I don't know whether she pulled the trigger or they pulled the trigger."

◆ ◆ ◆

Jane's middle son, Jamie Whynot, also favours an inquiry into his mother's death because there are so many unanswered questions. "The police just tell you anything to keep you happy."

And he wants to know what happened to the expensive leather gloves he always kept in the Ford Tempo's console. "They were in the car and I asked the cops for them, but they said they never found them," says Jamie. "But I always left them there in case I had a problem with the car. If I had to scrape the window or anything, they would always be there. I kept them in the console because if I left them lying around, somebody would take them."

◆ ◆ ◆

Jane's sister Sandy Thomson, who lives with her family in Ottawa, says that after listening to the tape Jane made two days before she disappeared, "I honestly believe that Jane played a part in this.

"I listened to the tape a couple of times and I put it on pause and just really pondered some things. I'm convinced that Jane knew this was going to happen, that this was planned. There's a lot of things that don't make sense and I don't know if she pulled the trigger, but when I listen to that tape, I'm convinced."

Mona Donnelly says Sandy accepts that Jane wanted to die but believes others are involved. "Everything is assumption," says Mona. "There is no clear-cut proof."

Mona still wonders if Hell's Angels played any role in her sister's death. She recalls getting ready to go to the Halifax airport to return to Barrie after the funeral service and candlelight vigil for Jane. "Peter Astephen phoned and he wanted Joel to come and pick up the Ford Tempo," she says. "He and Jamie went down to get it." Joel approached her on his return.

"Did you know that territory where Jane was found is considered Hell's Angels' territory?" he asked.

"No, I didn't," said Mona.

"Well," said Joel, "I mentioned that to Peter Astephen and he said, 'You want to keep that under your hat — you don't want that kind of stuff getting out.'"

On a subsequent visit, Mona says she heard from two other sources that Hell's Angels know what happened to Jane. "So that's three references to Hell's Angels."

◆ ◆ ◆

On Saturday, December 5, 1992, the day before the third anniversary of what has become known as the Montreal Massacre, the Halifax *Chronicle-Herald* dedicated a full page to the commemoration, including a three-column photo and two lengthy articles reflecting on Jane's "troubled life" as Canadians "remember the 14 young women killed by a gunman in Montreal."

In one of the articles, Mona Donnelly repeated that she could not be convinced that her sister killed herself, and she said the police investigation was shoddy.

Mona insists that her reluctance to accept suicide as the cause of Jane's death is based purely and simply on the fact that many of her questions remain unanswered. "People might say, 'You just don't want to believe your sister committed suicide,' but if someone gave me the facts and said, 'Here, there's this, this, this and this,' I would accept it. I would like to know what really happened so that we can put an end to this.

"All I know for sure is that I don't think she pulled the trigger. To me, it's a very violent way to die, and violence is what Jane fought against. I think it would be a very difficult thing to do — to hold a gun to your chest and pull the trigger."

Mona is a religious person and, like Jane, a Seventh-Day Adventist. "The church doesn't have any stand on suicide," she says. "To me, only the Lord can judge something like that. Only He knows the motives behind your actions and only He knows what's in your heart at the time. We don't believe in hell.

"I feel that when I die, I'm going to meet my Maker and I look forward to the day that the Lord does come again and the righteous will be in heaven. And I'm looking forward to seeing Jane there."

◆ ◆ ◆

Five weeks short of a year after Jane disappeared, the RCMP announced they had no proof that the written and verbal threats against her were self-orchestrated. The results were released in January 1993, seven months after Halifax police had closed their files on the case. Tests had been conducted on two taped copies of telephone threats, and fingerprint and DNA tests on the stencilled threats and their envelopes. In all, four telephone threats and three written threats were reported against Jane between December and the time of her death. The police had only two telephone threats to work with because one wasn't recorded and one was erased.

"There is no firm evidence to prove where [the threats] came from," said RCMP Constable Dave Pike. He said whoever sent them obviously went to great lengths to remain anonymous.

The results were not what RCMP Sgt. Keith Crosland expected. He felt strongly that the DNA tests on the envelopes would match Jane's DNA.

The RCMP said the lack of DNA on the envelopes indicated a liquid dispenser was used to seal them. And no fingerprints were found on the stencilled threats or the envelopes they came in. Police had removed a stencil set from Jane's house, but it did not match the one used to write the threats.

Although RCMP lab technicians weren't able to prove the telephone threats were made by a man or a woman, Pike said they did determine that they were prerecorded and then played over the phone. Initially, police thought the voice had been mechanically distorted, but the lab analysis indicated no mechanical devices were used.

"It is possible the prerecorded message was made by a female," said Pike. "As the lab results have not offered us any new information, there is nothing further police can do at this time."

Despite doubts by the experts, Staff Sgt. Don Thomander says "it's definitely a female voice. These voice analysts are not going to come to any conclusion unless they're one hundred percent sure. I think the Mounties have definitely gone a couple of steps more than they had to, because of the public outcry."

Sgt. Keith Crosland, who also listened to the taped threats, admits he's not an expert "but my opinion is that it is a female disguising her voice as a male. That's just my opinion."

(Liz Forestell, Kathleen Jennex, and Margaret Rodger, who works with Jennex at Coverdale, are convinced the threats were made by a male.)

◆ ◆ ◆

Jane's friends and associates were as divided over the value of a public inquiry into her death as they were over how she died. Some felt an inquiry might somehow turn the police view of suicide into murder, or determine whether others assisted or encouraged Jane to take her own life. Others felt an inquiry would "drag her name through the mud," sully her reputation and image, and detract from her legacy.

Dr. Malcolm MacAulay says the possibility of an inquiry was raised with residents in his classes at Dalhousie University. "We discussed this with the residents as an example of the issues," he says, "and they uniformly concluded that certainly Jane's interests and the family's interests would not be served by having all this come up again. All the things she achieved would be undone."

MacAulay says the thrust should be for society to put an end to abuse in the home. "It's on account of the spousal abuse that she ended up in this situation."

XXII
• • •
WHISPERS

MUCH OF THE ABUSE and sexual degradation Jane Hurshman was subjected to, including bestiality, was related in *Life With Billy*, but she told me and others that there were incidents and practices she did not divulge and that she had suppressed other memories. After her death, it was whispered among some of Jane's friends that she may have been a victim of ritual abuse by others, in concert with Billy, and she may have been "triggered" to kill herself.

Liz Forestell considers that a possibility. "Laying out the whole scenario to someone [Donna Smith], leads me to believe she could have been triggered," she says. "Either she was triggered to do it herself or it was a set-up to look like suicide. We know that it happens. We know that people are programmed and that there are ways of triggering them.

"It's so difficult, because there is still so much unknown about the whole phenomenon, but there are a lot of common denominators with victims."

Like ritual assault victims, Jane had trouble sleeping at night because darkness was associated with the terror and abuse she went through.

Jane was sexually abused as a child by someone close to the family and she quit seeing John Curtis apparently because she did not want to learn the extent of that abuse, or because recalling it was so painful.

It seems unlikely that Jane was the victim of Satanic or ritual abuse as a child, but in her five years with Billy Stafford she went

227

through experiences similar to those of ritual abuse victims. In his own crude way, Billy Stafford was a one-man cult, and the abuse he inflicted on Jane was certainly as severe and structured as that reported by ritual abuse victims. He didn't wear black robes of a Satanist, but he wouldn't allow a Bible in the house, he banned church-going, and he often said he was sent by the devil or that he was the devil.

Wendy Annand says she has been studying ritual abuse survivors. "Boy, so many things just fall into place. Just the way Jane's eyes were sometimes, I would say she was dissociating. Although it could be caused by other kinds of trauma, it's so typical of ritual abuse survivors."

And Ann Keith says "there's always that little nagging thing about Satanic stuff, and if you're programmed, and scared, it's amazing how you can be triggered."

Kathleen Jennex, of Coverdale, says that people who experience the kind of severe abuse Jane did "have to compartmentalize to survive, and that's how split personalities develop. They're finding that multiple personality is related to sexual abuse, and it makes so much sense. If you're a little kid and someone's doing those things to your body, your mind can't handle it, so it goes someplace else."

Some of Jane's friends wondered if Jane was afflicted with a mild form of multiple personality disorder. All of them witnessed her eyes bulging abnormally when she was dissociating, and Carrie Rafuse and Donna Smith occasionally witnessed the rigid, near-robotic state, so noticeable to Alan Ferrier, Jane's former lawyer.

"There were definitely different Janes," says Carrie. "I'm not saying she had different personalities. We don't know that. But after Jane's death I talked to Donna Smith, and the person Donna told me about and the person I knew were different."

A week before her death Jane was quick to deny to Carrie that she had a split personality, saying John Curtis had diagnosed her as having a dissociative disorder. But multiple personality disorder is a dissociative disorder — the most extreme form.

Dr. Marlene Hunter, a Vancouver hypnotherapist, told *Maclean's* magazine, in November 1989, that developing multiple personality disorder is "a very creative, sophisticated way of coping with an intolerable situation."

The coping method may work for a time, but Dr. Colin Ross, director of the dissociative disorders clinic at Winnipeg's St. Boniface General Hospital, said, in the same article, that more than seventy percent of multiple personality disorder patients attempt suicide. According to Curtis, although multiple personality disorder appears to be the worst of the psychological conditions, "it's the one you seem to be able to do the most for." The drawback is, treatment can take up to six years.

Curtis said the personalities within a person with the disorder can have marked differences in the way they speak, dress, and act — and even in their handwriting.

When Carrie Rafuse and Ann Keith went through Jane's diary on the weekend Jane went missing, they noticed extreme changes in her handwriting.

"There were at least three different types of handwriting," says Keith. "It was almost like she was different people. I was wondering about dissociation and multiple personalities."

Jane's normal handwriting slants to the right and is free-flowing and open. But in late January and early February, before her death, her diary writing was often tight and straight up and down. Keith says, "It started to change around February and then became erratic."

Many victims of ritual assault are preoccupied with the phases of the moon, and ritual ceremonies often take place when the moon is full. Carrie and Keith noticed that Jane kept track of the phases of the moon in her diary. In its full stage she drew an open circle and wrote "Full Moon" beside it. She did this on January 19 and again on February 18, three days before she went missing. On January 4 she drew a circle, filled it in, and wrote "New Moon" beside it.

It's quite possible Jane was recording the moon phases out of habit, left over from her days with Billy Stafford, who had been obsessed with astrology, horoscopes, and the devil. Astrology played a large role in his life, and he kept up-to-date horoscope books in the house. Jane was required to read the daily predictions for his zodiac sign.

"Okay, old woman, let's see what today holds in store for me," he would say.

Jane would read his horoscope and Billy would sit back and think about it. If the reading was positive, he would smile smugly and say something like: "Well, the old devil is going to be with me today. I can do as I please and nothing will happen to me." He would scowl darkly if the reading was negative. "The old devil gave me his warning. I'll be good today." Being good usually meant staying around the house and getting drunk or high. Jane dreaded the negative readings because they meant she and Darren would be abused more than usual. "Being cruel to us gave him a sort of satisfaction or revenge for having to stay home," she said.

Jane was a very religious person and would never willingly be drawn into Satanism, or anything that smacked of evil or an affront to her belief in God or the Lord. Her fear of being involved in anything like that was demonstrated in the spring of 1990, when she was invited to speak at a seminar on women's issues in a town sixty miles from Halifax.

"Jane called me up and wanted me to go with her," recalls her sister Mona. "She told me it was supposed to be a real good seminar." Mona was unable to attend the seminar and Jane went on her own. "When I was down at Christmas, Jane told me she was very concerned because all of the women that were at the seminar were witches and they wanted her to be their leader.

"She said she had a very eerie feeling and some things were going on that she felt uncomfortable about."

Jane was so fearful that she slipped away to her room and stayed there for the evening. Mona related the incident to Liz Forestell, who had friends in the town check out the group.

"She told me these women call themselves white witches," says Mona, "but they're really quite harmless. They do things with their minds to relax. Elizabeth Forestell said it was no big deal."

It appeared to be an overreaction on Jane's part, but it's possible the very thought of a coven of witches conjured images, or memories, of evil — perhaps relating to Billy Stafford, or to an incident or incidents of ritual abuse in a group setting.

On January 19, 1992, one of the days on which Jane drew a circle and wrote "Full Moon," Darren found the stencilled threat on her windshield. Jane mentioned the threat in her diary and, on the same day, wrote the farewell note to her family.

Was it happenstance that there was a full moon on the same day the threat was received and the note was written? Did Jane choose a full moon to orchestrate the threat against herself? Or was the threat real and someone else used the full moon to magnify her fear?

At the time of the threats against Jane, Liz Forestell remembers her talking a lot about Billy "and how the police never seemed to be able to get a grip on him even though they know he was doing all this stuff."

"Do you have information that they would be frightened by?" she asked Jane.

"I was in places where strange things were going on, and there were people there who just weren't appropriate to be there," replied Jane.

"Do you know things that they're afraid you're going to start talking about now?"

"I don't know. There was a lot of stuff going on and I've pushed it all out of my mind and I don't even know what I remember anymore."

Forestell found the comments cryptic and curious, and Jane didn't expand on them. "That was all she told me. She was really uncomfortable talking about it. She was nervous about how much information to give because she didn't know who to trust."

XXIII
• • •
DISINTEGRATION

THOSE WHO BELIEVE THAT Jane Hurshman was murdered say she wouldn't have killed herself without leaving a note. The reality is, Jane left many messages, including a will, a tape, and letters. And, in her daily journal on January 19, she wrote the brief good-bye to her family, expanding on it in the audio tape recorded two days before she disappeared. She also left detailed instructions, allocating chores to be shared by Darren, Jamie, and Joel in the event of her death.

Jane believed her affairs were in perfect order and that upon her death all of the family bills would be paid, including the mortgage on the house; Darren would go to live with Mary and Paul Jacquart; the Arklow Drive house would be jointly owned by Joel, Jamie, and Darren; Joel and her three sons would each receive $25,000; and Joel's life insurance would list Jamie and Darren as beneficiaries.

Jane was confident that Joel would look after her sons as if she were still around, and she even suggested that he, Darren, and Jamie take a trip to Alaska, with Allen and Charlene perhaps joining them. "Take time to get to know each other and to love each other," she said in her audio message.

The live-happily-ever-after ending she envisioned for Joel and her sons proved to be an elusive fairy-tale.

The last will she drew up was ruled invalid; most of her insurance claims were rejected; her sons received virtually nothing; Joel and her family don't speak to each other; Darren is living with his grandparents; and Joel lives with another woman, who also has three sons, two of them at home.

Jane would be devastated if she knew that the dream of home and family that she worked so hard to nurture had disintegrated within weeks of her death.

The disintegration had its roots in simmering resentments between Joel and some members of her family. Jane was the dominant force in her family, and as long as she was alive the resentments were held in check.

Jane never said anything negative about Joel to her family or friends. In a letter to Jo Sheridan, written the day before she disappeared, Jane said, "I am really enjoying being married, and Joel is just a wonderful, fantastic partner and friend."

However, it's the consensus of Jane's family and many of her friends that although she was the dominant personality in the relationship, Joel could be a different person when she wasn't around.

Mary Jacquart says, "I don't think Jane realized or saw the other side of Joel."

Victoria Jones, who lived for a time with Jane and Joel, did see his other side, which included many angry outbursts. "But he didn't do it in front of Jane," she says. "He's a scary person when he gets going."

Joel says he occasionally loses his temper, "but that's normal — that's life. And I can't say I agreed one hundred percent with everything Jane wanted done."

Jones says Joel was "very boisterous, which was another thing I could never understand, because Jane was a very quiet person. Just before she died, neither one of them would be home on their days off. Either she'd send him down to her parents or she'd be gone."

Jones says Jane supervised and budgeted the family funds, deciding how hers and Joel's paycheques would be distributed among their accounts and which bills would be paid. "She even filled out Joel's bankruptcy papers and sent them in. She did everything for him."

Jane's sister Sandy says she has trouble understanding her sister's marriage to Joel. "There was absolutely no respect in that relationship. He jumped at every little thing she wanted. Jane was certainly the boss. I honestly don't believe she loved him."

When she listened to Jane's taped message to the family, Sandy thought, "Jane, how could you be so blind to think that he would follow any of your wishes?"

Carrie Rafuse says that Jane once told her not to worry about Joel. "He'll be okay," she said. "He'll find someone else. He's young and he will be all right. I know that. And he'll look after the kids, I know that."

◆   ◆   ◆

Jane's family was upset that although Joel knew Jane had a gun he didn't tell any of them about it.

"He didn't tell us abut it until almost two weeks later," says Gladys Hurshman.

Joel says he would not have told anyone about the gun if someone from the Bridgewater area hadn't told police that Joel had been looking for a gun. He says he wouldn't have told anyone about the gun because Jane, in strong terms, told him not to tell anyone and he remembered her anger when she learned he had shown the gun to Darren.

But Mona Donnelly feels strongly that when Jane went missing, Joel should have said something about the gun — if not to the police at least to the family.

Jane's son Jamie initially did his best to maintain a civil relationship with Joel, hoping Joel wold comply with the terms of Jane's will by setting up a joint bank account with him, transferring ownership of the house to the two of them and Darren, and transferring the Mustang over to him. He says Joel continually put him off, saying they had to wait for more information.

"Jamie wanted to keep on the good side of Joel because he was living at the house," says Allen. "So I was the one in conflict with him. He hated me because I was the one getting in his way. He was on a one-way road and I was the one with the stop sign. I would say, 'You can't do it this way. Mom wouldn't want this.'"

The dislike between Joel and Allen intensified when Jane's will was declared invalid and it became obvious that the bulk of her estate would go to Joel.

On November 2, 1991, Jane brought out two wills while Carrie was visiting her. Joel was there at the time.

"Now that Joel and I are married, I'd like you to witness our wills," said Jane.

"You keep them here in the house?" asked Carrie.

"Yes. I got them in a stationery store."

"But maybe they're not legal."

"No, no, they're fine."

"Jane, look," said Carrie, "I just had a will drawn up and all it cost was $100. Why don't you have yours done like that?"

"It's fine," insisted Jane.

"Well okay, I'll sign, but I don't know if I'd trust it."

Jane's will was invalid because she named Joel as executor and, as such, he shouldn't have signed it as witness.

"I didn't know I wasn't supposed to sign it, but I did," says Joel. "I didn't know any better."

Jane eventually scrapped it and drew up another will.

"I wasn't aware that she had redone the will," says Joel. "I vaguely remember her saying, 'Here, sign this,' so I signed, not reading it. I had no reason not to trust her."

The will he signed was the one Jane signed and took to Mary Jacquart, who also signed it and kept it. Joel didn't know about that will until he called Jacquart to tell her Jane was dead. Jacquart began to cry and told him about the will.

"Well, I'll get the will from you," said Joel.

"No, you won't," said Jacquart.

"Well, what are you going to do with it?"

"I'm going to make a couple of photocopies, and one will go to the police and one to the lawyer handling Darren's custody case, and I'll always have one."

"Well, I'm her husband," said Joel. "I should have that."

"Well, I'm her friend and she gave it to me for a reason," said Jacquart. "I'll do with it whatever I damn well please."

She says Joel then slammed the phone down.

Because Jacquart and Joel didn't sign the will in each other's presence, it was eventually ruled to be invalid.

◆ ◆ ◆

Debbie Sangster, who worked with Jane on the special committee on incarcerated women, had met Joel at Jane's funeral. "I told him how I felt about Jane, and who I was and who I worked for," she says. "I got the feeling that he felt very comfortable talking to me."

Sangster was living in Sackville, with two sons, aged seventeen and six, when she met Joel. A third son, age twenty-two, was away at university.

Joel says he called Sangster sometime in March and asked if he could visit her after he dropped Darren off at his tutor, Mary Jacquart, who lived nearby.

"We spent a lot of time talking and as far as I was concerned, I would just be there as a support person for him," says Sangster. "But then he got this funny idea in his head that he really, really cared about me and loved me."

Joel eventually moved in with her and her sons.

◆   ◆   ◆

Three weekends after Jane's death, Joel and Jamie drove down to Danesville to visit the Hurshmans and then to Bridgewater to see one of Joel's friends. Later, they ended up in a Bridgewater tavern where Jane's friend Jeff worked as a bartender.

"I was playing pool all night," says Jamie. "I'd come over and sit down and get a beer and go back and play pool. Joel was sitting talking to a couple of girls he knew."

Jamie says he and Joel spent the night with them. The next day, Joel told him not to say anything about being with the women. "He said he didn't know if anything was going to come of it — if they were going to get together again or not."

"I don't want to cause any pressure with other people finding out," Joel told him.

A week later, Joel began seeing Debbie Sangster, and the word was soon out among Jane's family and friends.

Debbie Sangster believes that Joel loved Jane very much and that "he had all this love tied up and nowhere to put it. He still has a very special place for Jane in his heart and will always love her. He speaks of Jane freely and I encourage this."

She says Joel saw a psychologist who told him he's able to go on with his life, and "it's not that he's replacing Jane, but he's able to meet somebody new. But the boys, they can't replace their mother."

"And so they're striking out at me," says Joel, "because I have to go on with my life. I can't just say, 'Okay, I've got to live with Jane.' Jane's dead, and I've got to live with her death."

Joel says others "can't put a time limit on any person's feelings on when it's time to move on." And Sangster believes that if she and Joel had waited until two years after Jane's death, "people would still say, 'It's only been two years.'"

Joel says, "I can't live in the past, because anyone who lives in the past is consumed by it."

◆ ◆ ◆

Allen Whynot says the "bad blood" between him and Joel Corkum intensified at his grandfather's house in Danesville shortly after Jane's death. "We were down at Nan and Gramps' for the weekend and Joel was there, and I told him maybe Charlene and I should have custody of Darren, and he blew up."

"No fucking way," said Joel. "You fight me on this and I'll see that this whole thing goes to probate court and nobody will get a thing."

Joel says Jane specifically said she wanted Darren to live with Mary and Paul Jacquart or to stay with him and Jamie.

The Jacquarts, meanwhile, were being frustrated in their attempts to gain custody of Darren as Jane had asked them to. Mary Jacquart says that after Joel hung up on her when she refused to give him Jane's will, her access to Darren was cut off.

She wrote Darren a letter telling him how much she and her family cared for him and that there was a place for him in their home. After the funeral service at the church in Mahone Bay, she went into the vestibule, where the family had gathered, and handed Darren the letter.

A couple of days later, Jacquart called the house and talked to Darren. "He was just as cold and distant as he could possibly be. It was not the Darren I knew."

The Jacquarts wanted him to become part of their family, but the boy's coolness toward them continued. Eventually, Mary Jacquart talked with Allen, and he and Jamie brought Darren over to the Jacquart house about two weeks after the funeral.

Darren cried and said he missed his mother. "He thought that she didn't love him," she says. "I said, 'No, Darren, you're wrong. Your mother loved you very much and she wanted to make sure you were cared for.'"

Jacquart says Darren agreed to move in, and she and her husband commenced family court proceedings to gain custody. Joel was also seeking custody, against the wishes of the family, and he was angry when he learned of the Jacquart's intentions.

Mary Jacquart said that after the third hearing of Darren's case, Joel "became real nice to me. He called and said he wasn't going to contest it. We could have Darren and he thought it was great, because he was starting a new life and Allen and Jamie were crazy and they thought that he had killed Jane and he had had enough of them."

"Joel," said Jacquart, "they're boys. You're supposed to be an adult. Let them go. They lost their mother. You lost your wife, but you've got another woman. They lost their mother — they don't have another mother."

Sangster says "it's really sad as far as Darren was concerned, because from what I observed, he and Joel got along very, very well. Joel wanted to adopt him."

But Allen, Jamie, and Jamie's girlfriend, Anita Bruce, tell a different story. They say Darren was often on his own running the streets and Joel tried, more than once, to have him charged by the police. And when Darren took the Mustang without permission and got into an accident, Joel was livid. "You touch another set of keys in this house and I'll blow your fucking head off."

"That's how he dealt with Darren," says Anita Bruce. "He had Darren really scared. Whenever he stepped out of line he threatened to beat him up. He was always wanting to charge him for stupid things."

Joel says he and Darren "got along most of the time — but hey, he's a kid. I could handle Darren. I could deal with Darren. But with Allen's constant meddling, I couldn't do nothing with him. Allen would fill his head full of shit. What he wanted Darren to do was not necessarily what Darren wanted."

While Joel continued to seek legal custody of Darren, Allen was making arrangements for him to go to his aunt Sandy's in Ottawa, in mid-April.

"I got pissed off at Allen when he decided to send him up there without telling me," says Joel.

Initially, it was planned that Darren would stay in Ottawa, but he returned after one week. The matter of his custody became academic when he decided to live with a friend, rather than with Joel or the Jacquarts. After four or five weeks at his friend's place, Darren moved down to his grandparents' in Danesville and has remained there ever since.

Both the Jacquarts and Joel ended their efforts to seek custody.

"When Allen shipped him down to his grandparents," says Joel, "I just called up my lawyer and told them to withdraw my application for custody, because no matter what I tried to do for Darren it was never good enough. I just wiped my hands of it."

◆　◆　◆

With the growing animosity between them and Joel, the family became increasingly concerned about what would happen to Jane's personal possessions, the house, insurance, and her car.

Whenever Jamie pressed Joel to establish a joint bank account or put the house in both their names, Joel would rebuff him. Meanwhile, in Barrie, Mona was becoming alarmed at the deteriorating relationship between Joel and Jane's sons. She was particularly upset by a telephone call from Joel.

"If Allen don't fuckin' leave me alone, I'm either going to kill him or kill myself," said Joel, "or I'm going to take the money and run."

The RCMP had returned the guns they took from the house after Jane's death, and Mona was worried. She immediately telephoned Allen, who got in touch with Jamie.

"Jamie took it upon himself to remove all the guns from the house, including mine," says Joel, "because he thought I was crazy. He refused to give it back to me. I reported it stolen to the RCMP and they didn't do anything about it."

Allen says the pump-action shotgun was in Joel's name but Jane had purchased it to eventually give to Darren.

The situation deteriorated to the point that Joel changed the locks and boarded the windows, forcing Jamie to spend one night sleeping in the woods.

"I went to the police the next day but they wouldn't do anything," says Jamie.

Joel says he took the action because items were being taken from the house without his permission. Jamie was eventually allowed back into the house, but the situation remained tense.

Eventually, Mona flew down to Halifax to see if she could calm the situation and to see if some of Jane's personal effects could be retrieved.

"I remember, probably the day after Jane's death, me, my mom, and Joel were sitting in the bedroom talking, and he said he was going to take all Jane's jewellery and divide it between the boys," she says. "But that didn't happen."

When Mona arrived, she spent the first night at the Arklow Drive house. "Joel came home around supper and we were talking and I asked him if the kids could have certain things."

"Well, there's things that I want," said Joel.

"Why don't you tell me what you want and then maybe we can have what's left," said Mona.

But the next day when she went to meet Joel at the house, the locks had been changed again. She said she waited and waited, but Joel didn't show up.

Joel says he decided to change the locks again after a conversation with Jamie. "It was Jamie's fault for that one," he says. "Every time I came home from work, something else was missing from the house — different ornaments and stuff like that. Jamie said he didn't know anything about it, and it finally got to the point where I said 'fuck it.'"

Mona said she finally got in touch with Joel at work the next day. "He said he wasn't going to put up with any more. He said an ankle bracelet and Darren's radio were missing. He gave me a very hard time over the phone. Finally he agreed he would bring some photo albums down to my parents'. I really had to beg the man for those things — to the point that I was crying. I was so upset that he would do this. He was blaming everything on the boys — doing this, and taking that."

She says he dropped off some boxes for her. "Some of it was just junk and some was family photographs. I wasn't at all satisfied, but I'm just glad we got some of the family photo albums. I was hoping he might have brought a few books."

◆ ◆ ◆

When Joel changed the locks to the house, Jamie was forced to stay with friends. He was unemployed and was having a difficult time financially. He also had clothes and other personal belongings that he wanted out of the house.

He contacted the RCMP at Cole Harbour and they recommended he arrange with Joel to get into the house and remove his things. He told Joel he was moving out and wanted to pick up his belongings. They agreed on a time and Jamie went to the house.

"He had packed four green garbage bags with my things," he says. "He had another guy with him. He was going through all the books on the shelves."

"I thought you weren't allowed to give any of this stuff away," said Jamie.

"I'm not giving nothing away," said Joel.

As Jamie looked around the house to see if there were other items that belonged to him, Joel followed wherever he went.

"I was mad, and I left a lot of things behind," Jamie said. "On the way out I saw a pile of books all stacked up. I know he was giving them away."

Jamie arranged one more visit to the house, to pick up an expensive leather jacket he had left behind. This time he saw two women going through his mother's things. Joel told him his jacket was out on the back patio.

Jamie and the rest of the family were incensed when they learned the women were Debbie Sangster and her mother. The family was furious at the thought of strangers going through Jane's things.

"Joel invited my mother over just to see the house one time," says Sangster. "And, in fact, I was helping Joel take an inventory after so many things went missing."

Joel says that if the boys had asked permission to take items from the house "most likely I would have said yes."

Jamie says he asked permission many times, but Joel always told him nothing could be removed from the house until all the legal and financial matters were settled.

Under increasing pressure from the family, Joel eventually rented a cube van and took "a bunch of stuff that was Jane's before I knew her" down to her parents' place.

Jamie says that through the years, his mother told him, Allen, and Darren that certain of her things would be theirs one day, but because nothing was written down, "Joel can say it's bullshit."

Joel says that most of Jane's jewellery was removed from the house by her sons. "They just up and removed it," he says. He singled out Darren and called the RCMP at Cole Harbour.

"I called the police and told them I wanted to charge him," says Joel. "But they said there was nothing they could do because it was a gift."

Joel says as far as he's concerned, the family would never be satisfied "unless I give them one hundred percent of everything."

◆   ◆   ◆

Increasingly, the RCMP detachment at Cole Harbour saw itself caught in the middle of a nasty family argument with Joel claiming to be under siege on all sides and Jane's family claiming he was greedy and didn't care about Jane or her wishes and that he was only after her possessions. The fact that he was already with another woman, the family said, proved that he didn't care about Jane.

The family found it particularly galling and insensitive that Jane's ashes continued to sit in an urn at the house. Jane had said she wanted her ashes to be spread at Rainbow Haven, a public beach at the entrance to Cole Harbour. She loved to go there to walk her dogs.

The family thought the ashes should be spread as soon as possible after the memorial service, but Joel gave no indication when he planned to do that. He says he and Jane agreed that if she died before him he would spread her ashes on the beach, but he would do it when he felt ready to do it.

But the family thought it was sacrilegious that her ashes weren't being immediately spread on the beach.

◆ ◆ ◆

On August 2, 1992, the Arklow Drive house was broken into and vandalized, and the urn with Jane's ashes was stolen.

An axe was used to cut up the hardwood floors in the living room and hall. And the walls, chesterfield, chairs, tables, and pictures were sprayed with black and gray paint. Sprayed on one of the walls was the message "J.C. - Murder" and on a counter, the numbers "666" — the sign of the devil.

"It was my initials and they called me a murderer," says Joel.

Jane's sons were questioned as part of the RCMP investigation of the break-in. The intruders were never found.

Joel had the house up for sale at the time and he says "you don't have to be smart to figure out who the hell did it. The axe that cut up the hardwood floor and Jane's ashes are all that's missing."

He says wallpaper had to be stripped, the walls painted, and the floors covered with carpeting. The repairs, covered by insurance, cost close to $10,000.

The house was sold in September 1992.

Since Jane's will was invalid, any estate assets not specifically signed over to Joel were subject to probate. Initially, Joel and Jamie were to be co-administrators of the estate but, after the break-in, Joel was angry and petitioned the court to name him as sole administrator.

Jamie and Allen were prepared to oppose his petition at a hearing in mid-September. The night before the hearing, Mona telephoned Joel and released some of the pent-up frustration she had been harbouring. She saw his move to be named sole adminstrator as yet another attempt to shut out the family. She hasn't spoken to Joel since.

Joel says the call from Mona left him with a migraine headache and he decided he didn't need any further stress. He had his lawyer agree to a proposal whereby both he and Jamie would step down as administrators and leave it in the hands of a public trustee. "I said fine, let the public trustee do it," says Joel. "They can take all the shit and nobody needs to call me for nothing — and that's it."

There is apparently little left in the estate. It includes a small piece of wilderness property, Jane's final paycheque, $1,400 from Canada Pension, two GST rebates, rebates of about $500 in insurance premiums, and, possibly, a rebate on Jane's 1991 taxes.

Joel says the property "is in the middle of nowhere" and "isn't worth much at all." He says the estate will have to pay legal fees and two small loans in Jane's name. "By the time the bills are paid, I'll probably end up owing them."

◆ ◆ ◆

Following Jane's instructions, Joel went to the bank on Monday morning, February 24, the day after her body was found. He closed their joint accounts and opened a chequeing account in his name. He says about $2,200 was transferred to him. Later that week, as Jane had instructed, he paid $1,620 to discharge his bankruptcy.

Joel also received $54,000 as beneficiary of Jane's insurance policy at the rehab centre and a monthly payment of $153 for life. And he was listed as the beneficiary on her RRSP. He says about $4,000 from her plan was rolled into his plan.

Because the insurance claims were rejected, the house was not paid off, and Joel says he was facing a monthly mortgage payment of $725, which he couldn't afford. After a pay-out penalty and legal and real estate fees, he says he netted about $1,700 on the sale of the house. "I got shafted real big time," he says.

In all, Joel received about $62,000 in cash and RRSPs, the lifetime monthly payment of $153, and Jane's 1987 Mustang.

The Ford Tempo, in which Jane died, was in Joel's name, although Jamie drove it most of the time. It was sold for $400, of which half went to Jamie.

◆ ◆ ◆

Because Joel was listed as Jane's beneficiary and most of the life insurance claims were rejected, he is legally entitled to the monies that he received. Moral entitlement is another matter. It's obvious from the audio tape Jane left that she wanted her estate divided fairly between Joel and her sons. That has not happened.

The family feels strongly that if Joel really cared about Jane he would have kept the house, paying the monthly mortgage from the $54,000 insurance monies from the rehab centre. Jamie, and eventually Darren, could have contributed once they completed school or found full-time employment.

They also believe that Joel should have sat down with the family while they went through her books, clothing, jewellery, photos, and so on and divided them up fairly.

The family finds it inexcusable and insensitive that he would allow others, but not them, to go through Jane's things.

Joel says he was the beneficiary of Jane's RRSPs and insurance policies, "just like she was beneficiary of my RRSPs and my life insurance. That's normal.

"I could have kept the house for a while, until the funding run out," he says. "It was like I was sliding. Jamie never contributed five cents. I bought the food. I put the roof over our heads. I paid the lights, the phone — everything. I changed the locks after everything got stolen. And I put the house up for sale, not to spite them — I couldn't afford it.

"I could see them being bitchy if Jane owned the house before I came along, but she didn't. We bought the house together."

The family scoffs at Joel's claims, pointing out that Jane paid the down payment for the house, that his bankruptcy had not been discharged, and the only reason his name was on the title was because she insisted on it.

Jamie says Joel seldom bought food, and when Mona was in the house, the day before the locks were changed, "there was no food in the house."

◆ ◆ ◆

The break between Jane's family and Joel is probably permanent.

"I haven't heard from any of them," says Joel. "If they could talk civil to me, I could talk civil to them. But all that comes out of Allen's mouth is verbal diarrhoea. He makes me so angry — I could probably get myself in a deep pile of shit . . ."

Maurice and Gladys Hurshman say they never want to see Joel

again, and Allen says he can never forgive him. "Even though Mom probably loved him, I'm not sure if she didn't figure she was involved in something she couldn't get out of, and she was so down and depressed, she got married right quick — just wham, bang.

"Joel could have at least given my two brothers a thousand dollars each out of all he got. I can't forgive him. There's a hate in me that will always be there."

XXIV
• • •
LEGACY

THERE ARE MANY NOVA SCOTIA WOMEN, some of whom knew Jane Hurshman better than others, who vow that the contribution she made to end violence against women will never for forgotten.

Mary Haylock, the counsellor and chaplain who works with Coverdale Court Work Services, says that working with Jane "was a blessing and a privilege — one I'll never forget. She has given women the courage to heal and has raised consciousness and awareness that not only does abuse happen but that it must be stopped. I believe her call went out to society because it is a societal issue."

Haylock has counselled so many battered women that she no longer accepts that term *domestic violence*. "It's not domestic violence," she says. "It's *criminal violence* that happens in intimate relationships. Until we name it that bluntly, it will go on. *Domestic* means it's protected by the sanctity of the home and all that jazz. I never call it that anymore — I call it criminal violence."

Jane's former parole officer, Wendy Annand, says Jane touched every woman in Nova Scotia. "I can say that without any hesitation at all. People came up to me for months, it took that long just to accept that she was dead. The way everything happened with the police and the media, it didn't help the healing process at all."

Annand says Jane worked tirelessly to help battered women. "She was remarkably helpful with the transition houses. I know she often dropped in down here at Bridgewater and she spoke in Yarmouth and Halifax. And she would often advertise her phone

247

number for women to call, whether they were kleptomaniacs or whether they were battered.

"Jane always wanted to learn more. Sometimes she would attend conferences just to meet people and listen and learn. She sometimes turned down requests to speak when she didn't feel up to it, but I don't know that she ever turned away an individual. She would either see the woman herself, or she would refer her to the crisis line she helped out with. She was always there for people."

Ann Keith says some "incredible goodness" has come out of the sadness over Jane's death. "And I think it has brought people closer together and has given us a real strength to carry on her mission. Jane's body is gone but not her spirit. She was such a wonderful woman — very gentle, soft-spoken. But behind that was a real strong lady, with a mission to help women who had been abused. It was a ferocious mission, and she devoted her whole life to it.

"Jane was a real good friend with wonderful sense of humour, and until after her death, I never realized how much she had done for other women and what she meant to them. She touched women who had never even met her — they had read her story, or they had met other women who had gathered strength from her. So many women called SSAV, it was just incredible."

Liz Forestell says Jane was a strong and positive influence. "I think she felt really hopeful about the work we were doing both on the committee and at Elizabeth Fry," she says. "One of the ways she really helped me a lot was that I could check with her about what was okay and what wasn't. There are many people in corrections who don't believe inmates who say they've been physically or sexually abused — that they just say it to get sympathy. To have Jane at the table to counter that was really important. Jane was a very valuable witness for women in that situation. She blossomed in that process.

"Jane's contribution was vitally important. She showed women that there was a way to survive and that they weren't to blame for the situations they found themselves in."

The committee on imprisoned women thought so much of Jane that its final report, released a few weeks after her death, was dedicated to her, stating that "she generously contributed her time and expertise to bring us to an understanding of the lives of incarcerated women. In many ways, she was our guide on the journey. She taught us that, while her strength and survival were remarkable, her story was not unique."

And the report of the Dartmouth task force on violence against women, released a week after Jane's death, said: "Whenever we struggled with a recommendation we simply remembered the voice and presence of Jane Hurshman as she spoke to our community in our final public meeting. Quietly and with great dignity she challenged us as a community to critically assess how we participate in the process of discrimination and abuse. For Jane Hurshman . . . and those women and families who suffer as a result of violence against women, we are called as a community — *first mourn, then work for change.*"

◆   ◆   ◆

Besides raising the public's consciousness about widespread violence against women, Jane, in a very real way, helped change the law as it applies to battered women who kill their spouses.

The Crown successfully appealed the jury's not-guilty verdict in Jane's 1982 murder trial. The appeal division of the Nova Scotia Supreme Court ruled that the evidence of Billy Stafford's brutality against Jane, her children, and others "served only to create sympathy for the Respondent [Jane], and for this reason should have been excluded." The appeal court also ruled that the defence of self-defence was improper in Jane's case because Billy was asleep in the truck at the time she shot him.

"In my opinion, no person has the right in anticipation of an assault that may or may not happen, to apply force to prevent the imaginary assault," said Mr. Justice J.A. Hart, who delivered the court's unanimous judgement in 1983. "The jury should not have been permitted to consider a possible assault as a justification of her deed, and Section 37 [self-defence] of the code should not have been left with them."

But in May 1990 the Supreme Court of Canada unanimously ruled that a battered woman should be allowed to use a plea of self-defence as a reason for killing her abuser, even if an attack against her was not in progress or imminent. It also ruled that evidence of the battered-wife syndrome and evidence of the deceased's character were admissible to support the self-defence plea.

The court made the ruling in the case of Angelique Lavallée, a Winnipeg woman who, in 1986, shot her common-law husband in the back of the head as he was walking away from her. Like Jane, she had been severely abused over many years and believed if she didn't kill her tormenter, he would kill her. On September 22, 1987, after deliberating for more than nine hours, a jury found her not guilty of second-degree murder.

Lavallée's defence was based on the battered-wife syndrome. At her trial, Dr. Peter Markesteyn, Manitoba's chief medical officer, testified that a woman trapped by the syndrome "finds herself in a situation of physical, emotional, sexual — or a combination of — abuse. This occurs in all levels of society. It does not only occur in lower socioeconomic classes. It can occur in the professional strata of society."

Markesteyn described it as a condition "characterized medically" by getting worse without intervention and "very seldom becomes better." He said women in this situation usually attempt to hide their bruises and injuries from their friends.

Lavallée's lawyer, G. Greg Brodsky, introduced evidence that proved the battered-wife syndrome is recognized as a psychiatric diagnosis.

The Supreme Court ruled that battered women themselves are in the best position to assess whether a lethal attack against them is likely to take place. It also rejected arguments that evidence from experts on battering is improper. And the Court said experts were necessary to explain the dynamics of the battered-wife syndrome so jurors would understand why abused women are unable to leave their situation.

"We would expect the woman to pack her bags and go," said the judges. "Where is her self-respect? Why does she not cut loose and make a new life for herself? Such is the reaction of the average person confronted with the so-called battered-wife syndrome. We need help to understand it, and help is available from professionals."

Brodsky wrote in *Crown Counsel's Review*, in 1987: "To understand Angelique Lyn Lavallée's response, it was of prime importance to explain the 'learned helplessness' of a battered spouse.

"Random and unpatterned assaultive behaviour . . . will produce a learned helplessness. This condition promotes coping responses rather than escape responses in order to survive the relationship."

Explaining all of this, says Brodsky, is necessary when "presenting the defence of self-defence. Firstly, so that the jury should not feel that the battered spouse should have retreated from the menacing situation. Secondly, to convince the jury that in her mind the battered spouse felt she had no other option but to respond in the aggressive fashion set out in the indictment.

"Thirdly, to show to the jury that the violence of the moment, even if it be minimal or non-existent, must be taken with the historical background that made up the relationship between the battering spouse and the battered spouse."

Jane Hurshman's lawyer Allan Ferrier said after her 1982 acquittal and before the Crown's appeal that he thought the verdict "shows that our system of punishments isn't flexible enough to take into consideration abuse like this. By finding her not guilty, I think the jury was maybe telling the world that they didn't want this woman to be incarcerated for twenty-five years and perhaps not at all.

"She was prepared to go to jail for a couple of years. But the attorney general's office evidently did not want to be seen engaging in plea bargaining on a murder trial, and they made the decision to go for first-degree murder and let the jury decide. Now they're not too pleased with what the jury decided."

At the appeal, Jane, with the Crown's consent, pleaded guilty to the lesser charge of manslaughter — the result Ferrier had sought all along.

Today, Ferrier says "we were essentially trying to argue the battered-wife syndrome, although we didn't know it and we didn't call it that. I guess the significance from a legal perspective was the law was out of sync with the feelings of the people. We all know what the jury felt and what the public felt. It took a lot of those types of cases, in which cumulative provocation couldn't be used, to force the Supreme Court to say, 'well, we've got to have an out here.'"

The Nova Scotia attorney general who ordered the appeal of

Jane's acquittal was Harry How, who went on to become chief provincial court judge. Before retiring in 1988, he told reporter Cathy Nicoll, of the Halifax *Chronicle-Herald*, that he "agonized" over Jane's case because the law at that time had not developed to the point of recognizing any defence "other than self-defence, which has a narrow definition."

"Self-defence only covers an immediate action or confrontation," he said in the September 1987 interview. "It doesn't take into account the accumulation of provocation. I searched in vain for any precedent in Canadian or British law. The law hadn't caught up with the growing phenomenon of wife abuse."

How said gross abuse, over a long period, eventually becomes intolerable and the victim becomes violent. "Society's attitude in Liverpool was that this lady [Jane] had suffered enough — beyond human endurance — but the law provided no defence."

Nicoll interviewed How a few days after the Winnipeg jury accepted the battered-wife syndrome as a defence and acquitted Lavallée.

"I'm now watching to see if the principle enunciated by that judge will be appealed and if it will survive the appeal," said How. "It's a reversal of law applied in the Stafford case."

He told Nicoll he had listened to the taped evidence from Jane's trial several times. "The provocation was absolutely inconceivable in its brutality and degradation."

How said he was advised that he had to go ahead with the appeal of the not-guilty verdict in Jane's case "because the courts were not prepared to accept any other provocation than instantaneous."

He met Jane after she was released from jail "and told her of my agonizing over whether the appeal should go ahead."

The meeting between Jane and How took place at a criminal justice workshop in March 1985. It was there that Jane, encouraged by Wendy Annand, made her first public speech. She wrote about that experience in a letter to Jo Sheridan on April 30, 1985.

"I was very, very nervous when I spoke to all those professionals. When I got done, I really felt I got my point across, because as I looked out at my audience, I knew I touched their hearts. I knew for a moment in time, that each and every one there felt a bit of my hurt. I knew it as I watched tears run down their faces — even the men. They gave me a standing ovation and later presented me with a pair of gold earrings.

"That evening the attorney general was the guest speaker at the dinner. He is the same guy who ordered my appeal. The dining room was full to capacity and I had no idea he was going to speak. When he stood up and introduced himself, I was not impressed. In fact, I got up from my table and walked out."

At about ten o'clock a woman from the provincial parole service telephoned Jane in her room and asked her if she could go to the inn's main entrance to meet Attorney General How, who wanted to talk to her before he left.

"I hesitated, but told her I would be down," wrote Jane. "Well Jo, what a surprise. He shook my hand and introduced himself and he gave me a formal apology — but stated he had to do what he did at the time."

She said they talked for a time, "and then, right out of the blue," How said, "now Jane — off the record — I want to say, that cock-sucker should have been shot a long time ago."

Jane wrote Sheridan that those were How's exact words and she was "shocked, amazed, and flattered."

"It gave me a new outlook on lot of things," said Jane.

◆ ◆ ◆

In the months before her death, Jane told friends that she thought the movie, *Life With Billy*, was important because battered women who didn't have access to the book might see the movie (scheduled to air on CBC in late 1993).

"If it helps even one battered woman get out of her situation, it's worthwhile," said Jane.

Shooting for the movie was supposed to begin in April 1992, but Jane's death left the project in doubt. The film's producer, Michael Donovan, of Salter Street Films in Halifax, attended the funeral service at Mahone Bay and it was there that he decided the project should go ahead. "I felt very badly and confused, but when I heard the eulogy by Reverend Margie Whynot, I felt much better. She pointed out the way in which Jane had touched various people's lives, including hers. Jane clearly wanted a sharp, bright light focused on this issue and I think she felt that a movie would help that even if it exposed, once again, her own story."

The role of Jane went to Nancy Beatty, a television and film actor from Toronto who built her reputation in the theatre. Nova Scotia-born, Stephen McHattie, a New York actor who recently moved to Los Angeles, was chosen to play the role of Billy Stafford.

"It had to be done right," says Beatty, "not only because it's an important story, but because Jane cared enough to tell it."

She says all of the elements of the battered-wife syndrome "were very clearly there in Jane's life, and the audience, hopefully, is going to be saying, 'I understand this feeling.' I hope that will be illuminated, instead of sensationalizing the story."

Jane too was wary about how her life would be portrayed, telling one interviewer, "I don't want it to be sensationalized just to get an audience."

But she also wanted the movie to be brutally honest, even more so than the much-acclaimed television movie, *The Burning Bed*. "There should be more movies like *The Burning Bed*," she said. "I read the book before I saw the movie. The movie was excellent, but it didn't show enough of what that woman went through."

Jane's friends, Carrie Rafuse and Ann Keith, who were invited to the set, said it was uncanny how similar Beatty's mannerisms were to Jane's.

"I felt close to Jane when I was around her," says Carrie. "But I didn't have good feelings on the set. It felt weird, like a real dark blanket went over me. They did a scene where she was going to tell Darren that Billy was dead. Well I couldn't handle that at all. I had to get out of there."

The half-ton Jeep truck used in the film was the same one in which Billy was shot by Jane. Jane's father, who is very good at repairing motors, had kept the truck, and the film company put in a new radiator and rented the truck from him for $250.

"People of the South Shore are ultimately very practical, and despite the tragedy of Billy, he [Hurshman] did have a good truck and found no reason to get rid of it," says Michael Donovan.

The second unit took the truck off to shoot on location in Bangs

Falls where Billy was killed. "The truck had been working perfectly well up to that point," says Donovan. "But when they went to leave the location, it refused to start and required a tow truck. When they checked it out later they could find nothing wrong with it. I'm a superstitious type, and when I heard that, I felt that getting the truck was a mistake."

Beatty says driving the truck, "felt right. I don't know why people found it so shocking that Jane or her father kept the truck. It was practical, so what's the point of making it spooky."

◆ ◆ ◆

In addition to all of the oral and written tributes that had poured in since Jane's death, a non-profit organization, called Jane's Fund* has been established in her memory. It was set up by Wendy Annand and three other friends and admirers of Jane, including Dianne Cromwell, an activist on women's issues and operator of a fish plant in Yarmouth County; Janus Naugler, a lawyer and former chair of Second Story Women's Centre in Bridgewater; and Deborah Herman-Spartanelli, a close friend of Jane's since her Bangs Falls days.

"We were the legal four founding co-chairs," says Annand. "We did it that way so we could get away from having a hierarchy and bureaucracy. Now there are about eight of us involved, including Ann Keith. The first year has been mostly hammering out the legalities and deciding where we think we'd like to go."

Annand says the group keeps in touch with Jane's sister Mona Donnelly through Deborah Herman-Spartanelli. "They call and write to each other."

Jane's Fund will have five general goals:

1. To assist in the healing of abused women and their children.

2. To raise public awareness of the effects of abuse, including sexual, physical, and emotional violence.

3. To educate women in need, as well as professionals and others

---

* See Appendix 3.

who work with survivors.

4. To work toward a society in which women have alternatives to remaining in abusive relationships and are supported in speaking out about their experiences.

5. To empower women by carrying out this work using a feminist process, based on co-equality among board, committees, staff, volunteers and women who use the services of Jane's Fund.

Annand says the fund's objectives are broad-based "to leave ourselves as flexible as possible. We might want to set up a retreat centre for abused women, or we might want to offer a scholarship fund for women who want to continue their education, or we might want to offer second-stage housing. Until we know which grants to apply for, or how much fund-raising we'll be able to do, we don't want to restrict ourselves."

Jane often said she one day wanted to build a rural retreat for battered women and their children.

Wendy Annand says that no matter how Jane died, "she's still a hero and we all need to remember that, because women have so few heroes of whom we can say, 'Look at what this woman did,' and it's not because she had money behind her, and it's not because she had powerful friends. It's because of what she lived through and her own grit and determination."

SOCIETY

Observe the child
Raised on hate and misunderstanding
Taught that rules are tools for fools
Nourished on pain, seeking escape
With society failing to provide the means

How can you, society, judge my crime
When you committed the greatest sin of all
Killing the innocent child
Disfiguring the beauty
Distorting the image of the emerging woman
The innocence is forever gone
But let her learn a sense of self
And taste the sweetness of a simple life
That you, society, dangled enticingly
But steadfastly kept from her through the years

Isn't it her birthright to be loved, not destroyed
I may sound bitter, society,
But I am that child, you see
Like ice cream made with society's sour milk
I tasted the pain that tears apart inside

I am now the mother, sensitive and giving
The plea I make today, society,
Is to give this child a chance
Is it too much to ask to let us live
Is it too much to ask

— Jane Hurshman

XXV
∙ ∙ ∙
PROBLEMS AND
SOLUTIONS

IN THE DECADE FOLLOWING Billy Stafford's death, Jane Hurshman dedicated herself to the struggle to end violence against women and children. Jane made a huge contribution, but the problem remains.

"While there's much publicity generated, we seem in Canada to lack the social consciousness and political will to put an end to it," says Bonnie Diamond, director of research for the Canadian Panel on Violence Against Women. "It often appears to many of us that the life of a woman is worth less than the valuables in your house. It appears that people who abuse the body of a woman are dealt with less harshly than people who rob.

"We owe an awful lot to the courage that Jane showed in exposing her life. As far as I'm concerned, the abuse of women is the top-priority issue in Canada. If you want to talk about women's health, it's the number-one health issue."

Diamond says what people "can't measure, and still don't understand, is the psychological abuse that goes with physical abuse — it's a concentration-camp syndrome.

"I can remember women who testified before us, who talked about really systematic torture — women who were required to come home at night, strip, and walk through dark apartments, not knowing when they'd be attacked or if they'd be attacked. They could not anticipate, it was just absolute uncertainty."

She says society cannot separate the way men generally treat women from the eventual abuse that women suffer. "It's an absolute

259

continuum. The individual who is harassing a woman in the office is setting that whole stage in which the terror is played out. It's all connected."

The Panel on Violence Against Women released its report in July 1993, and Diamond says it was cast "in terms of the fact that inequality is dangerous and there is no point in only trying to contain the hurt. Until we take equality in a very serious way, gender relationships aren't going to change.

"There must be equality in wages, power — business and corporate — and women's full political participation so there's a different focus in the political agenda. I really believe that that's absolutely the only way to reduce the violence. Until that time all we are doing is restraining."

Finally, says Diamond, there must be massive education and re-education until the dynamics of abuse are understood and recognized. "We must get through the wall of absolute denial in Canada because there are many men who would never batter but very much condone and reinforce the behaviour of men who do by not challenging it."

◆　◆　◆

Many feminists and others were furious when the federal government created the Panel on Violence at a cost of $10 million. They say the problems have been well defined for years and action to solve them is what is lacking. That $10 million could have helped the grossly underfunded transition houses.

The problems and solutions were clearly defined for the government in June of 1991, when the House of Commons Standing Committee on Health and Welfare, Social Affairs, Seniors and the Status of Women turned in its report, *The War Against Women*, which included twenty-five recommendations.

"The incidence of violence perpetrated against women in this country received a considerable amount of attention from many witnesses," stated the report's introduction. "They presented the committee with a shocking array of statistics derived from official data sources, victimization and public attitude surveys, and special studies of emergency service providers."

Some of the findings included in the committee's report:

- In 1989, 12,970 sexual assaults were reported to the police. Between 1983 and 1989, the number of complaints of sexual assault made to the police increased 93 percent.
- Every seventeen minutes there is a sexual assault committed in Canada. Ninety percent of the victims are female. One in four women will be sexually assaulted at some time in their lives, half before the age of seventeen. There are between 14,000 and 18,000 sexual assaults in the province of Quebec every year.
- Of aboriginal women surveyed in a study by the Ontario Native Women's Association, eighty percent had been assaulted or abused.
- At least fifty percent of women are afraid to walk unaccompanied on their own streets at night.
- At least one in ten women are physically and/or sexually assaulted each year by a husband, ex-husband, or live-in partner. A woman is assaulted by a husband or partner an average of thirty times before she even calls the police.
- In 1989 in Ontario, seventy-eight transition houses accommodated 9,838 women, accompanied by 11,000 children. Eighty-seven percent of the families were in an emergency shelter because of domestic violence.
- The husband is the victim of battering in no more than five percent of all spousal assaults. Of the adults and juveniles charged by the police for crimes of violence in 1989, eighty-nine percent were males.
- Of children who have lived in a shelter, twenty-five percent indicated, before counselling, that it was appropriate for a man to strike a woman if the house was messy.
- The rate of wife beating was a thousand times higher for men who had observed violence in childhood than for men who had not had similar experiences.
- In 1989, 119 women were murdered in Canada by current or former husbands or partners. Of all women murdered in Canada, sixty-two percent were killed by their partners.
- There has been a marked increase in the number of women killed after they have gone through counselling, the legal system, and custody battles for the children.

◆ ◆ ◆

The then minister responsible for the status of women, Mary Collins, informed the committee that male violence against women is a form of discrimination that exists on a continuum that includes sexist jokes, pornography, sexual harassment, prostitution, emotional, psychological, and physical wife assault, date violence, child abuse, incest, and individual, serial, and mass murders,

The committee was told that the violence against women was analogous to the aggression toward women that occurs during wars. Women in war locations are raped, threatened, harassed, beaten, and killed. Rape crisis centres and shelters were likened to war-time Red Cross shelters for women where the physical and psychological wounds of the survivors are treated.

Pat Freeman Marshall, who would later co-chair the Panel on Violence, reiterated the war analogy to the committee: "I said this was a war on women. There is a need for a war budget."

Instead of a war budget, the government decided on further study.

The problem is also being studied in the U.S., where the rate of injury to women from battering surpasses that of traffic accidents and muggings combined, and the surgeon general reports that battering is the largest single cause of injury and death to women. A report released by the Senate Judiciary Committee estimates that there were 1.13 million violent domestic crimes against women in 1991, with at least 3 million more going unreported. It identified violent crime as murder, rape, aggravated assault or simple assault.

The Canadian *War Against Women* report outlined the cost to society of the widespread violence against women:

- Taxpayers pay significant sums in medical costs to doctors, hospitals, and mental health clinics; in criminal justice costs for police, courts, and corrections; and in social service costs for welfare, housing, and daycare. There is also a cost to employers in high absenteeism and low productivity.
- Women who have been sexually assaulted are about five times more likely to have a nervous breakdown and eight times more likely to commit suicide or die prematurely.

- Ninety percent of women in psychiatric wards of Toronto general hospitals suffered from severe sexual and/or physical abuse in their childhood.
- More than eighty percent of federally sentenced women interviewed for a study submitted to the committee had been abused physically and/or sexually.

◆ ◆ ◆

Among the committee's recommendations to the government:
- Develop and promote strong and consistent violence-prevention education in schools across the country. Such education should expressly address sexual-equality issues and be a mandatory part of the school curriculum in all elementary, junior, and high schools.
- Require mandatory gender-sensitivity training and refresher courses for the federally appointed judges and the RCMP. The courses should be developed in consultation with front-line agencies that work with female victims of violence.
- Urge provinces and municipalities to require similar training for personnel in law enforcement, social, and health sectors. The provinces would also be urged to require their judges to take the same courses.
- Invite the Canadian Advisory Council on the Status of Women to conduct gender-sensitivity programs for members of Parliament.
- Require federal prosecutors to take courses on violence against women and be directed to recommend mandatory counselling and treatment for abusers, in addition to criminal penalties that apply. Provincial governments would be urged to do the same with their Crown prosecutors.
- Take a lead role to ensure stable, adequate funding for treatment programs for violent men.
- Develop a legal policy that would allow a judge, on a request from a Crown prosecutor, to issue an order removing a man charged with assaulting his wife or partner from the family home. This policy should ensure that the police and the courts provide adequate protection to the victim and enforce the court order.

- Coordinate the development of a housing policy and providing tangible support to resolve the crisis in affordable and accessible accommodation confronting low-income earners and the poor, particularly for women who are not safe in their homes.
- Stress the importance of the mandatory charging policy in cases of physical and sexual assault and abuse by directing the RCMP to assiduously follow the policy, and urge the provinces to do the same with their police forces.

◆ ◆ ◆

Ann Keith, of Services for Sexual Assault Victims, sees some progress in the past ten years, but, she says, the slow pace of reform is discouraging.

"When I look back from 1983 to now, the changes are quite incredible," she says. "The first year, we used to go around and talk to the police, doctors, the media, and others and say, 'Hey guys, we're here — sexual assault does happen.' And I remember a doctor saying, 'I can't believe you people, I thought you'd be coming in braless, with a peasant blouse on, eating green curd,' and I thought, *Oh boy, have we got our work cut out.* And it was the same with the police back then. Basically patronizing us, and saying sexual assault and abuse don't happen here. But I must say, we've come a long way."

Keith says that despite the awareness, the problem is still there. "We figure that eighty to ninety percent of sexual violence is not even reported or disclosed, so all we're seeing is the tip of the iceberg.

"It's getting worse because we don't have the extended family anymore. You don't have that built-in support. People are isolated and they don't have role models or values, so what the hell do you expect. It's very scary.

"Normally I'm an optimist, and I wouldn't be here this long if I wasn't. You can't keep dwelling on the rotten, but you have to be a realist too. Society has to change. We have to go to the government and say 'we're not going to put up with this anymore.' We really have to emphasize preventive education. It's the key. Otherwise we're just doing band-aid stuff. It has to start with little kids and primary socialization. Little boys have to learn that it's all right to feel and to cry."

Wendy Annand sees the justice system close up in her job as a parole officer and believes it is a major part of the problem because "it's run by old men whose attitudes are back there," she says. "All you have to do is compare drunk driving convictions and what they get compared to what a guy gets for beating up his wife. That's wrong."

Annand says that at current levels of spousal battering there aren't nearly enough transition houses in Nova Scotia. "There's the additional problem of transportation," she says. "For some women to get to a transition house is a major, major event."

She says there is more public awareness of domestic violence, and attitudes are slowly changing, particularly among professionals and the media. "The problem is really deep-rooted, but because of Jane and other women who've been through it and are willing to speak out, it's slowly filtering through all levels of society."

Annand favours removing an abuser, and not the victim, from the home. "There's no reason that women should be the ones constantly disrupted. It's outrageous."

That message was heard over and over again from women who appeared before the Panel on Violence Against Women. "We've heard that as a common recommendation across the country — that men should have to leave," said Pat Freeman Marshall, the panel's co-chair. "Having to leave home is an incredible cost to pay, having a lot of the basic comforts taken away. Why is she being made to bear the incredible cost of this violence? We're certainly going to have to look seriously at this."

The problem of women being forced to flee, and then look for alternative housing after her stay in a transition house, is compounded when children are involved. Counsellors report seeing seven- or eight-year-old children suffering from ulcers as a result of being uprooted from their schools and friends.

Many feminists believe where there is evidence of abuse, the man should be removed to a hotel or halfway house where he goes immediately into treatment. He would be allowed no contact with his spouse or any of her relatives, but would be permitted to continue working.

A batterer could be required to wear an electronic ankle bracelet, monitored by police, to ensure he does not attempt to return to the home. And a new silent "panic button" system, developed in the U.S., would permit women to alert police without the knowledge of their attackers if they attempted to return.

The battered woman and her children would also get immediate treatment so they could come to understand what has happened to them and that it is not their fault.

The male spouse would be required to continue support payments for the upkeep of the house. If he respected court-imposed restrictions and completed therapy, those factors would be taken into consideration when he went to court. If an abuser refused treatment — and the chance at mitigating his sentence — his case would be heard quickly.

There should be a new class of criminal offence making an assault more serious when it occurs in the home, because of the breach of trust involved. The courts must deal harshly with abusers. Treatment must be mandatory in prison and must be continued during probation.

If an abuser chooses instead to stay in a hostel or halfway house, he must wear the electronic ankle bracelet, and attempting contact with his spouse or her family constitutes a new offence with harsh, mandatory penalties.

When a batterer is jailed and is not supporting his family, the government should help with mortgage or rental payments to allow the family continuing stability until other suitable arrangement can be made.

When counsellors deem that a batterer understands and is able to control his impulses, it will be up to the victim to decide if she wants to attempt reconciliation or begin divorce proceedings.

Those men who are successfully treated need not spend time in jail, but they should be put on two or three years' probation, during which they would do community work — which, whenever possible, should entail working as a volunteer at the hostel or halfway house to counsel new offenders.

And for those men who default in their support payments when a relationship ends, there should be a Canada-wide uniform tracking and collection system to force them to pay up.

None of this will work without full integration of social services, police, and the courts.

Too often, a man who has abused his spouse for years hits or punches one time too many and a woman dies. Inevitably, the charge is manslaughter or second-degree murder. That practice must end.

Judges and prosecutors must understand that there is nearly always a long history of violence in households where a man kills his partner. It is a deliberate process that escalates step by step until the ultimate violence occurs.

Femicide should become a separate offence, with the same penalties as first-degree murder. Femicide would mean that whenever a woman is killed and there is a history of abuse, the charge must always be femicide — no more second-degree murder or manslaughter charges and the light sentences that often go with them.

Likewise, in the case of severe abuse or attempted femicide, the new law must have harsher penalties when there is a history of abuse.

◆ ◆ ◆

As Bonnie Diamond says, until there is true equality in employment, wages, and decision making, the root causes of abuse will remain.

Only 2.7 percent of the top jobs of Fortune 500 companies were held by women in 1990, according to a study that blamed sex discrimination and the old-boy network. The study, conducted by the Feminist Majority Foundation, a women's rights advocacy group, looked at the jobs at the level of vice-president and up. Only 175 of the 6,502 corporate officers employed at the five hundred largest U.S. companies were women; all but five chief executive officers were men; and only 4.7 percent — 254 out of 5,384 — of directorships were held by women.

Eleanor Smeal, head of the foundation, said that at the current rate of increase, it will take "more than four hundred and fifty years to reach equality with executive men."

A Canadian survey of 676 public and Crown corporations

showed that women accounted for less than 5 percent of the 7,076 company directors listed in 1990, up from 2.7 percent in 1985. Sixty-four percent of the companies had no female directors at all, and one in six had no female senior executives. In all, 6.7 percent of the 5,091 top executives were female in 1990.

And in Canada in 1990, women who worked full-time earned only 67.6 percent of what men did, according to a report from the National Action Committee (NAC) on the Status of Women. Women earned an average of $24,923 annually compared to $36,863 for men.

Former NAC president Judy Rebick said a small number of educated, mostly white, women, "are doing better . . . but the majority of women are getting poorer, and their lives are getting harder."

The seventeen-page NAC annual assessment said fifty-seven percent of single-parent families headed by women live below the poverty line — a figure that has not changed since 1974. In addition, about seventy-five percent of women lived out the last quarter of their lives in poverty. The report said the political playing field also remains far from level, with only thirty-nine women holding seats in the 295-seat House of Commons. That's 13.2 percent in a country in which more than half the population is female.

Despite the positive influence of the women's movement, men still consider women emotional and dependent and believe that their role in society should be centred in the house. This attitude persists, even though at least three of four women will be on their own financially at some point in their lives and most Canadian families require two incomes to live decently.

These built-in systemic inequalities mean that far too many Canadian women are socially and economically dependent on a male provider — a dependency perpetuated by a lack of economic choices and by the emphasis on marriage, family, and the home as a woman's "proper place."

In fact, though, the home is no sanctuary for a large number of Canadian women who, instead, find it a place of violence and a place where they are more likely to be killed than anywhere else. This violence is the most obvious and tragic symptom of women's dependency and subordination. Because of structured inequality, the options available to women in this situation are extremely limited. It is this lack of control over their lives that must be redressed by society.

◆ ◆ ◆

The right of the accused to a fair trial in our system takes precedence over all. The rights of women who have been subjected to physical and sexual violence in the home are considered secondary. This must be changed.

The legal system in practice makes exceptions — when the court thinks a suspect might flee or commit another crime — by refusing to grant bail or setting bail impossibly high.

Usually the battered woman is the only witness to the crime and it becomes her word over that of the accused. (Unless her injuries are so obvious there is no question that an assault took place.) In one study, ninety-two percent of respondents thought a woman who was sexually assaulted in a parking lot by a stranger was raped, but only 18.5 percent thought it was rape if the woman was assaulted after kissing a man she was dating.

The problem is not restricted to the attitude of judges, lawyers, and police officers. As former Supreme Court Justice Bertha Wilson said in 1990, the law itself, in some areas, is at fault. "A distinctly male perspective is clearly discernible and has resulted in legal principles that are not fundamentally sound . . . Sound aspects of the criminal law, in particular, cry out for change since they are based on presuppositions about the nature of women and women's sexuality that, in this day and age, are little short of ludicrous."

Speaking at Osgoode Hall Law School in February 1990, Wilson said men and women have a very different sense of ethics and morality. She said men see moral problems "as arising from competing rights — the adversarial process comes easily to them. Women see moral problems as arising from competing obligations . . . because the important thing is to preserve the relationship, to develop an ethic of caring.

"The goal . . . is not seen in terms of winning or losing but rather in terms of achieving an optimum outcome for all individuals involved in the moral dilemma."

At the time of Wilson's speech there were 849 federally appointed judges in Canada, but only 73 — nine percent — were women, among them two others on the Supreme Court.

"If women lawyers and women judges, through their differing perspectives on life, can bring a new humanity to bear on the decision-making process, perhaps they will make a difference," Wilson said. "Perhaps they will succeed in infusing the law with an understanding of what it means to be fully human."

And in April 1991, another female Supreme Court justice, Beverley McLachlin, criticized the law's gender bias, charging that male-dominated parliaments have passed discriminatory criminal laws that have the effect of denying women equality. She cited abortion and prostitution laws that ignore the social and economic reasons why women terminate their pregnancies or sell their bodies on the streets. "The history of the so-called feminine crimes suggest that they impact mainly against women, and often unfairly so," she said.

◆ ◆ ◆

Police attitudes toward violence against women are changing but there is still a long way to go. Kathleen Jennex, of Coverdale Court Work Services, cites the example of a woman who was before the court in Dartmouth. "The woman was a victim of abuse and it was one of those disputes where both of them were accused of assault and the Dartmouth police officer said right in front of my court worker, who was assisting the woman, 'Yeah, if she was my wife, I'd slap her around too.' So when you have attitudes like that on the police force, women don't stand much of a chance."

◆ ◆ ◆

A lot of men get upset and angry when they are told that the killing of fourteen women by Marc Lepine was more than just the action of a crazed individual. The best response to that anger was stated in a report on violence against women for *Ms.* magazine (September/October 1990) by Jane Caputi and Diana E.H. Russell:

Canadian novelist Margaret Atwood once asked a male

friend why men feel threatened by women. He replied: "They are afraid women will laugh at them." She then asked a group of women why they feel threatened by men. They answered: "We're afraid of being killed."

However disproportionate, these fears are profoundly linked, as was demonstrated on December 6, 1989, at the University of Montreal. That day, 25-year-old combat-video aficionado Marc Lepine suited up for war and rushed the school of engineering. In one classroom, he separated the women from the men, ordered the men out, and, shouting, 'You're all fucking feminists', opened fire on the women. During a half-hour rampage, he killed fourteen young women, wounded nine other women and four men, then turned the gun on himself. A three-page suicide note blamed all of his failures on women, whom he felt had scorned him. Also found was a hit list of fifteen prominent Canadian women.

Unable to complete an application to the school of engineering, Lepine felt humiliated by women he defined as feminists, because they had entered traditional male territory. His response to the erosion of white male exclusivity was a lethal one. It was also an eminently political one.

In the massacre's aftermath, media reports regularly denied the political nature of the crime . . . despite Lepine's clear explanation of his actions. Whether individual hate killers are demented is beside the point. In a racist and sexist society, psychotics as well as so-called normals frequently act out the ubiquitous racist and misogynist attitudes they repeatedly see legitimized.

Lepine's murders were hate crimes targeting victims by gender, not race, religion, ethnicity, or sexual orientation. When racist murders — lynchings and pogroms — occur, no one wonders whether individual perpetrators are crazy or have had bad personal experiences with African Americans or Jews. Most people understand that lynchings and pogroms are motivated by political objectives: preserving white and gentile supremacy. Similarly, the aim of violence against women — conscious or not — is to preserve male supremacy.

Caputi and Russell say that like rape, "the murders of women by husbands, lovers, fathers, acquaintances, and strangers are not the products of some inexplicable deviance. Murder is simply the most extreme form of sexist terrorism."

That terrorism includes rape, torture, mutilation, sexual slavery (prostitution), child sexual abuse, physical emotional battery, sexual harassment, and forced motherhood (criminalizing abortion). "Whenever these forms of terrorism result in death, they become femicides," said Caputi and Russell.

The extent of the violence against women becomes obvious when we realize there are about 340 transition houses and emergency shelters for women in this country and many of them are overcrowded.*

"Everybody I talk to says that they have a waiting list and that they turn people away," says Bonnie Diamond.

In 1992 alone, about 95,000 women and children sought refuge in transition homes and shelters in Canada. About a third stayed between eleven and twenty days; another third stayed for ten days or less.

Most of the homes and shelters offer crisis counselling, a crisis telephone line, and transportation services. Most residents are referred out for psychological treatment, addiction treatment, medical services, and legal advice and support.

In 1990, it was reported in Montreal that two of every three women going to a shelter were turned away for lack of space. Despite that, the province cut the budgets of one third of the shelters in the previous year.

And it wasn't as if Montreal didn't have a problem. In a single month that year eleven women and six children were killed. Former husbands and lovers did the killing. In almost every case, the woman who was slain had left her partner.

One clinical psychiatrist described the killings as desperate acts of control by fiercely jealous men, while the children were killed as acts of revenge to punish spouses for their new-found autonomy.

Claude Roy, director of Pro-Gam, a counselling group for violent men, said at the time: "There is an unprecedented concentration of domestic murder, a killing spree like we've never seen in this country before. I think that part of the blame for the high number is the publicity they are getting in the media. To a certain extent they

*See Appendix 2.

are copy-cat crimes."

After the killings, Anne McGrath, chair of the violence committee of the National Action Committee on the Status of Women, said the murders, coming so soon after the Montreal Massacre, "has caused a real sense of dread in the women's movement. We are being asked to live with the knowledge that most women victims of violence are turned away from shelters, and that's creating a real hysteria.

"The public has to realize that the system is not working — the safety of women is not being guaranteed."

And the light sentences handed out to many spouse killers are certainly no deterrent. A study of the judicial treatment of forty-four Montreal men charged with killing their spouses between 1982 and 1986 revealed that not one was convicted of first-degree murder. The exhaustive study by former Montreal law professor, Andrée Côté, found that seventy per cent of them pleaded guilty to lesser charges and did not even go to trial. Eight were convicted of second-degree murder, twenty-nine of manslaughter, and two of lesser offences. Five were acquitted.

Almost half of those found guilty were sentenced to less than five years in prison, 18.5 per cent received suspended sentences, a fine, or less than two years in jail. The eight convicted of second-degree murder could be parolled after serving ten years.

"These were intentional homicides," Côté told a 1992 symposium on equality. "I'm talking about stabbing someone twenty-five times...fifty times, sexually mutilating her, strangling her."

By agreeing to withdraw charges in exchange for a guilty plea on a lesser offence, some Crown attorneys are helping spouse killers get away with murder, Côté contends. "The excuse most frequently stated is that the victim provoked her aggressor."

Côté said Crown attorneys often ignore months or years of abuse that usually precedes a woman's death. Many of them were killed after they left their spouses or had threatened to leave. "The Crown is substituting itself for the jury. These cases should go to trial. We should put it to a jury."

On the first anniversary of the Montreal Massacre, a judge in Quebec City gave a suspended sentence to a man who strangled his wife because she made him mad.

Helter-skelter decisions and sentencing, and outrageous utterings from judges, are not restricted to Quebec:

- A jury acquitted an Ontario man on murder charges after he stabbed his estranged wife twenty-one times.

- In Alberta a man was fined $500 for punching, kicking and choking his common-law wife to near unconsciousness.

- In Prince Edward Island a prominent lawyer was given an absolute discharge after being convicted of assaulting his wife and, in another case, a judge said the death of a woman by her estranged husband, at close range with a rifle, was "at the lower end of the spectrum" of brutal crimes because she was killed instantly. The killer was given the minimum sentence for second-degree murder and can be freed after ten years.

- A B.C. Judge characterized a three-year-old girl as "sexually aggressive" in a 1988 sexual assault case and a Manitoba judge said sometimes all a wife really needs is a good slap.

- In Nova Scotia, a drunken man who butted out a cigarette on his wife's hand, picked her up crudely, and pushed her against a wall, claimed he thought she was a sack of potatoes. He was acquitted of assault, but a higher court overturned the decision.

- A man who axed and stabbed his estranged wife to death — inflicting thirty-four wounds — was sentenced in Ontario to ten years in prison. He will be eligible for parole after serving less than three and a half years.

- Also in Ontario, a forty-year-old man who kicked his wife to death was sentenced to six years (eligible for parole in two), and a man who caved in his wife's skull with a baseball bat during an argument was sentenced to ninety days, to be served on weekends.

- A former Bay Street broker who killed his wife with a butcher knife was released after serving only three and a half years in prison. After stabbing her, he left her body to freeze in a car in a hotel parking lot, and returned later to scrape her fingernails with his car keys to remove any flesh she had scratched from his face trying to defend herself.

The list of similar cases could fill volumes. A December 1989 seminar for Ontario police officers and social workers was told that many judges are insensitive and poorly educated on the devastating impact of physical and sexual assaults against women.

Dr. Peter Collins, a forensic psychiatrist at the Clarke Institute, suggested judges and others in the justice system take sensitivity courses to better understand the trauma victims go through.

Insomnia, nightmares, and feelings of anger and disgust are some of the symptoms that linger long after an attack, he told the seminar.

Although 7,722 cases of sexual assault were reported in Ontario in 1988 alone, many thousands more went unreported because women are afraid others will think the crime was their fault. And for many, repeated court appearances can be as traumatic as the actual assault they experienced.

◆ ◆ ◆

Bonnie Diamond says we have to change the way men and women relate to each other in society. "It has to start at a very early age. From the time that boys decide that acting out is an appropriate way to behave and little girls are socialized into sitting on the sidelines and watching, it's reinforced in all of our social institutions and structures.

There's no doubt in my mind that abuse of women is socially constructed, even though it's always individually willed by the person who does it. It is cyclical, although we can't broad-brush it, because there are many people who have been abused who have chosen to live peaceful lives.

"And the proof of that is, with the very widespread abuse of women, women lash back very, very seldomly, and when they do the full force of the law seems to fold in on them. Jane was a perfect example of that. When a woman has been abused and there is no way out — except to lash back — there should be full protection in the Criminal Code that recognizes that abuse and the behaviours that flow from desperation."

◆ ◆ ◆

Jane Hurshman often spoke about some of the myths surrounding spouse abuse: "That wife abuse is always the result of an argument that got out of hand. That women provoke the attack. That women enjoy being abused. That alcohol is always involved. None of this is true."

Another immediate concern of Jane's was that "there needs to be much more readily available information for battered women. Society needs to be educated and made more aware that domestic violence is an unacceptable criminal behaviour, punishable by law.

"My purpose in speaking out is to tell other battered women not to be silent screamers. Do not keep it behind closed doors. Come out and be heard. The more that come forward and speak out the sooner society's attitudes will change and there will be an end to this cycle of violence.

"Since the beginning of time, women have belonged to their men, to be used and abused. I say it's time they stopped treating us as their property. Publicly tell your story no matter how shocking or unbelievable it may sound. Be honest and sincere and help and support will be there for you.

"I want to stress that there are other means available for women in violent situations, without having to reach the point of desperation that I did and acting upon that by taking the law into their own hands. Every victim needs to know that they have a real choice — the choice of being able to live without violence."

EPILOGUE
◆ ◆ ◆

THE PREPONDERANCE OF EVIDENCE indicates that Jane Hurshman fired the bullet that killed her, but there can be no doubt that society loaded the gun and helped squeeze the trigger.

Jane was a fighter, and her instinct to survive brought her through a loveless childhood, a depressing, numbing marriage to an alcoholic, and five years of severe physical, emotional, and sexual abuse with Billy Stafford.

Describing what can happen to severely battered women like Jane, Winnipeg psychiatrist Dr. Fred Shane says there comes a point "that an act or a series of acts crosses that line of total unacceptability. It may be precipitated by a violent act of a sexual nature, or of an aggressive nature . . . or some behaviour toward their children which becomes totally revolting.

"Once they felt that this line has been crossed, and also that their sense of hope has been obliterated, the need to do something to escape and to mitigate the threats becomes overwhelming. Suddenly, there is energy that was not available before and the primal need to survive asserts itself."

It was that energy and need that led Jane to kill Billy Stafford.

"Paradoxically," says Shane, "after the death of the spouses of those women involved in homicide, is often a deep, profound remorse, a difficulty in accepting that they have been part of this act."

There can be no argument that Jane was a tireless fighter against criminal violence in the home and that she touched the lives of hundreds, perhaps thousands, of women across Canada. She had the toughness to survive and eventually work out her inner turmoil. What she couldn't survive was the kleptomania. She couldn't understand it and she couldn't control it. It was like a train bearing down on her. There was no escape and now she is dead.

Jane was convinced that if her body was found with a bullet wound and no gun present, the case would unquestionably be treated as murder. But as often happened in her life, someone let her down.

Regardless of how Jane died, the reality is that if she had not been a battered spouse raised in a society that has always accepted abuse and treated women as inferior, she would not have died as she did.

◆ ◆ ◆

There is an image of Jane, in 1963, when she was fourteen, a strong and determined cross-country runner, facing a hundred competitors from three Canadian military bases in a seven-mile race through the German countryside. She came second and won a medal. At the same meet her basketball team won a first-place ribbon and her volleyball team a second-place ribbon.

Jane won other athletic awards. At the same time, she was excelling at school as she always did. It was this grit and intelligence that helped her survive the emotional and physical brutalities for as long as she did.

Considering the cards she was dealt in her abbreviated life, Jane's accomplishments are remarkable. The tragedy of her death is the unfulfilled promise of this spirited, intelligent, and brave woman.

Imagine the possibilities if she had grown up loved and self-assured in a society where women and men were equal, where women and children were not forced to live in fear.

APPENDIX I
FEMICIDE IN NOVA SCOTIA, 1989-1992
◆ ◆ ◆

VICTIM	DATE/LOCATION	PERPETRATOR(S)	RELATIONSHIP
Suzanne Dube, 22, 2 children	Disappeared November 17, 1988; body found March 25, 1989 Halifax	Unknown	
Janice Faye Johnson, 2 children	February 20, 1989 Shelburne County	Clayton Norman Johnson, 46, school teacher	Husband
Catherine Lee Doyle, 34, 2 children	August 6, 1989 Eastern Passage	Donald Michael Doyle, 35	Husband of 15 years
Gale Laura Naugler 34, 3 children, school bus driver	September 18, 1989 Bridgewater	Darrell Wayne Lowe, 23	Ex-boyfriend, separated one month earlier
Jean Hilda Myra, 31, 3 children	April 5, 1990 Halifax	Unknown	
Deborah Ann Neary, 32	August 13, 1990 Glace Bay	Gregory William Pittman, 36	Tenants in same apartment building; Pittman's wife suspected him of having affair with victim
Barbara Baillie, 42, 5 children	October 19, 1990 Spryfield	Dennis Ira Baillie, 43	Husband of 24 years

METHOD/CHARGE/SENTENCE	NOTES
Unknown	Victim's body found in Bedford Basin; exhumed April 24, 1991, for forensic testing.
Husband charged with first degree murder on April 2, 1992, following a lengthy RCMP investigation.	
Victim shot 3 times in the chest with a 30-30 rifle while sleeping. Originally charged with 1st degree murder, reduced to 2nd degree murder at preliminary inquiry, pleaded guilty. Sentenced to life with no parole for 10 years; increased on appeal to no parole for 17 years (Justice David Chapman). Leave for appeal to Supreme Court of Canada denied.	Perpetrator believed his wife was being unfaithful. A long history of physical and emotional abuse.
Shot with .22 calibre rifle; perpetrator then shot himself in the head, died at Victoria General Hospital.	Perpetrator granted a conditional release the previous week on charges of threatening to shoot victim and her children. Also had prior conviction for indecent exposure.
Strangled	Victim last seen leaving a tavern at 11:30 p.m. on April 4; found dead near grain terminals in early morning of April 5 naked from the waist down.
Stabbed several times and throat cut; charged with second degree murder; sentenced to life without parole for 15 years (Chief Justice Constance Glube). Accused has appealed sentence and parole eligibility (to be heard January 16, 1992)	Couple had been drinking heavily. Victim told perpetrator she had given statement to police regarding her involvement in a break and enter. Perpetrator was on probation for break and enter.
Strangled with shoelace. Charged with 2nd degree murder; sentenced to life with no parole for 13 years (Justice David Gruchy)	History of abuse. Perpetrator had prepared death note prior to murder explaining his actions; attempted suicide prior to arraignment

VICTIM	DATE/LOCATION	PERPETRATOR(S)	RELATIONSHIP
Yvonne Margaret Donovan, 28, 2 children	October 24, 1990 Sydney Mines	Lawrence Alexander Young, 32, fish plant worker	Had dated on and off for 5 years; victim had tried to end the relationship the day of the murder
Barbara Anne Parrish, 34, clerk at Cobi Foods	January 4, 1991 Kentville	Donald Roy Neaves, 57, sanitation worker at Cobi Foods	Common-law husband
Theresa Maureen Carrick, 21, receptionist at Jani-King Canada	February 12, 1991 Dartmouth	Derrick John Holmes 18, Dartmouth High School senior	Boyfriend's best friend
Kelly Whynot, 17, prostitute	February 27, 1991 Dartmouth	Stephen Dale McMaster, 24 or 25; Nina Marie McMaster, 37, mildly mentally disabled	No prior relationship
Bernice Bridget Whiffen, 17, 1 child	March 6, 1991 Sydney	Kevin George Wainwright, 20	Dated for several months; separated for one year during which time Whiffen received hate mail and threats from Wainwright
Carla Gail Strickland, 20, university student	Disappeared June 3, 1991; body found June 5, 1992 Dartmouth	Unknown	
Emma Anne Paul, 25, 3 children	September 26, 1991 Sydney	Norman Woodrow Francis, 45	Boyfriend
Marilyn Rose Sabean, 44 2 children, personal care worker	January 7, 1992 Halifax	Carl Franklin Sabean, 55	Husband

METHOD/CHARGE/SENTENCE	NOTES
Stabbed 27 times with kitchen knife. Charged with second degree murder; sentenced to life with no parole for 14 years (Justice Robert MacDonald)	Victim had announced she was moving back in with husband. Perpetrator had history of alcohol abuse; has consumed eight tranquilizers a few hours prior to murder.
Shot in the nech with .35-calibre rifle. Charged with second degree murder; sentenced to life with no parole for 10 years; appeal rejected.	Perpetrator had history of alcohol abuse. Released on $5,000 bail until he violated bail conditions (drinking).
Shot with .270 bolt-action hunting rifle. Perpetrator committed suicide.	Victim had an affair with suspect which ended in November 1990. Perpetrator also wounded two male employees of Jani King.
Manually strangled by Stephen McMaster during intercourse, struck on the head eight times with metal pipe by Nina McMaster, then strangled with pantyhose by Stephen.	Perpetrators had been drinking and watching X-rated videos prior to hiring Whynot. Her body was left in a garbage can outside McMasters' apartment.
Stabbed approximately 43 times. Charged with second degree murder; found not guilty by reason of insanity (Justice William Kennedy); remanded indefinitely to Nova Scotia Hospital under Lieutentant Governor's Warrant.	Satanic bible and other materials found on the accused and in his rooms.
Not released, believed to have been strangled.	Victim last seen leaving Halifax nightclub at 3 A.M. Partially clothed body found in a wooded area near Dartmouth.
Strangled in bathtub.	Francis arrested in Los Angeles in December 1991 on provisional warrant; extradition pending.
Rifle; perpetrator committed suicide at scene.	Perpetrator had prior conviction for two counts of pointing a gun at victim; served two-month sentence; prohibited from owning weapons for three years; placed on two years' probation. According to family, perpetrator was depressed because he was no longer the breadwinner.

VICTIM	DATE/LOCATION	PERPETRATOR(S)	RELATIONSHIP
Mary Anne Lamrock, 26 (in 1990)	Disappeared April 6, 1990; body found January 29, 1992 East Pubnico	Unknown	
Marie Lorraine Dupe, 47, store clerk	March 22, 1992 Sydney	"White man, late 20s...seen in the area at the time."	"Victim apparently did not know her attacker."
Margaret Lorraine (Mills) Halnuck, 24, 2 children	April 30, 1992 Sydney	Paul Joseph Halnuck, 29	Separated since fall 1991
Deborah June Harvey, 38, 2 children	May 17, 1992 Windsor	Dane Robert Harvey, 41	Estranged husband; separated for two months
Unnamed woman, 39	June 2 or 3, 1992 Belle Cote, Inverness County	Male, 17 (identity protected under Young Offenders Act)	Unknown
Daisy Jean Jefferson, 50	August 30, 1992 Digby	Albert Frank Jefferson, 53	Estranged husband

METHOD/CHARGE/SENTENCE	NOTES
Stabbed at least twelve times	Victim last seen walking along highway; body found in woods by hunters. Formerly of Shelburne, she often hitchhiked back and forth from Pubnico.
Stabbed	Victim working her first night shift at a convenience store murdered in robbery attempt.
Stabbed	The day before victim had made court application for a peace bond against Halnick who she said had threatened to kill her on April 21. Victim had previously been a resident at local transition house.
Murder-suicide with gun	
Gunshot. Charged with second degree murder; remanded to N.S. Hospital for psychiatric assessment	Body found in woods near the family farm.
Head injuries. Perpetrator killed in gas explosion which destroyed house.	Victim had obtained a peace bond against her husband in February 1992. Police were called four times subsequently, once when victim complained Jefferson was damaging her house.

Prepared by the Nova Scotia Advisory Council on the Status of Women, September 1992

APPENDIX 2
CANADIAN WOMEN'S SHELTERS
◆ ◆ ◆

This list was provided by the National Clearinghouse on Family Violence (Ottawa). For security reasons no addresses are included. Call the shelter or transition house nearest you for emergency accomodation. For immediate protection call the police.

ALBERTA

Calgary Women's
Emergency Shelter
Calgary
(403) 232-8724

Discovery House
Calgary
(403) 277-0718

Sheriff King Home For
Battered Women
Calgary
(403) 266-0707

Camrose Women's Shelter
Camrose
(403) 672-1035

Lurana Family Centre
Edmonton
(403) 424-6872

W.I.N. Houses I And II
Edmonton
(403) 471-6709

W.I.N.G.S. of Providence
Edmonton
(403) 426-4985

Sucker Creek Women's
Emergency Shelter
Enilda
(403) 523-4357

Crossroads
Fairview
(403) 835-2120

Unity House
Fort McMurray
(403) 743-4691

Grande Cache
Transition House Society
Grande Cache
(403) 827-5055

Dr. Margaret Savage
Women's Crisis Centre
Grande Centre
(403) 594-5095

Odyssey House
Grande Prairie
(403) 532-2672

Safe Home Network
High Level
(403) 926-3899

Yellowhead Emergency Shelter
Hinton
(403) 865-4399

Hope Haven Society
Lac Labiche
(403) 623-3100

Harbour House
Lethbridge
(403) 329-0088

Lloydminster Interval Home
Lloydminster
(403) 875-0966

Medicine Hat Women's Shelter
Society
Medicine Hat
(402) 529-1091

Stoney Women's Shelter
Morley
(403) 881-3871

Peace River Regional
Women's Centre
Peace River
(403) 624-3466

Central Alberta Women's
Emergency Shelter
Red Deer
(403) 346-5643

A Safe Place
Sherwood Park
(403) 464-7232

St. Paul and District Crisis Assoc.
St. Paul
(403) 645-5132

Wellspring Women's Crisis Centre
Whitecourt
(403) 778-6209

BRITISH COLUMBIA

Marguerite Dixon House
Burnaby
(604) 298-3454

Annelmore House
Campbell River
(604) 286-3666

Ann Davis Transition House
Chilliwack
(604) 792-3116

Act 2 Society — Safe Choice
Program
Coquitlum
(604) 254-3479

Comox Valley
Transition House Society
Courtney
(604) 338-1227

Kootenay Haven
Cranbrook
(604) 426-5222

Mizpah House
Dawson Creek
(604) 782-9176

Somenos House
Duncan
(604) 748-7273

Meope Transition House
Fort St. John
(604) 785-5208

Golden Safe Homes
Golden
(604) 344-5317

Kamloops Emergency Shelter
Kamloops
(604) 374-6162

Kaslo Home Support Services
Kaslo
(604) 353-2518

Central Okanagan Emergency
Shelter Society
Kelowna
(604) 763-1040

Ishtar Transition Housing Society
Langley
(604) 530-9442

Han Kna Kst Transition House
Lytton
(604) 455-2284

Cythera Transition House
Maple Ridge
(604) 467-9966

S-yem/yi. 'm House
Merritt
(604) 378-0881

Mission Transition House
Mission
(604) 826-7800

Nakusp and District Family Services
Nakusp
(604) 265-3674

Haven House
Nanaimo
(604) 754-2452

Nelson Safe Homes
Nelson
(604) 352-3504

Haven Safe Homes
Parksville
(604) 248-2093

South Okanagan
Women in Need Society
Penticton
(604) 493-7233

Port Alberni Transition House
Port Alberni
(604) 724-2223

Coquitlam Transition House
Port Coquitlam
(604) 464-2020

North Island Crisis Centre Society
Port Hardy
(604) 949-8333

Powell River Safe House
Powell River
(604) 483-3200

Phoenix Transition House
Prince George
(604) 563-7305

Prince Rupert Transition House
Prince Rupert
(604) 627-8588

Amata Transition House
Quesnel
(604) 992-7321

Revelstoke Women's Shelter Society
Revelstoke
(604) 837-4362

Nova House
Richmond
(604) 270-4911

Shuswap Area Family
Emergency Society
Salmon Arm
(604) 832-9616

Xolhemet House
Sardis
(604) 858-0468

Sunshine Coast Transition House
Sechelt
(604) 885-2944

Evergreen Transition House
Surrey
(604) 584-3301

Three Sisters Haven Society
Telegraph Creek
(604) 235-3120

K'san House
Terrace
(604) 635-6447

W.I.N.S. Transition House
Trail
(604) 364-1543

Emily Murphy House
Vancouver
(604) 987-1773

Kate Booth House
Vancouver
(604) 872-7775

Munroe House
Vancouver
(604) 734-5722

Powell Place Shelter
Vancouver
(604) 683-4933

Vancouver Rape Relief and
Women's Shelter
Vancouver
(604) 872-8212

Vernon Women's
Transition House
Vernon
(604) 542-1122

Victoria Women's
Transition House
Victoria
(604) 380-7527

Atira Transition House
White Rock
(604) 531-9151

Women's Shelter
Williams Lake
(604) 398-5658

MANITOBA

L.E.A. Wife Abuse Committee
Ashern
(204) 768-3016

Westman Women's Shelter
Brandon
(204) 727-3644

Parklands Crisis Centre
Dauphin
(204) 638-8707

Evergreen Spouse Abuse
Committee Inc.
Gimli
(204) 378-5200

Killarney Committee on Wife Abuse
Killarney
(204) 523-4667

First Nation Healing Centre
Koostatak
(204) 645-2750

Portage Women's Shelter
Portage la Prairie
(204) 239-5234

Mamawehetowin Crisis Centre
Pukatawagan
(204) 553-2198

Russell Committee Against
Family Violence
Russell
(204) 773-2895

Nova House
Selkirk
(204) 482-7882

Wechinin Waskigan
Shamattawa
(204) 565-2548

Snow Lake Centre
on Family Violence
Snow Lake
(204) 358-7141

Agape House
Steinbach
(204) 326-6062

Swan River Committee on the
Abuse of Women
Swan River
(204) 734-9369

Aurora House
The Pas
(204) 623-7497

North W.I.N. House
Thompson
(204) 677-2723

Genesis House
Winkler
(204) 325-9957

Ikwe-Widdjiitiwin Inc.
Winnipeg
(204) 772-0303

Osborne House Crisis Shelter
Winnipeg
(204) 942-7373

Women In Second Stage Housing
Winnipeg
(204) 786-4440

NEW BRUNSWICK

Maison du Passage House
Bathurst
(506) 546-9540

La Maison Notre Dame
Campbellton
(506) 753-4703

L'Escale Madavic
Edmunston
(506) 735-4580

Women in Transition
Fredericton
(506) 455-1498

Crossroads for Women
Moncton
(506) 853-0811

Miramichi Emergency Centre
for Women
Newcastle
(506) 622-8865

Hestia House
Saint John
(506) 634-7571

Second Stage House
Saint John
(506) 632-9289

Fundy Region Transition House
St. Stephen
(506) 466-4485

Sussex Vale Transition House
Sussex
(506) 433-1649

Accueil Sainte Famille
Tracadie
(506) 395-2212

Woodstock Sanctuary House
Woodstock
(506) 325-9452

NEWFOUNDLAND

Corner Brook Committee on
Family Violence
Corner Brook
(709) 634-4199

Iris Kirby House
St. John's
(709) 722-8272

LABRADOR

Libra House
Happy Valley
Goose Bay
(709) 896-8251

Labrador West Family Crisis
Shelter
Labrador City
(709) 944-5450

NOVA SCOTIA

Cumberland Transition House
Amherst
(902) 667-1344

Naoimi Society
Antigonish
(902) 863-3807

Harbour House
Bridgewater
(902) 543-3665

Bryony House
Halifax
(902) 423-7183

Chrysalis House
Kentville
(902) 582-7955

Eastern Shore
Safe Home Association
Musquodoboit Harbour
(902) 889-2146

Tearmann House
New Glasgow
(902) 752-1633

Leeside Society
Port Hawkesbury
(902) 625-1990

Cape Breton Transition House
Sydney
(902) 539-2945

Third Place Transition House
Truro
(902) 893-4844

Juniper House
Yarmouth
(902) 742-4473
742-8689

ONTARIO

La Montée d'Elle
Alexandria
(613) 525-5338

My Sister's Place
Alliston
(705) 435-9400

Atikokan Crisis Centre
Atikokan
(807) 597-2868

Yellow Brick House
Aurora
(416) 727-1944
(416) 773-6481 OAKRIDGE

Maggie's Resource Centre
Bancroft
(613) 332-3010

Women and Children's
Crisis Centre
Barrie
(705) 728-1362

Mississauga Resource Centre
Blind River
(705) 356-7800

Muskoka Interval House
Bracebridge
(705) 645-4461

Family Life Resource Centre
Brampton
(416) 451-4115

Nova Vita Women's Shelter
Brantford
(519) 752-4357

Leeds and Grenville Interval House
Brockville
(613) 342-4724

Family Crisis Shelter
Cambridge
(519) 653-2422

Lanark County Interval House
Carleton Place
(613) 257-3469

Chatham Kent Women's Centre Inc.
Chatham
(519) 354-6360

Women in Crisis
Cobourg
(416) 372-0746

My Friend's House
Collingwood
(705) 444-2511

Maison Baldwin House
Cornwall
(613) 938-2958

North York Women's Shelter
Downsview
(416) 635-9630

Hoshizaki House
Dryden
(807) 223-3226

Avoca Foundation
Eganville
(613) 628-2154

Women's Crisis Centre
Elliot Lake
(705) 461-9868

Women's Habitat of Etobicoke
Etobicoke
(416) 252-1785

Three Oaks Foundation
Foxboro
(613) 967-1416

Geraldton Family
Resource Centre
Geraldton
(807) 854-1529

Survival through Friendship House
Goderich
(519) 524-5333

Marianne's Place
Guelph
(519) 836-1110

Pavilion Family Resource Centre
Haileybury
(705) 672-2128

Martha House
Hamilton
(416) 523-8895

Hamilton Native
Women's Centre
Hamilton
(416) 522-1501

Hope Haven Homes
Hamilton
(416) 547-8110

Inasmuch House
Hamilton
(416) 529-8149

Interval House of
Hamilton/Wentworth
Hamilton
(416) 547-8485

Maison Interlude House
Hawkesbury
(613) 632-1131

Habitat Interlude
Kapuskasing
(705) 337-1122

Kenora Family
Resource Centre
Kenora
(807) 468-5491

Women's House of Bruce County
Kincardine
(519) 396-9814

Kingston Interval House
Kingston
(613) 546-1833

Anselma House
Kitchener
(519) 742-5894

Mary's Place
Kitchener
(519) 744-0120

Women's Community House
London
(519) 439-0755

Northshore Family Resource
Centre
Marathon
(807) 229-2222

Family Resource Centre
Matheson
(705) 273-2339

Mattawa Family Resource Centre
Mattawa
(705) 744-5567

Rosewood/Huronia Transition
Homes
Midland
(705) 526-4211

Halton Women's Place
Milton
(416) 878-7757

Haven House
Manitoulin Island
Mindemoya
(705) 377-5160

Interim Place
Port Credit
(416) 271-1861

Weechahewin Centre
Moosonee
(705) 336-2456

Nelson House
Nepean
(613) 225-0533

Nova House
Niagara Falls
(416) 356-3933

Crisis Centre North Bay
North Bay
(705) 474-1031

Nipissing Transition House
North Bay
(705) 476-2401

Ojibway Family
Resource Centre
North Bay
(705) 472-7828

Hillside House
Orangeville
(519) 941-1433

Green Haven Shelter for Women
Orillia
(705) 327-7319

Apple House
Oshawa
(416) 576-8880

Higgins House
Oshawa
(416) 576-8880

The Denise House/Sedna
Women's Shelter
Oshawa
(416) 728-7311

Harmony House
Ottawa
(613) 233-3386

Interval House
Ottawa
(613) 234-5181

La Présence
Ottawa
(613) 233-8297

Amity House
Ottawa
(613) 234-7531

Grey Bruce
Women's Shelter
Owen Sound
(519) 371-1600

Esprit Place
Parry Sound
(705) 746-4800

Bernadette McCann House
for Women
Pembroke
(613) 732-7776

Y.W.C.A. Crossroads I And II
Peterborough
(705) 743-3526

New Starts for Women
Red Lake
(807) 727-3303

Ernestine's
Women's Shelter
Rexdale
(416) 746-3701

Womens Interval Home
Sarnia
(519) 336-5200

Women In Crisis
Sault Ste. Marie
(705) 759-1230

Emily Stowe Shelter
for Women
Scarborough
(416) 264-4357

Haldimand-Norfolk Women's
Shelter
Simcoe
(519) 426-8048

Women In Crisis
Sioux Lookout
(807) 737-1438

Women's Place
St. Catharines
(416) 684-4000

YWCA Women's Place
St. Thomas
(519) 633-0155

Optimism Place
Stratford
(519) 271-5550

Sturgeon Falls
Family Resource Centre
Sturgeon Falls
(705) 753-1154

Genevra House
Sudbury
(705) 673-4754

Beendigen House
Thunder Bay
(807) 622-5101

Community Residence
Thunder Bay
(807) 625-2430

Faye Peterson House
Thunder Bay
(807) 623-6600

Native Women's Shelter
Toronto
(416) 920-1492

Interval House
Toronto
(416) 924-1491

Nellie's
Toronto
(416) 461-1084

Stop 86
Toronto
(416) 922-3271

Street Haven at
The Crossroads
Toronto
(416) 967-6060

Bloor House
Toronto
(416) 533-1175

Spadina House
Toronto
(416) 967-5227

Woodgreen Red Door
Family Shelter
Toronto
(416) 469-4123

YWCA Women's Shelter
Toronto
(416) 693-7342

Chadwic House
Wawa
(705) 856-2848

Women's Place
Welland
(416) 732-4632

Shirley Samaroo House
Weston
(416) 249-7095

Naomi's Family Resource Centre
Winchester
(613) 774-2838

Hiatus House
Windsor
(519) 252-7781

Woodstock Women's
Emergency Centre
Woodstock
(519) 539-4811

PRINCE EDWARD ISLAND

Anderson House
Charlottetown
(902) 368-8658

QUÉBEC

La Passerelle
Alam
(418) 668-4671

Maison Mikana
Amos
(819) 732-9161

Maison Anjou
Anjou
(514) 353-5908

Maison Fafard
Baie St-Paul
(418) 435-3520

Maison des Femmes de Baie-Comeau
Baie-Comeau
(418) 296-4733

Le Clair de l'Une
Buckingham
(819) 986-8286

Urgence-Femmes
Cabano
(418) 854-7160

Auberge Camiclau
Chambly
(514) 658-9780

La Re-Source de Chateauguay
Chateauguay
(514) 698-1598

Centre féminin du Saguenay
Chicoutimi
(418) 549-4343

Horizon pour Elle
Cowansville
(514) 263-5046

Halte-Secours
Dolbeau
(418) 276-3965

La Rose des Vents
de Drummond
Drummondville
(819) 472-5444

L'Amie d'Elle
Forestville
(418) 587-2533

Maison Unies-Vers-Femmes
Gatineau
(819) 568-4710

Centre Mechtilde
Hull
(819) 777-2952

La Traverse
Joliette
(514) 759-5882

La Chambrée
Jonquière
(418) 547-7283

Le Havre des Femmes
L'Islet-sur-Mer
(418) 247-7622

La Montée
La Malbaie
(418) 665-4694

Le Toît de l'Amitié
La Tuque
(819) 523-7829

La Bouée Régionale
du Lac-Mégantic
Lac Mégantic
(819) 583-1233

Le Parados
Lachine
(514) 637-3529

La Citad'Elle
Lachute
(514) 562-7797

Le Prélude
Laval
(514) 682-3050

Carrefour pour Elle
Longueuil
(514) 651-5800

La Jonction pour Elle
Lévis
(418) 833-8002

Corporation Halte Femmes
Haute-Gatineau
Maniwaki
(819) 449-4782

Le Gigogne
Matane
(418) 562-3377

La Passe-R-Elle
Mont Laurier
(819) 623-1523

Assistance aux Femmes
Montréal
(514) 270-8291

Auberge Madeleine
Montréal
(514) 597-1499

Auberge Transition
Montréal
(514) 481-0496

Escale pour Elle
Montréal
(514) 351-3374

Flora Tristan
Montréal
(514) 939-3463

Inter-Val
Montréal
(514) 933-8488

La Dauphinelle
Montréal
(514) 598-7779

Le Chainon
Montréal
(514) 845-0151

Maison du Réconfort
Montréal
(514) 768-8648

Maison Marguerite
Montréal
(514) 932-2250

Multi-Femmes
Montréal
(514) 523-1095

Secours aux Femmes
(hébergement pour femmes
immigrantes)
Montréal
(514) 593-6353

Maison d'hébergement de Pabos
Pabos
(418) 689-6288

La Maison la Montée
Pointe au Pic
(418) 665-4694

Centre femme
Québec
(418) 683-2548

Expansion-femmes de Québec
Québec
(418) 623-3801

La Maison d'accueil Marie Rollet
Québec
(418) 688-9024

Maison de Lauberivière
Québec
(418) 694-9316

Maison des Femmes de Québec
Succursale Haute-Ville
Québec
(418) 692-4315

La Débrouille
Rimouski
(418) 724-5067

L'Auberge de l'Amitié
Roberval
(418) 275-4574

Alternative pour Elles
Rouyn
(819) 797-1754

Refuge pour les Femmes
de l'Ouest de l'Ile
Roxboro
(514) 620-4845

La Maison le coin
des Femmes
Sept-Iles
(418) 962-8141

La Séjournelle
Shawinigan
(819) 537-8348

L'Escale de l'Estrie Inc.
Sherbrooke
(819) 569-3611

La Source
Sorel
(514) 743-2821

Maison Havre L'Éclaircie
St-Georges Ouest
(418) 227-1025

Pavillon Marguerite
de Champlain
St-Hubert
(514) 656-1946

La Clé sur la Porte
St-Hyacinthe
(514) 774-1843

Le Coup d'Elle
St-Jean-sur-le-Richelieu
(514) 346-1645

Maison d'Ariane
St-Jerôme
(514) 432-9355

L'Ombre Elle
Ste-Agathe-des Monts
(819) 326-1321

Centre Louis Amélie
Ste-Anne-des-Monts
(418) 763-7641

Maison des Femmes Immigrantes
de Québec
Ste-Foy
(418) 652-9761

Maison Hélène Lacroix
Ste-Foy
(418) 527-4682

Maison d'accueil le Mitan
Ste-Thérèse de Blainville
(514) 435-3651

La Gitée
Thetford Mines
(418) 335-5551

Résidence de L'Avenue "A"
Trois Rivières
(819) 376-8311

Maison de Connivence
Trois-Rivières
(819) 379-1011

Le Nid
Val-d'Or
(819) 825-3865

L'Accueil du sans-abri
Valleyfield
(514) 371-4618

L'Entre-Temps
Victoriaville
(819) 758-6066

Centre Amical de la Baie
Ville de la Baie
(418) 544-4626

Centre des Femmes
Ville-Marie
(819) 622-0111

Maison Vallée-de-la-Gatineau
Wakefield
(819) 827-4045

SASKATCHEWAN

Flin Flon/Creighton
Crisis Centre
Creighton
(204) 687-5517

Qu'Appelle Haven
Fort Qu'Appelle
(306) 332-6882

West Central Crisis and Family
Support Centre
Kindersley
(306) 463-6655

Laronge Family Service Centre
Laronge
(306) 425-3900

North East Crisis Intervention
Centre
Melfort
(306) 752-9455

Moose Jaw Transition House
Moose Jaw
(306) 693-6511

Battleford's Interval House
North Battleford
(306) 445-2750

Emergency Shelter for Women
Prince Albert
(306) 922-2800

Isabel Johnson Shelter
Regina
(306) 525-2141

Saskatchewan Treaty Indian
Women's Safe Shelter
Regina
(306) 757-2096

Regina Transition House
Regina
(306) 569-2292

Sofia House
Regina
(306) 565-2537

Saskatoon Interval House
Saskatoon
(306) 244-0185

Southwest Safe Shelter
Swift Current
(306) 778-3692

Shelwin House
Yorkton
(306) 783-7233

NORTHWEST TERRITORIES

Katimavik Centre
Cambridge Bay
(403) 983-2055

Sutherland House
Fort Smith
(403) 872-4133

Safehome Network
Hay River
(403) 874-3311

Nutaraq Place
Iqaluit
(819) 979-4500

Crisis Shelter
Rankin Inlet
(819) 645-2214

Ikajuqtauvvik
Crisis Centre
Spence Bay
(403) 561-5902

Crisis Centre
Tuktoyaktuk
(403) 977-2526

Alison McAteer House
Yellowknife
(403) 920-2777

YUKON

Dawson Shelter
Dawson City
(403) 993-5086

Help & Hope
for Families
Watson Lake
(413) 536-2221

Kaushee's Place
Whitehorse
(403) 668-5733

APPENDIX 3

◆ ◆ ◆

Jane's Fund is a non-profit organization established to help battered women. It's charitable tax number is 0943829-09. Anyone wishing to become a member of Jane's Fund as a volunteer or as a financial contributor (tax receipts for donations over $5), can write to Jane's Fund, 99 York Street, Bridgewater, Nova Scotia, B4V 1B2.

A portion of the Canadian hardcover royalties from *Life After Billy* will be donated to the fund by the author to honor Jane's memory.

CHAPTER NOTES
◆ ◆ ◆

PROLOGUE

Page xiii: "A light rain was falling on April 14, 1984,..." *Life With Billy*, Seal Books, 1986, page 208.

CHAPTER II

Page 10: "The first time my parents ever told me they loved me." *Life With Billy*, Seal Books, 1986, page xii.

Page 10: "One of Jane's few childhood memories..." *Life With Billy*, Seal Books, 1986, page 20.

Page 10: "when Jane came home from school..." *Life With Billy*, Seal Books, 1986, page 231.

CHAPTER IV

Page 18: "I was full of hope for a new and better life." *Life With Billy*, Seal Books, 1986, page 51.

Page 19: "40 percent of spousal assaults..." *Globe and Mail*, December 5, 1992.

CHAPTER VI

Page 37: "Jane considered Valery's home to be an oasis..." *Life With Billy*, Seal Books, 1986, page 24.

CHAPTER VII

Page 47: "It wasn't the first time Jane had taken on..." *Life With Billy*, Seal Books, 1986, page 210.

Page 51: "In Metropolitan Toronto for example..." *Globe and Mail*, September 12, 1992.

Page 51: "But by 1988, police laid charges in only fifty-eight percent..." *Toronto Star*, November 10, 1989.

Page 51: "The Canadian Panel on Violence Against Women..." *A Progress Report*, Canadian Panel on Violence Against Women, August 19, 1992, Page 1.

Page 51: "for police forces, the adoption of zero tolerance..." *A Progress Report*, Canadian Panel on Violence Against Women, August 19, 1992, Page 23.

Page 51: "Adoption of zero tolerance for hospitals will mean..." *A Progress Report*, Canadian Panel on Violence Against Women, August 19, 1992, Page 24.

CHAPTER VIII

Page 56: "the Solicitor General's Special Committee..." *Blueprint For Change*, report of the solicitor general's special committee on provincially incarcerated women, Province of Nova Scotia, April 1992.

CHAPTER IX

Page 68: "I never had no more to do with her..." *Life With Billy*, Seal Books, 1986, page 147.

Page 69: "and Roger Manthorne helped Allen Whynot..." *Life With Billy*, Seal Books, 1986, page 108.

Page 70: "She also told Oickle..." Vernon L. Oickle, *Life and Death after Billy*, Nimbus Publishing, 1993, page 80.

Page 71: "On March 23, 1984, Jane wrote a letter..." Vernon L. Oickle, *Life and Death after Billy*, Nimbus Publishing, 1993, page 81.

Page 72: "It triggered memories of Christmas..." *Life With Billy*, Seal Books, 1986, page 68.

CHAPTER XI

Page 83: "They went to Zellers..." *Life With Billy*, Seal Books, 1986, page 69.

Page 95: "Hurshman fined for theft..." Halifax *Mail Star*, July 4, 1991.

Page 96: "Shoplifting — kleptomania is a disease..." Halifax *Chronicle-Herald*, July 9, 1991.

CHAPTER XIV

Page 116: "Toronto writer Donna Laframboise wrote..." *Globe and Mail*, December 6, 1991.

Page 124: "(On the night she shot Billy Stafford..." *Life With Billy*, Seal Books, 1986, page 107.

CHAPTER XV

Page 135: "Two or three months after I got there..." *Life With Billy*, Seal Books, 1986, page 85.

CHAPTER XVIII

Page 176: "Billy was killed by a slug..." *Life With Billy*, Seal Books, 1986, page 149.

Page 176: "In his 1982 autopsy report..." *Life With Billy*, Seal Books, 1986, page 8.

CHAPTER XIX

Page 183: "The news media reported both statements..." Halifax *Daily News*, February 26, 1992. Halifax *Chronicle-Herald*, February 27, 1992.

Page 195: "In an interview with Vernon Oickle..." Liverpool *Advance*, March 4, 1992.

CHAPTER XX

Page 206: "Three days after Jane's body was found..." Halifax *Daily News*, February 27, 1992.

Page 206: "Judy Hughes, Nova Scotia's representative..." Halifax *Daily News*, February 27, 1992.

Page 208: "Jane told Oickle that she did not like..." Liverpool *Advance*, February 26, 1992.

CHAPTER XXI

Page 210: "And Mona Donnelly, in a telephone interview..." Liverpool *Advance*, June 17, 1992.

Page 211: "Liz Forestell was also sceptical..." Halifax *Chronicle-Herald*, June 10, 1992.

Page 225: "There is no firm evidence to prove where (the threats) came from..." Halifax *Chronicle-Herald*, January 14, 1993.

CHAPTER XXII

Page 228: "and he often said he was sent by the devil..." *Life With Billy*, Seal Books, 1986, page 90.

Page 229: "Astrology played a large role in his life..." *Life With Billy*, Seal Books, 1986, page 72.

CHAPTER XXIV

Page249: "The appeal division of the Nova Scotia Supreme Court ruled..." *Life With Billy*, Seal Books, 1986, pages 190-91.

Page 250: "Brodsky wrote in Crown Counsel's Review, in 1987..." G. Greg Brodsky, *Crown Counsel's Review*, Vol. 5 No. 11, December 1987, page 1.

Page 251: "She was prepared to go to jail for a couple of years..." *Life With Billy*, Seal Books, 1986, page 191.

Page 254: "Jane too was wary..." Liverpool *Advance*, February 26, 1992.

CHAPTER XXV

Page 261: "Some of the findings included in the committee's report..." *The War Against Women*, First Report of the Standing Committee on Health and Welfare, Social Affairs, Seniors and the Status of Women, June 1991.

Page 262: "The problem is also being studied in the U.S...." *Journal of the American Medical Association (JAMA)*, June 17, 1992, Vol. 267 No. 23.

Page 267: "A Canadian survey of 676 public and Crown..." *Globe and Mail*, June 30, 1992.

Page 268: "women who worked full-time earn only 67.6 per cent..." *Globe and Mail*, May 30, 1992.

Page 269: "In one study, ninety-two percent of respondents..." *Toronto Life*, Holiday 1991, page 77.

Page 269: "As former Supreme Court Justice Bertha Wilson..." *Toronto Star*, February 9, 1990.

Page 270: "And in April 1991, another female Supreme Court Justice, Beverley McLachlin..." *Toronto Star*, April 18, 1991.

Page 272: "In 1992 alone, about 95,000 women and children..." *Statistics Canada*, Transition Home Supplement Residential Care Facilities Survey 1991-92.

Page 273: "study of the judicial treatment..." Andrée Côté, *La rage au coeur*, Rapport de recherche sur le traitement judiciaire de l'homicide conjugal au Québec. (Baie-Comeau: Regroupement des femmes de la Côte Nord, 1991,) page 139.

Page 273: "These were intentional homicides..." *Toronto Star*, February 13, 1992.

Page 273: "On the first anniversary of the Montreal Massacre..." *Toronto Star*, December 7, 1990.

Page 274: "A jury acquitted an Ontario man..." *Globe and Mail*, November 10, 1992.

Page 274: "In Alberta a man was fined $500..." *Canadian Press*, May 14, 1992.

Page 274: "a prominent lawyer was given an absolute discharge..." *Globe and Mail*, September 3, 1991.

Page 274: "A B.C. judge characterized a three-year old girl..." *Toronto Star*, December 10, 1991.

Page 274: "In Nova Scotia, a drunken man..." Halifax *Daily News*, February 27, 1992.

Page 274: "a forty-year-old man who kicked his wife to death..." *Toronto Star*, March 11, 1989.

Page 274: "A former Bay Street Broker who killed his wife..." *Toronto Star*, September 10, 1991.

Page 275: "many judges are insensitive and poorly educated on the devastating impact..." *Toronto Star*, December 3, 1989.

EPILOGUE

Page 277: "Describing what can happen to severely battered women..." Dr. Fred Shane, *Crown Counsel's Review*, Vol. 5 No. 11, December, 1987, page 3.